Psychoanalysis, Feminism, and
the Future of Gender

Psychiatry and the Humanities, Volume 14

Assistant Editor
Gloria H. Parloff

Published under the auspices of the
Forum on Psychiatry and the Humanities,
The Washington School of Psychiatry

Psychoanalysis, Feminism, and the Future of Gender

Joseph H. Smith, M.D., *Editor*
Afaf M. Mahfouz, Ph.D.,
Associate Editor

The Johns Hopkins University Press
Baltimore and London

The Johns Hopkins University Press
2715 North Charles Street
Baltimore, Maryland 21218-4319
The Johns Hopkins Press Ltd., London

Library of Congress Cataloging-in-Publication Data
will be found at the end of this book.

A catalog record for this book is available
from the British Library

Contributors

Sander L. Gilman
Goldwin Smith Professor of Humane Studies, Cornell University

Wendy Harcourt
Editor, *Development:* Journal of the Society for International
Development

Afaf M. Mahfouz
Vice President, Society for International Development and Chairperson of its Women in Development Program; Psychoanalytic Psycho-
therapist, Mobile Medical Care, Inc.; former Chairperson, Department
of Law and Political Science, University of Helwan, Cairo, Egypt

Angela Moorjani
Professor of French, Department of Modern Languages and Linguis-
tics, and Associate Vice President for Academic Affairs, University of
Maryland, Baltimore

Richard Rorty
University Professor of Humanities, University of Virginia

Roy Schafer
Training and Supervising Analyst, Columbia Center for Psychoanalytic Training and Research; private practice in New York City

Barbara Shapard
Instructor, Child and Adolescent Psychiatry, Georgetown University;
faculty, Couple and Family Therapy, Washington School of Psychiatry

v

Joseph H. Smith
Psychoanalyst and founding Editor, *Psychiatry and the Humanities*

Wilfried Ver Eecke
Professor, Philosophy Department, Georgetown University

Kathleen Woodward
Director, Center for Twentieth Century Studies; Professor, Department of English and Comparative Literature, University of Wisconsin, Milwaukee

Contents

Introduction

Afaf M. Mahfouz and Joseph H. Smith

La théorie, c'est bon, mais ça n'empêche pas d'exister.

Theory is good; but it doesn't prevent things from existing.
—Charcot replying verbally to an objection by Freud (*S.E.*
3: 13)[1]

More than fifteen years ago, following the 1975 International Women's Year, a group of men and women met every month for a year at the home of psychoanalyst Edith Weigert to reflect on what was then called the psychology of women. From January 1991 until October 1992 a few members of that group, with several others, started a seminar on gender and psychoanalysis. The goal was once again to explore, to discuss, to share thoughts, and to deepen members' understanding of the relationships among psychoanalysis, feminism, and broader questions of gender. The idea was for us to become more aware of how much we do not know or understand about gender and to take a fresh look at old and new writings in feminism, psychoanalysis, and related fields. The tool was a monthly discussion of some of these writings. The present volume is in part an outgrowth of those discussions.

The relationships between feminism and psychoanalysis are complex and difficult to understand. As Elizabeth Grosz comments, they can be approached in multiple ways, since "it is not clear which psychoanalysis needs to be addressed, [and] it is even less clear which feminisms best illuminate the merits and problems of psychoanalytic theory" (1990, 19). That is to say, the abundance of scholarship on feminism and psychoanalysis as well as the emergence of psychoanalytic feminism brought the two fields closer and yet added to the difficulty (*Signs* 1992).

Whether we think that the two fields are undermining, challenging, or nurturing each other, we need to use other fields of knowledge to shed more light upon their different perspectives and to further our understanding of the tense, often conflictual relationships between psychical and sociopolitical realities. Psychoanalysis has provided us with a theory, a methodology, and a clinical practice. It "help[ed] us understand power in its noninstitutional forms—how relations of domination become woven into the fabric of the self and how desire and domination become intertwined" (Flax 1990, 16). Feminism, on the other hand, has also offered us a theory as well as an analysis of gender and a plan of action. It has enabled us to deepen our thinking about power relations in male-dominant society.

Finally, psychoanalytic feminism has enriched us with fresh looks, from "within" the two fields in an attempt to integrate other fields of knowledge. Luce Irigaray, for example, "assumes psychoanalysis as the framework from which she can analyze other knowledge and representations (including those of psychoanalysis itself), examining their elisions and silences—examining them, that is, from the point of view of the repression of femininity" (Grosz 1990, 172). Without going into the notion of "truthfulness," or into Foucault's "games of truth" (1966 and 1971), we would only emphasize Grosz's further point that for Irigaray "psychoanalysis becomes a critical and deconstructive tool rather than a truthful or descriptive model" (172).

This book can be taken as rereadings or rewritings of Freud's sentence "When you meet a human being, the first distinction you make is 'male or female?' " (*S.E.* 22: 113). The oppressive heaviness of that sentence is the weight of emphasis given to its second half. Gender is destiny. Without changing a word, feminism has wrought a rewriting in which the emphasis instead is on the first phrase. In that reading the sentence is no longer the androcentric assertion that gender or sexual difference "is the most distinctive feature of a person," as Kathleen Woodward interprets it here. It is, instead, a comment about what goes on between strangers.

The first phrase could just as well be "Upon meeting a stranger." That would be true to Freud's meaning, but giving the first phrase the emphasis is different from his conscious intention and lightens up, opens up, and exposes to question the ponderous assertion of the second half. Would "male or female?" really be the first question to arise on meeting a stranger? Would not "friend or foe?"—"dangerous or not dangerous?"—underlie and motivate all initial questions regarding similarity or difference?

The sentence, in fact, can only be true—or at least come close to being true ("male or female?" may not be the first question, but, if not, it is close behind and, as we shall see, is probably always already interwoven with the first)—as a statement about an encounter with a stranger. It is patently not true if read as a statement that because it is the first question to arise in the encounter with a stranger, gender is therefore at all times and in all contexts always the most distinctive feature of a person. In this reading the possible future of gender—being "beyond" gender—would not mean to be beyond having a gender or beyond allowing sameness or difference of gender to be vitally important in certain contexts. Being beyond gender can instead be taken as meaning beyond being strangers to ourselves and with one another; men coming to know women in newly empowered roles; men and women being beyond the inevitably defensive reactions upon first meeting a stranger; beyond difference as fearful strangeness and similarity as a threat of engulfing sameness; a beyond wherein the creation of attributes of what it is to belong and to be human can be mutually fostered.

We know that such a beyond is never perfectly achieved. In some measure each person remains a stranger to herself or himself and to others. But acknowledging this does not invalidate the quest. That we in some aspects remain strangers to ourselves and others is instead the insight that arises from the convergence of feminism and psychoanalysis. It is the insight that saves the quest from being purely utopian and renders it more complex, paradoxical, interesting, and fruitful.

We do not enter the world as strangers. The strange is, first of all, anything or anyone other than the ministrations of the good mother (or good caretaker), whom we know right off by smell, taste, touch, sight, and sound. It takes time to come to know that this good mother is also the bad mother who fails us—that all along she[2] was also the stranger and separate, and so were we. The loss of the purely good mother calls for whatever mourning or defense a one-year-old can manage, but coming to know the mother and self as whole and separate is also an achievement, one that derives from a confrontation with the mother (and thus one's self) as stranger. This sequence is forever repeated. Getting beyond being strangers, getting to know someone more fully, requires an openness to aspects or potentialities not previously known and, in that sense, strange. The same is true of knowing one's self more fully.

The new self and the new other are born of loss and mourning, and the imprinting and effects of all past loss and mourning and the defenses arising in connection with them are carried forward into each new encounter. Defenses are inevitable. Because development is, among other things, always a product of mourning and defense against mourning, the statement "When you meet a human being, the first distinction you make is 'male or female?' " derives partly from the question to which no one ever achieves a final answer (though most persons believe they have), "Who is more the stranger, who is more frightening, my father or my mother?"

Each essay in this volume, explicitly or implicitly, considers the issues that lead one to look toward the future of gender, toward a beyond of gender. Roy Schafer's Weigert lecture on postmodern gender discourse discusses certain preconceptions about gender that analysts are always in danger of imposing on their material and applies the ideas thus developed to two frequently occurring clinical problems in the analysis of women.

For Schafer gender "should be approached as a construction; more exactly, it is a never-ending process of constructing ideas about male and female characteristics and differences." He assesses the binary conception of gender and criticizes its conservatism, its bias and its eventual support of fixed essences, phallocratic values and hierarchical difference. Schafer displays his ability to link fields of knowledge, enriching the clinical work of psychoanalysis with postmodern feminist contributions. After his summary of postmodern, largely feminist themes, Schafer applies his integrative ideas to the analysis of two jokes and a quotation from Freud in addition to the two clinical problems. While his analysis of the strength and weakness of the clinical setting is convincing, some readers would probably wish that he had also chosen a clinical problem to illustrate gender issues that occur frequently with men in treatment.

For Angela Moorjani a beyond of gender might derive from finding ways of barring the quick identification of the other in terms of gender, an identification that burdens every new encounter with the baggage of maternal or paternal transference. Moorjani's discussion of fetishism, gender masquerade, and the mother-father fantasy starts from the beginning: from Freud to Klein to Lacan with the archaic mother-father fantasy, which allows us "first to conceive of our bodies as sexually complete; then the denial of this powerful fantasy results in mourning the missing parts in others and in oneself."

Moorjani goes from the normal mourners of Freud's "Mourning and Melancholia" to the abnormal mourners, such as fetishists, who keep the lost object both alive and dead within a split-off unconscious region of the ego. Extending a concept from Abraham and Torok, Moorjani goes from cryptonym, or fetish-word, to fetish-sign to beyond fetishism.

Moorjani's literary yet multidisciplinary, multicultural approach bridges psychoanalysis and feminism thoughtfully. She illustrates the difficulty of our topic with a telling quote from Hélène Cixous:

> Men and women are caught up in a network of millennial cultural deter-
> minations of a complexity that is practically unanalyzable: we can no more
> talk about "woman" than about "man" without getting caught up in an ide-
> ological theater where the multiplication of representations, images, re-
> flexions, myths, identifications, constantly transforms, deforms, alters each
> person's imaginary order and in advance, renders all conceptualizations
> null and void.

Moorjani agrees with Catharine MacKinnon, "Sex, in nature, is not a
bipolarity; it is a continuum. In society it is made into a bipolarity." She
concludes with a renewal of Monique Wittig's call for a new personal
definition, which is possible only "beyond the categories of sex
(woman and man)."

Richard Rorty opens his discussion of feminism and pragmatism also
by quoting from MacKinnon, but he comments that she "sees feminists
as needing to alter the data of moral theory rather than needing to formulate principles which fit preexistent data better." His discourse reminds us of Irigaray's attempt "to begin to dismantle from within the
foundations of Western metaphysics" (Whitford 1989, 108). Rorty follows with the need to provide a "new language," "not just new words
but also creative misuses of language." He makes the case for the possible usefulness of pragmatist philosophy to feminist politics, since
pragmatism "redescribes both intellectual and moral progress by substituting metaphors of evolutionary development for metaphors of progressively less distorted perception." Pragmatist philosophy may be
more useful to feminists than both realism and universalism, which are
"committed to the ideas of a reality-tracking faculty called 'reason' . . .
and thus unable to make sense of the claim that a new voice is needed."
For Rorty the difference between pragmatism and Marxism can be
compared to the difference between radicalism and utopianism: "Pragmatists cannot be radicals, in this sense, but they can be utopians."
Rorty discusses his claim that a pragmatist feminist needs to help create
women rather than free them and makes a distinction between expression and creation.

For the pragmatist there is no "inviolable core," no "Nature of Human
Beings." But would not having been born into a language-speaking community, and thus having both language and shared practices of some
kind, *be* a (or the) core aspect of the nature of human being? That
would still leave a lot, but maybe not everything, up for grabs. Being
able to remember, know, and anticipate joys and sorrows are shared effects of language and the context for the creation of personhood, the
production of new social constructs, and of all other shared practices.

Having language, being a subject of language, being subject to language, would, in our view, be the basis for Kierkegaard's tenet that every person (the rub here is that he, of course, wrote "man") must be assumed to be in possession of what it is essentially to be a person. Would it be utterly oxymoronish to call having language and at least some of the shared effects of having language also a Rortyan or even Wittgensteinian view of the nature (without capitals) of human nature?

Wendy Harcourt traces in vignettes of her own history what it means to be a woman in what Julia Kristeva named the third generation of feminists—beyond the first, which demanded equality with men, and beyond the second, which stressed women's radical differences from men.

Harcourt's "Feminism, Body, Self: Third-Generation Feminism" includes three scenarios: giving voice to body, self; the search for power/knowledge; and the promise of female desire. Her account illustrates the poignant debate and reflection of her generation. Her discourse sheds light on many questions about the place of psychoanalysis not only in Western discourse but also in the Third World.

Woodward's tribute to the older woman holds hope for a calmer "beyond of gender" that might result from less emphasis on Freud's generational triangle (father, mother, and child) in favor of attending and enhancing the effects of the three-generational, linear relationship involving child, parent, and grandparent. Woodward here elaborates the issue of gender and generational identity presented in her *Aging and Its Discontents: Freud and Other Fictions* (1991).

Joseph Smith's essay considers a topic that the feminist literature sees as a major motive for injustice to women: the male's greater fear of the primitive mother. For Smith equality and difference stem from "the sense of unconditional worth of each individual." The language-related uniqueness (difference) of each is the equality that counts.

Wilfried Ver Eecke addresses the issue of unconscious articulations of gender and sexuality. He maintains that psychoanalysis must leave the patient the freedom to create his or her own life project but that the original link between gender and sexuality may not be denied or repressed. In Ver Eecke's view the awareness of human finitude is a fundamental theme of twentieth-century thought. Freud's unique contribution to this thought, Ver Eecke writes, "is that he connects the experience of finitude with the subjective experience of sexual difference." Other dimensions of Freud's thought on finitude are brought into relation with the connection Heidegger saw between finitude and death. Ver Eecke also discusses the link in Lacan and Derrida between finitude and the necessary structures of language.

Ver Eecke uses vivid illustrations to shed light on the three Lacanian concepts of the real, the imaginary, and the symbolic and their relationships. In Ver Eecke's reading of Lacan's linguistic reinterpretation of the Oedipus complex, the mother mediates entry of the child into the symbolic order. This is a painful process, since it is the confrontation of the child with his or her lack. Accepting the lack is for Lacan the origin of human desire. The mother's respect for the Name of the Father invites the child to accept the lack. "The male as the symbolic father has the task of representing rather than omnipotently being the law."

Sander Gilman's contribution is a study of the possible relationship between Freud's attitude toward women and his attitude toward his Jewishness. Gilman's "Freud, Race, and Gender" is most illuminating for any exploration of the issue of prejudice in general.

Barbara Shapard's essay, the only purely clinical study in the volume, discusses the meaning of gender stereotyping as it emerges in her work with couples. Shapard shows us the usefulness of clinical vignettes in a discussion of feminist psychoanalysis. Such examples demonstrate the complexity of motivations and how the treatment of men and women differs.

Possible motives for injustice toward women are addressed in this volume by Gilman, Harcourt, Moorjani, Schafer, Shapard, Smith, and Ver Eecke. Motives, however, inevitably remain partly a matter of speculation. Even though understanding motives could be of crucial importance to devising means of overcoming injustice, uncertainty about motive does not diminish certainty that injustice does exist. The impact of awareness of injustice to women, an awareness greatly enhanced by the feminist movement and here extended by way of thick description in essays by Harcourt, Moorjani, Rorty, Schafer, and Woodward, has led to different ways of thinking and being. Sometimes change occurs whether or not full insight has been achieved regarding a former way of being. We hope that the contributions assembled here both reflect and will foster such change.

Notes

1. Freud often used this quotation. See also Anzieu (1986, 561).
2. Or "he" where a father is the early caretaker.

References

Anzieu, Didier. *Freud's Self-Analysis.* Madison, Conn.: International Universities Press, 1986.

Flax, Jane. *Thinking Fragments: Psychoanalysis, Feminism, and Postmodernism in the Contemporary West.* Berkeley: University of California Press, 1990.

Foucault, Michel. *Les mots et les choses: une archéologie des sciences humaines.* Paris: Gallimard, 1966.

———. *The Order of Things: An Archaeology of the Human Sciences.* Unidentified collective translation. New York: Pantheon, 1971.

Freud, Sigmund. *The Standard Edition of the Complete Psychological Works of Sigmund Freud.* Edited and translated by James Strachey. 24 vols. London: Hogarth Press, 1953–74.

"Charcot" (1893), vol. 3.

"Femininity" (1933), vol. 22.

Grosz, Elizabeth. *Jacques Lacan: A Feminist Introduction.* New York: Routledge, 1990.

Irigaray, Luce. *L'éthique de la différence sexuelle.* Paris: Minuit, 1984.

———. *Speculum of the Other Woman.* Translated by Gillian C. Gill. Ithaca: Cornell University Press, 1985.

Signs. "A Review Essay on Psychoanalysis and Feminism: Current Controversies." *Signs: Journal of Woman in Culture and Society* 17 (Winter 1992): 435–66.

Whitford, Margaret. "Rereading Irigaray." In *Between Feminism and Psychoanalysis,* edited by Teresa Brennan. New York: Routledge, 1989.

Woodward, Kathleen. *Aging and Its Discontents: Freud and Other Fictions.* Bloomington: Indiana University Press, 1991.

1   On Gendered Discourse and Discourse on Gender

Roy Schafer

The bulk of postmodern discourse on gender has been developed by feminist scholars. Although their discussions are far from unified or harmonious, in my reading they center on, or at least imply, a set of interrelated themes. At the risk of appearing to be trying to impose closure on what gives every evidence of being a wide open, constantly evolving field of study and controversy, I begin with a summary of these themes. I do so because I believe that postmodern feminist studies bring to light much that present-day psychoanalysts should be aware of, and also because this course should establish a helpful context in which analysts may consider gendered discourse. In particular, I go on to emphasize certain implicit, unexamined, and disruptive preconceptions about gender that we analysts are always in danger of imposing on our material. Some of these preconceptions will be more evident in omissions than in the analyst's words, for discourse is made up of silence as well as speech. Following this lengthy introduction, I apply my summary to the analysis of two jokes and a quotation from Freud. Finally, I apply the ideas I have been developing to two clinical problems that occur frequently in contemporary psychoanalytic practice.

I

Gender should not be approached as an immutable, irreducible fact of nature. Instead, it should be approached as a construction; more exactly, it is a never-ending process of constructing ideas about male and female characteristics and differences. This constructionist process is likely to be regulated by, as well as expressive of, those discourses on gender that are most powerfully represented in one's cultural setting at

1

one or another historical moment. As a discourse-controlled process of construction, gender is an unstable mix of socially conformist beliefs and practices and individually varied, often hidden or marginalized forms of both submission to and rebellion against normative pressures.

Traditionally, we have employed a binary, or dichotomous, approach to discourse on gender: male and female. In poststructuralist critical theory, however, binary classifications have come under critical attack for their implying both absolute differences and a hierarchy of value, as in good-bad, high-low, white-black, and in this case male-female. The hierarchy of value is implied in the usual practice of implicitly putting the first term above the other in value. Thus, the binary approach to discourse on gender guides and licenses universalized and discriminatory conceptions of the sexes, and discourse itself becomes gendered. These biased conceptions presuppose that we both seek and find fixed essences in men and women rather than processes of gender development that remain in flux and are better approached as matters of degree and kind than of essence and value.

Additionally, the binary format obscures rather than highlights the relational aspects of gender. These relational aspects are both descriptive and prescriptive. Descriptively, the characterization of neither gender stands on its own feet, for the ways in which both sexes are characterized are interdependent; it does not do to set them apart. "Male" defines "female" and vice versa. Prescriptively, the implicit hierarchy of gender conveys directives for conforming to those patterns of interaction between the sexes that will support the traditional discourse of fixed essences and total, absolute, and hierarchical difference.

The binary conception of gender is also politically conservative in that it is based ultimately on taken-for-granted ideas about genital-reproductive anatomy. At least it is rationalized in the terms of the anatomical difference between the sexes. Briefly, either one has a penis or a womb or one does not, and that is what gender is all about. But that reasoning cannot comfortably accommodate biological variations within the anatomical realm, such as the various kinds of degrees of hermaphroditism. Nor can it comfortably accommodate subjective identities that do not correspond precisely to anatomy.

Another conservative consequence of this genital-reproductive focus is its reinforcing of the phallocratic values of our society. This it does by implying that being female absolutely requires heterosexuality and childbearing in the context of a traditional nuclear family. By assigning females to this stereotyped role, one places them closer to untheorized ideas of nature. As creatures of nature, females are simpler, more emotive or "hysterical," more inconstant and elusive, and their "destiny" is known in advance. In contrast, men are located higher in the order of things. They are beings who have emerged from nature to occupy a stable, complex, godlike position at the center of power, reason, language, and ordered change. They are plainly visible, whereas women are hidden in mystery or behind artifice. That's why *male* comes first in the verbal coupling; women, being less definable, are what's left over. At bottom, however, and just like women, men are captives of the dichotomy, for the sharp division implies that they, too, are expected to conform to heterosexual reproductive models. Thus, Freud (1905) concluded that being sexually polymorphous beyond early childhood is "perverse" and thereby advanced a prescription that normal sexuality should be classified in simple binary terms.

Contrary to conventional understanding, however, conceptions of gender and sexual practices have not been identical all through history, and they more or less vary from one culture to another. There are even discursive variations in how the biological body is represented (see, e.g., Laqueur 1990; Lewontin 1991). Once we adopt this historical, cultural, and discursive perspective, we are left with no good reason to argue "the truth of gender." Nothing is to be gained by defining gender in static, polarized, ahistorical ways. Consequently, the fruitful way to go seems to be to study the genealogies of conventional meaning and value in the realm of gender; that is to say, more is to be gained from studying in specific instances how "gender" has come to signify whatever it does signify and the consequences of that signification in the relevant areas of life: sexual practices, social roles, rules of decorum, occupational rewards, and so forth.

One last introductory word on gendered discourse: although the clinical work of psychoanalysis is assumed to be unconfined by conventional gendered discourse, everything that comes up in analysis being potentially open to analytic question, that work cannot avoid gender conservatism entirely. The reason for this lag is that to some extent the work of clinical interpretation cannot dispense with the terms of conventional discourse and, because the conventional conceptions of gender have ramified so extensively throughout our language, we must necessarily use problem-laden language to conduct analyses. This limitation includes analysis of the problems involved in the construction of gender, such as selective preferences for only certain metaphors and colloquialisms. This inherent tension of language—its inevitably enacting the very thing that it seeks to objectify and correct or change—has itself been much emphasized in postmodern thought, for example, in deconstructionist critical theory; consequently, discursive inconsistency need not invalidate an entire argument.

Here I conclude my summary of postmodern, largely feminist themes. Each of its prepositions is open to modification, articulation, elaboration, supplementation, and challenge. That openness itself testifies to the constructivist nature of gendered discourse. Indeed, the implications extend far beyond discourse on gender to all that we claim as our knowledge of reality and our way of getting to know reality, and what I have summarized itself draws on the work of many leading thinkers who have been developing philosophical orientations for purposes other than developing feminist critiques. Within all of these contemporary philosophical orientations, the chief working principle is that concepts are epistemological instruments. They are instruments for creating knowledge of the world of a certain sort. They are necessary master narratives that imply a limited set of story lines for specific instances. In other words, the world can be known only in the versions of it we narrate, and what we narrate is controlled by conventions of conceptualization. Each epistemological instrument, such as one or another master narrative (Schafer 1992), is limit setting, sometimes violently so. But the limits do not seem to be eternally fixed. Discursive systems are never totally closed to change; the stories change.

My summary itself is best regarded as an epistemological instrument; as such, it cannot lay claim to a forever-privileged position. It lays out just one way to go about the job of studying the discursive construction of gender; however, it can lay some claim to being a relatively coherent, active, and thought-provoking narrative of gender, and so it should help reduce the power of established sex-role stereotyping and its unhappy consequences in social and clinical practices and intellectual inquiry.[1]

II

This has been a heavy beginning. For some leavening I turn next to the two jokes and the quotation from Freud that I mentioned earlier. Not a whole lot of leavening, however, as my anatomizing of these jokes and the quotation will be a serious attempt to demonstrate how to detect some of the presuppositions of conventional gendered discourse and how to assess the consequences of these presuppositions. As I see it, the three instances I take up are not essentially different from a set of examples of clinical analysis, for that, too, may be described as a search for, and an assessment of, the presuppositions that enable the narratives that patients develop.

THE FIRST JOKE

In one of her writings Muriel Rukeyser retells and revises the popular version of the myth of Oedipus and the Sphinx:

> Long afterward, Oedipus, old and blinded, walked the roads. He smelled a familiar smell. It was the Sphinx. Oedipus said, "I want to ask one question. Why didn't I recognize my mother?" "You gave the wrong answer," said the Sphinx. "But that was what made everything possible," said Oedipus. "No," she said, "when I asked, What walks on four legs in the morning, two at noon and three in the evening, you answered, Man. You didn't say anything about women." "When you say Man," said Oedipus, "you include women, too. Everyone knows that." She said, "That's what you think." (1978, 498)

A joke it is, but at bottom not really a laughing matter and that not only because of the tragic destiny of Oedipus; for the story addresses seriously the way in which the male gender has been universalized and elevated in the hierarchy of beings. We surely have used *man* and *mankind* and similar words to refer to all human beings, just as we have used the pronoun *he* to refer to the singular form to persons of both sexes. Descriptively, *woman, womankind,* and the pronouns *she* have been put in a class of lower value, and, prescriptively, it is implied that that is as it should be in that woman make less of a difference in the world.[2] After all, as Oedipus would put it, "Everybody knows" that God is a he—that he is God the father and, as such, stands for the supreme omnipotent and omniscient male. And anyway, it is said, this common elevation of the he is merely an editorial convention; not to worry. No such luck, says the Sphinx.

Some feminists have argued that one major consequence of this universalization and hierarchization of maleness is the stripping away of women's identifying gender. In one argument the linguistic practice leaves women genderless, absent from gendered discourse or, at best, pushed to its margins and admitted into language only on an ad hoc basis. Language is for *him*, not for *her*. In another argument, one that moves in the opposite direction, the linguistic universalization of the male has so elevated him that it has removed him from gendered discourse altogether, leaving the female as the only gendered being and implying that gender is creaturelike. Thus, whichever direction we move in, we begin to detect in our male-centered conventions a built-in derangement of the "natural," that is, the presupposed and symmetrical order of things. The binary mode of thought that is supposed to reflect and insure order is creating disorder.

Further on Rukeyser's joke: it reminds us that in Greek mythology the Sphinx is a woman, and it highlights her as an empowered and potentially dangerous woman relative to the power-hungry male adventurer, the boy seeking manhood. Implicitly, she has made Oedipus pay for his masculinist answer, "Man." The joke implies that *Man* should be recognized to be merely a relational term. Taken in itself, the answer doesn't have a leg to stand on, and to fall back on the "Everyone knows" position—to rely on nothing more than powerful conventions in gendered discourse—is to enforce and reinforce a host of objectionable power-oriented, phallocratic assumptions. Postmodern feminists argue that the usages I have been discussing should be given up and replaced by individualized propositions and local formulations, that is, discourse that is specific to persons, practices, contexts, and methods of knowledge: which woman or women, in which cultural context, studied by which means (sociological, psychoanalytic, autobiographical, etc.), ascertained to be doing what, and so forth.[3]

THE SECOND JOKE

On the surface this joke seems to raise issues of a sort quite different from Rukeyser's; as I shall try to show, however, this appearance is mostly misleading.

> Two male friends meet and greet one another cordially. "How's it going?" "Fine, and you?" "Pretty good." The first man then asks, "How's your wife?" to which the second man replies, "Compared to whom?"

"Compared to whom?" is a clever response, one that unexpectedly shifts the context from friendly concern or social decorum to the bawdy. On first hearing many enlightened people, I among them, have found the joke quite funny. Upon reflection, however, those of us concerned with gender issues in general and with men's conventional degradation of women in particular, as I am, are likely to feel some shame that we laughed. For in the world of white male supremacy there can be no mistaking the wisecracker's phallocratic commitments: he dismisses conventional marital concern and decorum as well as respect for women's feelings by flaunting his role as philanderer and by using the occasion to engage in the kind of heterosexual braggadocio that indifferently reduces women to interchangeable objects.

Reflecting further, we may realize that the wisecrack may be damaging in other respects. Assuming that the question is intended personally and is not just a social nicety, we would take the wisecrack to be transforming a moment of actual or potential intimacy between male friends into a locker-room type of encounter. It would be creating distance from the questioner by adopting a competitive, "mine is bigger than yours" attitude. By assuming this more powerful and distant position, the respondent implicitly pressures the questioner to be just "one of the boys" instead of continuing to distribute his gender interests equally and trying to get emotionally closer. In other words, the questioner would do better to get back into line—the phallocratic line, the power line. Thus does the need of many men to assert supremacy over other men as well as over women disrupt relations between men.

In this view the wisecracker's response may be characterized as narcissistic rather than as interpersonally related. It is aggressively power-oriented rather than welcoming and egalitarian. It boasts of superior sexual appeal, potency, and connoisseurship and makes a positive value of consciencelessness. Additionally, we may suspect that the alacrity with which the respondent lays claim to a kind of masculine omnipotence betrays an insecure sense of masculinity, if not of overall personal impressiveness. And, as I indicated earlier, we may suspect that some of this insecurity is homophobic in that it could be spurning a male friend's caring approach by superimposing macho "hardness" on friendly "softness." All this at the same time as the wisecracker excludes tender personal concern from his relationship with his wife by reducing her to the status of one sexual object among others. It is an unpleasant, unfriendly joke, and, yet, at first hearing many do laugh.

In connection with the prevailing masculinist emphasis in our gendered discourse, we must note that ordinarily the joke would not succeed nearly as well if it were told about two female friends or about a man and a woman. Although some social change has already taken place in this respect, especially among the young, for the most part our superficially conventional society continues to put a premium on female modesty, passivity, and monogamy; it decrees that, to be ladylike, a woman should not engage in men's kind of locker-room bragging. In our cultural context people in general would be much less likely to laugh if the joke were to tell of one woman responding to another woman's question about her husband with a "Compared to whom?" wisecrack. One would be more likely immediately to assume an attitude that is questioning or even diagnostic. The spontaneous response might well be to wonder why the wisecracking wife was so predatory or even so open about it or so coarse or contemptuous or so intent on striking a pose of that kind. To begin with, the question would be, "What's her problem?"

I submit that these conventional responses, although different in form from laughing at the male-male story, would manifest the same phallocratic orientation in that the responding woman would be defined normatively as showing a lack or a fault or at the least a negation of values, that is, degrading herself by displaying a "failing" for all to see.

As I mentioned, there are now breaches in those conventions. For example, a feminist might ask, "Compared to whom?" in order to parody macho conversation or to make an ironic reverse allusion to men's philandering and the double standard. An entertainer of the Mae West variety relies heavily on this kind of parody and irony: enacting a feminist critique of the masculinist conception of gender relations, and relying on the role of the outsider—in her case, the pariah—she applies her wit to exposé and indictment.

And, finally, if the joke's cast of characters were to be a man and a woman, the man as respondent would conventionally be thought to be trying to embarrass the woman or to be propositioning her, or both, and the woman as respondent to a question about her husband would be thought of as being sexually inviting or at least teasing.

We may say that the second joke exposes the play of power in gendered discourse. The joke implicitly universalizes women by condescendingly putting them all in the class of sex objects and allowing them individuality only as better or worse sex objects, as judged by men. The joke also brings out the relational aspect of gender, the masculine being described and prescribed as the relatively more narcissistic, hostile, power-focused, and homophobic of the genders and the female as the repository of more primitive, creaturelike features. In general, the joke is a directive on how to behave in gendered settings and how to think about male and female social roles. Looked at in the present context, our laughing shows the pervasive, insidiously influential operation of our tendencies to retain these conventions of gendered discourse.

My discussion thus far has relied on a general principle of psychoanalytic understanding (as will all the discussions to follow). This principle concerns the importance of interpreting in context. In terms of gender relations, the principle specifies that with each change of local context—male-male, female-female, female-male, or feminist send-up—there occurs a change in the meaning of gendered rhetoric, such as we encounter in responses like "Compared to whom?" and "That's what you think." And with that change there occurs a change in the emotional and cognitive positions of males and females as well as a change in the distribution of power between them. Briefly, the principle states that what the concept of gender will be taken to refer to is context dependent. It should be added that whatever is said or done in a gendered context also modifies that context, if only by reinforcing it. Mae West shrewdly modified conventional contexts all the time. If, therefore, the choice of meaning to be ascribed to gender is not impervious to time, place, person, and rhetorical gesture, we can only gain in understanding by considering it an ongoing and context-dependent process rather than a static and universal attribute.

FREUD'S QUESTION

Freud asked, "What does a woman want?" (Jones 1955, 421) and, instead of immediately coming up with an answer, he has had a lot to answer for ever since. Postmodern thought is especially sensitive to the epistemological power of the kinds of questions that are asked, and it does not accept sharp distinctions between epistemological power and political power. In this context we may say that, unlike Oedipus, who *answered* in a biased way, Freud was *asking* in a biased way. Freud's question has become a shot heard round the feminist world. It has been responded to by the development of searching critiques of Freud's orientation to women, and to men too. Leading feminist theorists (e.g., Felman 1981; Jacobus 1986) have critiqued Freud's question. To develop that critique further I draw on those previous discussions, on general trends in the feminist literature, and on my 1974 article, "Problems in Freud's Psychology of Women."

Freud's question capsulizes a firm, traditional patriarchal orientation. In relation to theory his seemingly curious question tends to limit the possibility of a wide-ranging investigation and discussion. How is this so? The rhetoric of Freud's question is that of the empirical scientist feeling frustrated over his not yet having answered *his* research questions. It assigns a privileged position to the *male* investigator as the one who can ask the question; we may note in this regard Freud's 1933 discussion of femininity in which he states that women cannot resolve this problem, or answer his question, because they *are* the problem. To his mind the question is one for men to answer as well as to ask. Women are to remain silent on the subject of their "true" nature.

That this methodological prescription does not express cautious empiricism on Freud's part is evident once we note how far Freud privileged the male investigator in relation to men: He never even wondered how a man—to begin with, he himself—could hope ever to work out the psychology of men when men are the problem. "What does a man want?" For Freud that is a question that a man can both ask and answer; indeed, he believed he had already done just that. A man need never remain silent. After all, as Freud said (in one of his switches to nonanalytic discourse), men are more lucid, rational, and capable of impartial moral judgment than women (1920, 1925; see also Grossman and Kaplan 1988). The total history of psychoanalysis undermines Freud's confident position, for it shows that, in significant respects, Freud's answers to the question about men were both limited and contestable. Today's analysts have more questions to ask about men, and they have available to them more complex, varied, and individualized answers to these questions. It is old-fashioned to limit one's approach to men's psychology to that of Freud.

Further on Freud's question "What does a woman want?": it is arbitrary in its universalizing of the idea of "woman." Freud was not asking, "What does *this* woman want?" He was not asking, "What does she want under *these* conditions or *those* conditions?" Nor was he asking, "Have women *always* been this way? If not, how and why have they changed, and what are the consequences?" And so on. Freud's all-inclusive one-shot question presents women as interchangeable and fixed entities, as members of the species "woman," every member of which is predestined to "want" the same thing at bottom and to want it consistently enough to justify being classified at once. We can see that Freud's question follows the same line of thought as the "Compared to whom?" joke does.

True, Freud was never quite satisfied with the adequacy of the general answers that, over time, he had proposed: specifically, a woman wants a penis; she wants a child by the father, preferably a boy, as compensation for her penisless state; she wants assurance of the stability of being loved by the other; she wants narcissistically satisfying idealization by desirous and prostrate males. Later, and it seems largely in response to prodding by female analysts, Freud added that she wants revenge on mother for her seductions and deprivations beyond those in the oedipal sphere that he had already analyzed. It is not clear why Freud made a special point of being dissatisfied with his account of the psychology of women, for in the end his was not that simplistic an account. It is clear, however, that in his general theorizing he never questioned his presupposition that one could explain women totalistically—and, for that matter, men too. In his individual case discussions, however, and despite the biased generalizations he used, he did try to develop particularized portraits of women (see, e.g., 1905, 1920).

An additional restriction on knowledge imposed by Freud's generalized question is its presupposing that fundamentally a woman's desires must be different from a man's. His question does not convey what his own work prepared the way for: that sense of bisexual resemblance of the sexes, that unconscious androgyny they share, some of it by virtue of cross-projections and cross-identifications.

Yet another restriction stems from the implication that women can be defined by their wants. On my reading Freud consistently implied that men should be defined by their typical conflicts. Of course, their conflicts include their wants, but they are not exhausted by them; there are always the questions of the anxieties and guilt feelings associated with these conflicts and the characteristics of the defensive and adaptive psychic structures men develop to manage both these conflicts and the painful affects associated with them. Shouldn't the question about women have therefore read, "What are women's typical conflicts and painful effects, and what kinds of structures do they develop to manage them?" Freud's actual question seems to assign women to a position closer to untheorized "nature" and "the passions" and thereby to render women as being more simple and creaturelike than men. He said that he did not think they developed all that much psychic structure; he thought they had less reason to. This condescending conception is entirely consistent with his usual patriarchal outlook on women.

Finally, it is arguable that the question's rhetoric implies some exasperation over the alleged inconstancy of women. The question may have a tinge of "What do women want of me (or of men)?" There are other ways to state the problem; for example, "There are aspects of women's psychology that I have failed to work out to my satisfaction, and I wish I knew how to proceed further," or "I seem to have relatively more countertransference problems in my work with female patients." It is relevant to note in this context the abrupt, rejecting, and injurious way in which Freud ended his treatment of Dora (1905) and the so-called homosexual young woman (1920). Consequently, we may well ask whether, in these cases, the right question was "What did she want?" and whether the right or adequate answers, the ones he provided in these cases, were "Defiance" and "Revenge." And we may be justified in forming the impression that Freud did not take well to those women, or perhaps particularly those *young* women, who challenged his patriarchal authority, among other things by preferring women to men and not readily entering into an idealizing, sexual-oedipal transference to him. And so the question "What does a woman want?" may be more petulant and autocratic than curious.

III

The two common clinical analytic problems that I have chosen to examine are, first, the common practice of female patients privileging female analysts and, second, difficulties in the way of analyzing women for whom "the biological clock is ticking."

PRIVILEGING THE FEMALE ANALYST

Today it is common in the United States and perhaps elsewhere that women who are prospective patients seek out female analysts *because they are female*. I shall try to show that many phallocentric preconceptions enter into this preference, which, by the way, is shared by some analytic consultants. I emphasize in advance that my discussion does not support any general conclusions in favor of female patients being treated by male analysts. Not only does one error never justify another; in this instance, it would be the same error being committed in a different cause. Again, it is individualized judgments that are called for.

The privileging of female analysts is based on a number of highly contestable preconceptions. Foremost among these preconceptions is the idea of commonality of subjective experience among women. It is thought that the female therapist will understand more quickly, empathize more sensitively, and interpret more effectively when the patient is a woman. Having been exposed to the same inimical influences on girls and women in our phallocratic society, and having similar if not identical bodily experiences and concerns over the course of her development, the female analyst will be more identified with her patient and so should be closer to being an "ideal" therapist for her than a man could ever hope to be.

In its totalistic form this is not a strong argument. First of all, one could argue that the kind of identification in question will involve significant, disruptive countertransference potentials. Since the female analyst has experienced the same problematic societal and bodily impingements, and since subjective experience should be regarded as constructed rather than passively observed, her identification may well involve the same anxieties, self-esteem problems, and difficult moods as those plaguing her female analysand; thus, she might well have impaired vision for, and too greatly reduced distance from, just those problems that consciously matter the most to many women or that will come to matter the most in the thick of their analyses. And, to the rejoinder that the female analyst's own analysis will have helped her eliminate or greatly reduce her problems with being a woman, one could ask, "Treated by whom?" By a man—as is often the case? By this logic one would have to conclude either that female analysts have been left in too unanalyzed and conflicted a condition or that male analysts can analyze women effectively.

Even in those cases in which the female analyst has been treated by another woman, the same question arises, though displaced back one therapeutic generation; for, looking backward, it takes only a couple of generations to identify an almost totally male world of analysts. Furthermore, the evidence suggests that, with only a few partial exceptions, the women who practiced analysis in the early part of this century did not depart significantly from Freud's masculinist approach to gender differences.[4]

I turn now to a second general difficulty with the privileging of female analysts. Freud's view of gender development is that it is androgynous at its core, specific gender choices being resultants of fields of force occurring in the setting of ambivalence, loss, repression, and oblique returns of the repressed that signal, more or less, ambiguity of gender identity in psychic reality.[5] Analysts of both sexes should, therefore, have a common core of unconscious fantasy and trial identifications to draw on in their work. Female analysts encounter paternal transferences too (see, e.g., Goldberger and Evans 1985).

Further, male and female therapists commonly manifest features conventionally ascribed to members of the opposite sex. Looked at from the outside, their analytic work easily lends itself to a mixture of conventional masculine and feminine descriptions: caring, nurturant, empathic, forceful, active, passive, empowered, creature of nature, pillar of rationality, and so forth. With the help of their own analyses, analysts of both sexes are expected to have access to their own androgynous constructions of subjective experience in order to be ready to fill the bill as analysts in how they act as well as in how they empathize with and interpret their analysands' paternal and maternal transferences and their own gender-mixed countertransferences.

It must also be assumed that female analysands who present only "female" problems in analysis are not being fully analyzed. Similarly, female analysts who deal only with maternal transferences and feminine identifications and ignore androgynous, paternal, and homosexual transferences, in which they and their patients partly figure as male or male-equivalent, are also not carrying out complete analysis; in addition to defensive counteridentification, these analysts may have their own homophobic problems. Because analysis deals largely with psychic reality, one should never take it for granted that the analysand's biological femaleness limits her analysis to one specific, exclusive, and fundamental narrative of gender.

Women do vary among themselves in the strength and content of their masculine identifications and in their degrees of conflictedness in this area. These factors cannot be assessed except in relation to the strength and content of feminine identifications and conflicts over them. Particularly important in this regard is identification with the version in psychic reality of the mother with whom, from one's earliest days, one has built one's idea of being a woman; however, a counterpoised identification with the father will never be ignored if the analyst's approach to gender definition and subjective experience is conceived in the relational terms rather than binary terms.

And what of men in this context? Some male analysts would seem to have strong and well-integrated identifications with conventional maternal figures. It is certainly possible that, with these significant latent female identity components, such a male analyst may be in a less conflicted functional position as a "maternal" analyst than a woman with tons of "female" subjective experience, all of it conflicted. Should these men, too, be automatically ruled out by female patients?

I turn to one last argument against privileging the female therapist. Analysts analyze patients from varied cultural backgrounds. Sometimes they analyze patients much older than they are, sometimes patients who, unlike them, are married or single, with children or without, with chronic illness or severe experiences of object loss, and so on. Further, female analysts, of whom there are ever increasing numbers, do not regularly or frequently back off from analyzing men. There is no evidence that any of these differences regularly precludes effective analytic work. Indeed, it sometimes seems that the "outsider" has the advantage of observing and interpreting phenomena that do not touch her or him personally in any acute way and so can do the job with fewer disruptive countertransferences.[6]

I believe that my arguments in this context have been consistent with some of the feminist critiques of the binary approach to gender. What must be added now is that, when properly carried out, psychoanalysis helps free many attributes of being a person from conventional binary classifications, such as the ones that Freud used when he equated *female* with feminine-passive-submissive-masochistic and *male* with what he took to be their opposites. In our society the majority of women who are studied in analysis seem to be unconsciously haunted and confused by the idea that intellectuality, activity, assertiveness, leadership, power, nonconformity, and many other characteristics or ways of living are "masculine." Usually, they do not want to be masculine or to be thought to be that, and so they shrink back from being all they can be or else they suffer unnecessarily (Schafer 1984). Additionally, our culture seems to strengthen the link in unconscious psychic reality between these masculinized attributes and possession of the penis, and so to intensify envy of men (so-called penis envy) and to stand in the way of a woman's feeling and acting feminine or womanly in whatever way and to whatever extent she prefers to do so without disruptive ambivalence.

Upon reflection, even the primary genital-reproductive emphasis in the description of gender differences—that apparently most fundamental and undeniable component of the binary classification of gender, the anatomical difference—can be viewed as an expression of a choice of what to emphasize. In this view it is a choice that prejudges or precommits one to a certain outlook on social relations, and in particular the childbearing role, or destiny, of women. It is a value-laden choice. It is a perceptual-cognitive difference, a rhetorical difference, a historically rooted power difference that sets up prevailing hierarchies of biological "facts" (see, e.g., Laqueur 1990).

Cultural and political power being what they are, and interpretation and insight not possessing the omnipotence one might wish, total emancipation from sex stereotyping is difficult to achieve through analysis. But analysis can do some of the job; it often has. Modern feminist critiques point out, however, that much rethinking of gender issues remains to be done by psychoanalysts.

THE TICKING OF THE BIOLOGICAL CLOCK

Often enough these days the analysand is an unwed childless woman in her middle to late thirties who hears the "biological clock" ticking away and feels unable to establish satisfactory and stable relationships with the kind of man who is available for marriage and the responsible fathering of a baby. Feeling that her time for satisfying motherhood is running out, this woman introduces at the very beginning a transference-countertransference gender problem, for, as she emphasizes, she has turned to psychoanalysis, often after prolonged, ineffectual attempts at psychotherapy of various kinds, to help her realize her goal. Implied is the "natural" necessity and the urgent desirability to confirm or consolidate her "female identity" by bearing and rearing a child in an ongoing heterosexual relationship. Inevitably, it is implied that, in large part, it will be the analyst's burden to bring her to fruition. In an attempt to avoid serious misunderstanding, the analyst is obliged at the very beginning, when recommending analysis, to convey in some way that she or he can extend no such promise or guarantee and to explain that what analysis may accomplish is helping her reduce those disruptive conflicts that have stood in the way of her reaching the goals she has set for herself.

Frequently, it soon becomes clear that the initial clarification of what analysis is about has only served to drive the analysand's demands underground. Her readily and sincerely accepting the analyst's explanations of psychoanalysis proves to have remained pretty much on the level of conscious and preconscious understanding of the complex nature of identity formation, love relationships, and the life cycle. And so the demands resurface directly or are expressed indirectly. The patient may complain that all this analysis is interesting and even helpful, but still she has no man, no love, no heterosexual gratification, and no maternal prospects; or the patient may substitute detailed accounts of encounters with men, past and present, for free association, as though attempting to convert the treatment into premarital counseling; and so forth. Whatever the manifestations, the biological clock will be heard ticking in the analytic sessions.

Well aware of and empathizing with the patient's distress on this score, and knowing about men's narcissistic exploitation of overeager women and the like, the analyst will nevertheless be alert to the possibilities of constructing interpretations concerning: the patient's intense ambivalence over female identity; homosexual inclinations or intense fears of them; denied but powerful rage against men combined with much envy and competitiveness; deep-seated needs for omnipotent control; pervasive underlying depression with severe problems of self-esteem and self-assertion; major doubts about one's potential to be a good enough spouse and mother; reservations about motherhood owing to the disruptions, burdens, and risks it entails; and a host of unresolved problems with her own mother. These are common human problems, even in those who are well married and with children, but it is fairly likely that they are more severe in the woman we are considering. The problems are not unique to women. With few appropriate changes being made, the same list of problems applies to the average man in analysis too.

The analyst soon discovers that, among other things, the female analysand is using the ticking clock as a defense against analytic insight. It will be recognized that the analysand wants to mother a child in a heterosexual context *as an alternative* to looking into and resolving chronic personal problems that have made for a frustrating and painful life no matter what her occupational and other social achievements. Indeed, she may well be hoping that having a child will somehow cure all these other difficulties and resolve all her doubts. At this point a delicate phase of the analytic relationship will be reached, for interpretive approaches to this defensive use of the biological clock may readily be seen by the analysand as rigid, unempathic, withholding, blind, indifferent, even cruel, and certainly sexist.

In time the analyst will have grounds to interpret that the patient expects, symbolically if not literally, that the analyst will be the father of the desired child or the empowering and restorative mother who holds the power to fulfill or thwart the analysand's own maternal aspirations, or, in an androgynous way, both. The fantasy of the male analyst as father or co-father of the child is common in analytic work with women who want to get pregnant and do, and who deliver a baby during analysis, and that fantasy even comes up frequently in the analysis of women who already have children and bring up child-rearing problems during analysis. In the case of maternal transference to a male or female analyst, the patient may imagine the analyst to be the mother who might finally relent and no longer hinder the daughter's wholeness, separation, and oedipally colored gratifications.

I want next to indicate briefly the way the ticking clock is linked to my introductory remarks on the concept of gender. First, it is a powerful convention in our society that motherhood does confirm a woman's natural female identity. We idealize motherhood; we even sanctify it, as may be observed in the blissful and exalted way in which we tend to react to a woman's announcing that she is pregnant and to her swelling belly. We tend to forget how many women are deeply unprepared for womanhood as well as motherhood, just as many men are unprepared for manhood and fatherhood. We tend to forget the androgynous unconscious, the preoedipal fixations, the consciously repudiated but still influential identifications with sadistic and withholding mothers, the woman's rage at the baby who violates her body image, saps her vitality, and disrupts her career, and so on. In short, we do as the female patient of my example does: we defend in the name of motherhood, and thereby, from a societal point of view, we reinforce all the phallocentric, totalistic, binary-oriented reductions of women to the creaturehood of reproductive roles.

Upon analysis the countertransference will be found to express conventional emotional positions. For example, the analyst might unconsciously link the analysand to her or his own mother and thereby to familiar familial contexts, such as destructiveness toward real and imagined siblings, rivalry with the actual or potential father, and reparative aims in relation to the mother of psychic reality whom one has damaged in one way or another. The analyst is then in danger of feeling that she or he is the bad child who is not helping the mother to be a happy and fulfilled mother, and so a "good" mother, and may, in consequence, gradually shift into an attitude more appropriate to an eager midwife.

However solid our feminist convictions may be, in psychic reality we analysts remain more or less vulnerable to those countertransferences that will fit in with the analysand's defensively deployed demands and keep us feeling pressed, inadequate, guilty, or on the defensive. Insofar as we begin to collude with defensive use of the biological clock, we limit our effectiveness as analysts and reduce the woman's opportunity to accomplish enough working-through of her general problems to enhance her chances of living a satisfying life, with or without motherhood.

The analyst's ideal is to fortify the operation of the patient's reality principle. Then, the ultimate satisfaction of the pleasure principle will be achieved through the delays and the detours of thought as it tests inner and outer realities and assists one's coming to terms with oneself *analytically*. On this reality-principled basis the desire for motherhood will be reduced in ambivalence, and the desperate belief that one is a mother or nothing will lose much of its force. Obviously, not every childless woman who is significantly helped by analysis will become a mother, and there may be many circumstantial reasons for this. Whatever the reasons, these analysands will have some mourning to do for the child they have never had or, so to say, lost. Nevertheless, they will also know that they are sexual women, worthwhile grown-ups, with realistic opportunities for pleasure, pride, and love relationships available to them and with access to alternate routes to the gratification of at least some of their caretaking needs.

IV

In conclusion, I have tried to provide an orientation to postmodern, principally feminist thought about discourse on gender and gendered discourse and to show how this orientation helps us understand sex-biased use of language, story, joke, and the investigation and treatment of psychological problems. The psychoanalytic method and the postmodern approach to discourse abide by similar principles with respect to the recognition and interpretation of convention, rhetoric, belief, power, and gender. In every case we are examining the operation of epistemological instruments: scrutinizing (deconstructing) how knowledge and belief are constructed, revised, and rejected and how values are thereby enforced and reinforced.

I have applied my remarks in a critique of widespread assumptions concerning the female analyst's special competence to deal with female patients and in some reflections on the analysis of women preoccupied with becoming mothers before their time of fertility has run out. I have assumed that, in this respect, we psychoanalysts are not radically different from all members of our culture: having been steeped in the traditional biases of gendered discourse, we, female as well as male, must remain especially alert to how this discourse always threatens to induce countertransferences that control and limit the way we work. We must be aware of our tendency to believe that our ideas of gender refer simply to prelinguistic essences or fixed classifications in nature and that language merely describes these "facts of nature" in the only objective way possible. On this basis we may hope to move existing controversies concerning the conceptualization of gender onto a higher plane, a plane on which we may generate new and ever more fruitful dialogues concerning discourse on gender. By these means we may also achieve greater consistency in maintaining a truly analytic attitude in our clinical work with members of both sexes and those who resist binary classification altogether.

Notes

This chapter was originally presented as the Fifteenth Edith Weigert Lecture, sponsored by the Forum on Psychiatry and the Humanities, Washington School of Psychiatry, April 24, 1992.

1. In preparing this summary and in developing the argument of this essay, I have drawn especially on, and have been much helped by, the writing on gender and general feminist issues of Butler (1990); Culler (1982); de Lauretis (1984); Ellman (1968); Felman (1981); Flax (1990); Jacobus (1986); Moi (1985); and Scott (1988). These authors tend to refer to one another's work frequently and also to the work of other significant figures in this realm, such as de Beauvoir, Irigaray, Wittig, Nancy K. Miller, and Gallop, all of whose writings appear, along with many others, in such useful anthologies as those put together by Abel (1982); Belsey and Moore (1989); de Lauretis (1986), Miller (1986); Moi (1987); and Showalter (1985).

2. Even today male and female editors alike often object to an author's persistent use of *one* as an alternative to the all-purpose *he*. And many readers and writers still object to *he or she*, the alternation of *he* and *she*, and the use of *she* as an all-purpose pronoun.

3. This argument accepts the methodological recommendation of "thick description" emphasized by the noted anthropologist Clifford Geertz (1973) and illustrated in historical studies in an especially fine way by Joan Scott (1988).

4. Karen Horney (1967) is regarded as a special case by many feminists, and indeed she did attack some of Freud's phallocentric basic assumptions. In my view, however, she retained the male-modeled and misleading universalizing tendencies that impaired Freud's work. Melanie Klein is sometimes cited as another notable exception (Segal 1964); however, I read her foundational work as a compromise between, on the one hand, retaining Freud's flawed, overgeneralized propositions concerning gender and, on the other, subordinating them to other dynamic variables that did somewhat shift the emphasis away from Freud's steady focus on gendered sexuality. It would lead too far afield to pursue these issues here. In any case, Klein and Horney, between them, could not have analyzed great numbers of future female analysts and therapists.

5. It has frequently been noted that Freud himself did not adhere rigorously to the line of thought laid down by his theoretical emphasis on primary bisexuality and mixed gender identification in both sexes; all I can say in the present context is that his practice did not live up to his theory. It is however, toward Freud's theory, not his practice, that feminist thinkers have directed most of their critiques.

6. Those feminists identified with the "different voice" approach (see, e.g., Gilligan 1986) may reject this statement as the kind that only a man would make; there are, however, many other feminists who reject the different voice argument as misguidedly conservative in its manifesting all the faults of the universalizing, essentializing, binary mode of thought that, as they see it, has

helped to keep women over the course of history in an inferior position in this gender-hierarchized society. For present purposes I must note only that the matter is not settled. The different voice proponents do not have the last word; they speak only for one position among others.

References

Abel, Elizabeth, ed. *Writing and Sexual Difference*. Chicago: University of Chicago Press, 1982.

Belsey, Catherine, and Moore, Jane, eds. *The Feminist Reader: Essays in Gender and the Politics of Literary Criticism*. London: Blackwell, 1989.

Butler, Judith. *Gender Trouble: Feminism and the Subversion of Identity*. New York: Routledge, 1990.

Culler, Jonathan. "Reading as a Woman." *On Deconstruction: Theory and Criticism after Structuralism*. Ithaca, N.Y.: Cornell University Press, 1982.

De Lauretis, Theresa. *Alice Doesn't: Feminism, Semiotics, Cinema*. Bloomington: Indiana University Press, 1984.

———. *Feminist Studies/Critical Studies*. Bloomington: Indiana University Press, 1986.

Ellman, Mary. *Thinking about Women*. New York: Harcourt, Brace & World, 1968.

Felman, Shoshana. "Rereading Femininity." *Yale French Studies* 62 (1981): 19–44.

Flax, Jane. *Thinking Fragments: Psychoanalysis, Feminism, and Postmodernism in the Contemporary West*. Berkeley: University of California Press, 1990.

Freud, Sigmund. *The Standard Edition of the Complete Psychological Works of Sigmund Freud*. Edited and translated by James Strachey. 24 vols. London: Hogarth Press, 1953–74.

"Fragment of an Analysis of a Case of Hysteria" (1905), vol. 7.

"The Psychogenesis of a Case of Homosexuality in a Woman" (1920), vol. 18.

"Some Psychical Consequences of the Anatomical Distinction between the Sexes" (1925), vol. 19.

New Introductory Lectures on Psycho-analysis (1933), vol. 22.

Geertz, Clifford. *The Interpretation of Cultures: Selected Essays*. New York: Basic Books, 1973.

Gilligan, Carol. *In a Different Voice: Psychological Theory and Women's Development*. Cambridge: Harvard University Press, 1986.

Goldberger, Marion, and Evans, Dorothy. "On Transference Manifestations in Male Patients with Female Analysts." *International Journal of Psycho-Analysis* 66 (1985): 295–310.

Grossman, William I., and Kaplan, Donald. "Three Commentaries on Gender in Freud's Thought: A Prologue to the Psychoanalytic Theory of Sexuality." In

Fantasy, Myth, and Reality: Essays in Honor of Jacob A. Arlow, edited by Harold Blum. New York: International Universities Press, 1988.

Horney, Karen. *Feminine Psychology*. New York: Norton, 1967.

Jacobus, Mary. *Reading Woman: Essays in Feminist Criticism*. New York: Columbia University Press, 1986.

Jones, Ernest. *The Life and Work of Sigmund Freud*, 2 vols. New York: Basic Books, 1955.

Laqueur, T. *Making Sex: Body and Gender from the Greeks to Freud*. Cambridge: Harvard University Press, 1990.

Lewontin, R.C. "Facts and the Factitious in Natural Sciences." *Critical Inquiry* 18, no. 1 (1991): 140–53.

Miller, Nancy K., ed. *The Poetics of Gender*. New York: Columbia University Press, 1986.

Moi, Toril. *Sexual/Textual Politics: Feminist Critical Theory*. London: Methuen, 1985.

———. *French Feminist Thought: A Reader*. London: Blackwell, 1987.

Rukeyser, Muriel. *The Collected Poems*. New York: McGraw-Hill, 1978.

Schafer, Roy. "Problems in Freud's Psychology of Women." *Journal of the American Psychoanalytic Association* 22 (1974): 459–85. Also in Schafer 1992.

———. "The Pursuit of Failure and the Idealization of Unhappiness." *American Psychologist* 39 (1984): 398–405. Also in Schafer 1992.

———. *Retelling a Life: Dialogue and Narration in Psychoanalysis*. New York: Basic Books, 1992.

Scott, Joan. *Gender and the Politics of Historys*. New York: Columbia University Press, 1988.

Segal, Hanna. *Introduction to the Work of Melanie Klein*. New York: Basic Books, 1964.

Showalter, Elaine, ed. *The New Feminist Criticism: Essays on Women, Literature, and Theory*. New York: Pantheon, 1985.

2 Fetishism, Gender Masquerade, and the Mother-Father Fantasy

Angela Moorjani

The infantile fantasy of the phallic mother is closely related to fetishism, which in psychoanalytic terms is commonly described as a male perversion in which the phallus, missing where it is imagined to be on the maternal body, is replaced in fantasy by a fetish-object. The fetishist refuses to give up in fantasy the female phallus not found where it was thought to be. The loss of the imaginary part is "disavowed," setting in motion a process in which the phallic imago is displaced or condensed into a substitute sign—hair, a foot, a hand, a shoe, clothes, a doll, and so forth—which both points to and screens the loss. The constitution of a fetish, a material sign occulting an unconscious subtext, serves to replace the sexual attraction to women with the sexual fixation on a fetish-object. The word *fetishism* came to be used for such sexual obsession with partial objects because of its similarity to religious reverence for sacred articles and relics.[1]

The Mother-Father Fantasy

But how is one to explain the origin of this imaginary phallus whose traumatic loss and the trace it leaves in the psyche are of such consequence for subsequent gender perceptions? For the flight from women and their devaluation are part and parcel of phallic fetishism. Freud placed the mother with the phallus among infantile sexual theories (*S.E.* 7: 155 n. 2, 195) and in "Leonardo da Vinci and a Memory of His Childhood" (1910), in examining the importance of this fantasy for the artistic imaginary, mentions several preclassical depictions of phallic goddesses. Melanie Klein hypothesized that at the beginning of the child's oedipal period, which she dates roughly from six months to two years (the time of the Lacanian mirror stage), when children first see others as whole persons, the mother first, the father next, female and male body parts are attributed to one combined mother-father figure with whom the child identifies (1952, 78–79). At this stage, then, children imagine their own and others' bodies as sexually complete, with eroticized partial objects—breast, penis, and so on—attached to one childbearing figure. Given this archaic mother-father fantasy, it is not surprising that we find composite parent figures projected into myth, art, and literature. Phallic goddesses are only one instance of a recurrent iconography of the mother with a penis or the pregnant father with breasts. The Hindu god Shiva, sculpted as half-male and half-female, medieval Christian representations of a father god enfolding human souls in his lap, and African and Oceanic bearded and breasted phallic sculptures enwombing smaller figures inside themselves exemplify the ubiquitous mother-father fantasy.

If in accord with this fantasy—so closely repeated in the myth of the original hermaphrodite—we first conceive of our bodies as sexually complete, then the denial of this powerful fantasy results in mourning the missing parts in others and in oneself. As described in Freud's "Mourning and Melancholia," normal mourners, at first introjecting the lost object as both there and not there, simultaneously conceding and denying its loss, will eventually accept the object's disappearance. Other mourners, though, unwilling to admit the loss of the object, will cling to the mode of "disavowal" and maintain the article both alive and dead, there and not there, good and bad, within a split-off unconscious region of the ego. Freud found that fetishists adopt a similarly "artful" solution of keeping and giving up the object whose loss they cannot bear (S.E. 21: 152–57, 23: 275–78). Extending Freud's concept of an ego divided from itself, Nicolas Abraham and Maria Torok designate this unconscious site within the ego as a "crypt" and postulate that mourners refusing to mourn and fetishists screen their lost object by a fetish-word, or *cryptonym*. In my reading of literary and artistic works, I have extended the concept of fetish-words to fetish-signs, verbal and nonverbal, for time and again I have found in artworks cryptonyms or *cryptomorphs* screening the mother-father phantasm (Moorjani 1992, 27–40, 62–74). The manifestations of this figure encrypted in the ego are phallic and matric fetish fantasies.

Phallic Fetishism

The fetishist's disavowal of loss, or of a partial, gendered body, is closely associated with preoedipal terrors of a dismembered body, one's own, and the (m)other's, based on early separations and aggressive projections. The image of the missing maternal phallus results in feelings of guilt at having occasioned the loss by one's mutilating wishes against the mother-father's body. These guilt feelings, reinforced by earlier ones, are accompanied for the boy by the dread of reprisal (castration) and for the girl by rage at her mutilated state as a result of the mother-father's revenge (Klein 1928, 190–93).

In accord with the repetition compulsion, phallic male guilt and castration anxiety, as is well known, result in fantasies of severed limbs, hair, teeth, eyes, and so on, the stand-ins for the phallus. Such dismemberment fantasies are at times perversely enacted on the male's own body or on a woman's. At the same time male castration anxiety leads to envy of the father's phallic powers, male rivalry, and the compensatory need for virile display, which in the case of the fetishist manifests itself in a kind of macho masquerade, or "homeovestism."[2] The flip side of this (paranoid) phallic display is dread of the nonphallic (partial) woman and the devaluation of femaleness (misogyny). Fetishistic homeovestism (exaggerated phallic display to prove one has the phallus), on the one hand, and the fetish surrogates for the maternal phallus (the fetish-object or the phallic woman fetish), on the other, serve to repair the imaginary mutilations of self and mother, thus protecting the fetishist from his own anxieties of loss. (Readers will recognize in the formulations of this sentence echoes of the Lacanian distinction between the fetishistic "having the phallus," the male position, and "being the phallus," the female position, whose derealizing effects he stresses [1966, 694; 1977, 289].)

The female rage at phallic loss and partial gender gives rise to repeated scenarios (imaginary and acted out) of castration, such as surgical excisions, hair plucking, cutting into the body's surface, anorexia nervosa, and the dread of losing loved ones (Kaplan 362–407; Freud, *S.E.* 20: 143; Klein 1929, 213). The female fetishist, too, devalues femaleness (as a partial gender identity), envying the penis men have, wishing she could be a man (as well as a woman), and acting out phallic rivalry. She turns to transvestism, becoming a woman masquerading as a man, or the phallic woman. Such fetishistic transvestism, manifesting the wish to be both sexes, has as its other side female misogyny. In substituting a fetish surrogate for the fantasized maternal phallus (the fetish-child, -doll, etc.) or by being the fetish-phallic woman, female fetishists repair the imaginary mutilation (the mother's and their own) and undo their dreaded partial gender identity.

This quick summary of phallic fetishism has strayed—via Melanie Klein's concept of the combined mother-father fantasy—from considering it a largely male perversion to including both male and female

fantasies of a female phallus whose lack is disavowed by a fetish substitute. In his two-volume work on fetishism Wilhelm Stekel, in 1923,
held, in all seriousness, that female fetishists are exceptions because,
lacking the creative capacity of men, they are incapable of inventing
fetish surrogates (2: 341). And yet, among the cases he cites, there are
striking examples of female doll and cloth fetishism (1: 53–76). Freud's
former disciple is here guilty of the devaluation of women that I have
previously noted and that both Freud and he ascribe to the fetishistic
process.

More recently, a number of female critics have emphasized the existence of a "female fetishism," particularly in the form of the fetish-child
(the surrogate for the female phallus) and maternal collections of childhood memorabilia, each relic standing in for the child whose separation from the mother is thereby mourned. That the children thus
fetishized are males would appear to underscore the phallic nature of
the fetishism.[3]

Matric Fetishism

But what about infantile fantasies of the lost breast, the first part-object
attracting the child's love and hate, which is missing on the father's
body along with the other female features men lack? Do these absent
objects elicit the same feelings of guilt toward the imaginary mother-
father and anxieties for one's own bodily integrity as does the absence
of the maternal phallus? Why do we hear so little of a possibly matric
fetishism (fetish surrogates for the father's matrix) as compared to phallic fetishism (the stand-ins for the maternal phallus) or of male rage at
the lack of womb and breasts?

I use the word *matrix*, "womb," which is derived from the Latin *ma-
ter*, to indicate the fantasized nature of the father's childbearing capacities, that is, the "matric" father. In line with recent usage the terms
phallic and *matric* also include the power, both generative and social/
symbolic, that accrues to the father and the mother and with which the
child identifies and/or which it envies. In Lacanian terms the matrix
would be a signifier which along with the phallus points to the division
and loss that is each subject's grief on entering the symbolic order. Like
the phallus, the matrix too is out of reach and precipitates gender masquerades and the shams of "having" or "being" the matrix.

Awareness of the role of matric power would do away with a
uniquely phallic law and contest the Lacanian orthodoxy that it is the
law of the father that is needed to break up the mother-child dyad.
Could one not say that Lacan was in this instance fixated on a partial

explanation? For Freud realized as early (or is it as late?) as 1923, in *The Ego and the Id*, that he had "simplified" his discussion of the child's identification with the paternal law (based on phallic castration anxiety), when "perhaps it would be safer to say 'with the parents' " (*S.E.* 19: 31 n. 1). To make the child's law paternal, instead of parental, is an instance of phallic fetishism's defensive fixation on the phallus.[4]

Given that the iconography of the phallic woman is matched by that of the matric man, one would suspect that matric fetishism and mutilation anxiety and rage are as common as their phallic equivalents. And, further, one could suppose that each of the two types of fetishisms serves as a screen for the other. Is it perhaps the psychoanalytic overvaluation of the phallus, reinforced by and reinforcing societal gender myths of phallic power, that has kept matric fetishism from being named? It is, of course, the defensive insistence on phallic power (or the Lacanian exclusive focus on the phallic signifier) that is at the center of phallic fetishism based on anxieties of loss and fear of women. No doubt, we live in a society imbued with the perverse scenarios of phallic fetishism and paranoia.[5] But, at the same time, is it not perhaps the more archaic fear of matric power and more dangerous rivalry with the mother that keep matric fetishism hidden as the unconscious subtext of its phallic counterpart? For, if children imagine their parents' and their own bodies as sexually complete, then females would be traumatized by the missing parts on the paternal body and anxiously dread the loss of their own procreative capacities; males, on the other hand, would be horrified by the partial state of the father and mourn the loss of the female sexual attributes that had been theirs in fantasy.

Similar to phallic fetishism, in matric fetishism the missing childbearing powers of the father result in the child's feelings of guilt for having caused this partial and damaged state by mutilating wishes against the phantasmatic father-mother, that is, wishes to rob this figure of its contents, particularly of the children it is imagined to contain. Parallel to its male counterpart, female castration anxiety involves turning this emptying-out fantasy against one's own reproductive capacities (Klein 1929, 217–18). In *Female Perversions* Louise Kaplan also points out that "there is a female castration complex, but it is *not* about a genital not-there. The female castration complex concerns, among other things, anxieties that pertain to the damage or mutilation of *female* genitals" (1991, 88). This matric castration anxiety goes hand in hand with envy of the mother's childbearing capacities, rivalry with women, and the need for an exaggerated display of femininity, a kind of womanly masquerade, or female homeovestism, which, moreover, is accompanied by dread of the nonmatric (partial) male and the devaluation of maleness.[6] Female fetishistic homeovestism (the flaunting of womanliness to prove one has the matrix) and the fetish substitutes for the father's missing matrix, such as fabric (the stand-in for the body's linings), skin, dolls, stuffed objects, rooms, and houses, and, finally, the matric man fetish, make restitution in fantasy for imaginary losses.

Similarly, in matric fetishism, parallel to the female rage at phallic castration, there is male rage at the mother-father's vengeful deprivation of his female body parts. The male's dismay at his lost femaleness and partial gender comes to expression in fantasies or enactments of severed or damaged body parts that signify the female sexual organs (his own fantasized ones or a woman's). Although much has been made of penis envy and female rivalry with men (components of female phallic fetishism), womb envy and male rivalry with women (components of male matric fetishism) are little mentioned. And yet the desire to be a woman, envy of the procreative capacities of the mother, and grief over his lost female attributes are as powerful as phallic castration anxiety (if not more so), especially since this gynofetishistic mourning of loss repeats and builds on the earlier preoedipal identification with the mother. As expected, too, the male matric fetishist devalues maleness (as a partial gendered state) and fears the nonmatric (partial) male. To undo the gender division within himself and repair the matric father, he turns to transvestism, unifying the male and the female. With a male body in female masquerade, he turns himself into a matric man fetish.

Fetishist Fluctuations

Surely, once thought through in this way the parallels between phallic and matric versions of fetishism appear obvious. (See Table 1.) Male fetishism, although previously termed only phallic, has its matric shadow variant. Female fetishism, long thought not to exist, comes with phallic and matric facets. Both genders grasp at ways of disavowing the gender division demanded of them by oscillating between phallic and matric fantasies of completeness and denial of loss. The male fetishist's virile displays, or macho homeovestism, are but a screen for his transvestite wish to be a woman, and the female fetishist's womanly masquerade, or homeovestism, hides her transvestite wish to be a man, or vice versa. Theirs is an attempt to evade the oedipal double bind, which, in demanding that they be both like the mother and unlike her, both like the father and unlike him, places children into a paradoxical state of guilt, loss, and grief, no matter which of the contradictory commands they might attempt to obey.

These gender masquerades and reversals based ultimately on mother-

Table 1. Fetishism

Phantasms and Anxieties	Phallic Fetishism	Matric Fetishism
Archaic fantasy	*Mother-Father*	
	Phallic woman	Matric man
Imaginary object lost	Mother's phallus	Father's matrix
Imaginary or perverse mutilations	Severed or damaged body parts (own and other gender's)	
	Fetish phallic surrogates (limbs, eyes, etc.)	Fetish matric surrogates (skin, hair, etc.)
Anxieties/feelings		
Guilt	For mutilating wishes against the combined parent:	
	stealing the phallus	stealing babies
Dread	*Castration Anxiety*	
	Male loss of penis	Female loss of womb
Rage	Female rage at missing a penis	Male rage at missing a womb
Envy	Female penis envy/male envy of father's phallus	Male womb envy/female envy of mother's matrix
Rivalry	Rivalry with men (M/F)	Rivalry with women (M/F)
Devaluating fear	Fear of nonphallic woman; devaluation of femaleness (M/F)	Fear of nonmatric man; devaluation of maleness (M/F)
Disavowed wish	Female wish to be a man/ male macho wish	Male wish to be a woman/ female femininity wish
Imaginary restitutions	Female transvestism/male homeovestism	Male transvestism/female homeovestism
	Phallic fetishes; phallic woman fetish	Matric fetishes; matric man fetish

father identifications and fear of loss are further complicated by oedipal jealousies and interdictions: on the phallic side there is the male and female rivalry with the father for the love of the mother (i.e., wanting to be the phallus for the mother), and on the matric side there is the female and male rivalry with the mother for the love of the father (i.e., wanting to be the matrix for the father), which, when reactivated, bring with them overpowering guilt feelings for transgressive homosexual and incestuous wishes. A number of adult transsexual scenarios reiterate (and screen) both such oedipal sexual fantasies and the wish to reestablish male-female unity. Thus, the man in a man may love the woman in a woman and (or) the woman in a man; the woman in a man may love the man in a woman and (or) the man in a man; the woman in a woman may love the man in a man and (or) the man in a woman; and, finally, the man in a woman may love the woman in a woman and (or) the woman in a man. Of these eight possible transsexual reconnections, given the male/female masquerades and their reversals, none can be strictly defined as hetero- or homosexual, or even as bisexual, as commonly understood.[7]

Fluctuating gender masquerades, one the flip side of the other, and transsexuality, have been identified by more than one psychoanalytic thinker. In *Three Essays on the Theory of Sexuality* (*S.E.* 7) Freud points out that masculine men (male homeovestites) whose love objects are other men are attracted to the men's feminine qualities, thus making of the sexual object "a kind of reflection of the subject's own bisexual nature" (144). This notion is extended by Roy Schafer, who writes of a reversibility that includes "projecting the other side of one's bisexuality into one's partner and enjoying it there" (1978, 163). For Wilhelm Stekel every (male) fetishist wants to be a woman (1: 314), and beyond this wish the transvestite fulfills the infantile ideal of being both sexes (2: 318). For Joan Riviere, as we have seen, womanliness as masquerade functions to conceal masculine tendencies (1986, 38). Lacan, on the other hand, would have feminine masquerade, which draws attention to the absence of the penis, paradoxically turn a woman into the phallus for men, that is, the feminine mask conceals the phallic woman; and, conversely, Lacan finds that female refuge in the (transvestite) mask curiously results in making all virile displays appear feminine (1966, 825, 695; 1977, 322, 291).[8] More recently, Louise Kaplan writes that "the caricatures of masculinity and femininity expressed in the transvestite fantasy are a metaphor for any perverse strategy that makes evident and manifest one gender stereotype as a way of keeping hidden other gender stereotypes that are felt to be shameful and frightening" (1991, 249). Yet, even though the fantasies, anxieties, envies, rivalries, masquerades, and scenarios that I have shown as accompanying both female and male versions of phallic and matric fetishisms have been amply chronicled in psychoanalytic literature, the view has prevailed that there is only one type of fetishism. Even Kaplan, in her 1991 *Female Perversions*, an admirable discussion of the fragility of gender identifications and of the perverse scenarios and masquerades linked to the wish to be both sexes, continues to conceptualize a uniquely male phallic fetishism.

An exception to the single-gendered view of fetishism is Sarah Kofman's influential essay on Jacques Derrida's *Glas*, "Ça cloche" (1981), in which she combats Freud's phallocentric discourse on femaleness and fetishism by positing that an oscillation between genders results in un-

decidability and a generalized nongendered fetishism: "neither feminine nor masculine, neither castrated nor noncastrated, not because
bisexual but because shuffling between the sexes" (107; my translation). Hers is an optimistic valuation of fetishism whose perverse effects she does not bring into the discussion. On the other hand, if one
accepts the radical feminist view that gender, as currently defined, is an
arbitrary and oppressive political category that the gender masquerades of fetishists are doomed to caricature (even as they resist their
reduction to one gender), then a fluctuation between genders is difficult to celebrate (Wittig 1981; MacKinnon 1987, 32–45).

As an illustration of the caricatural (and reactionary) nature of male
transvestism, for instance, one might mention Warhol films, such as
Harlot (1964) and *Lonesome Cowboys* (1968), in which actors playing
female impersonators exaggerate the conventional gestures of Hol-
lywood femininity (Gidal 1991, 101, 112–13). Warhol finds that "drag
queens are living testimony to the way women used to want to be, the
way some people still want them to be, and the way some women still
actually want to be. Drags are ambulatory archives of ideal moviestar
womanhood" (1975, 54). Similarly, Warhol's portrayals of stars (Marilyn, Liz, Elvis) make the same point by exaggerating the flaunting of
stereotypical femininity and masculinity in homeovestism. The (conventional) gender oscillation Kofman seeks to validate for her nongendered, generalized fetishism is after all what has been happening all
along, despite attempts to explain fetishistic masquerades in strictly
phallic terms.

Before continuing this discussion on the future of fetishism (or a future without fetishism), I would like first to illustrate matric fetishism
with further examples from modern art and literature. Phallic fetishism, I feel, needs no such illustration, because the literature has focused
extensively on it.

Male Matric Fetishism

The German surrealist artist Hans Bellmer (1902–75), who is known
for his construction of life-size "child-woman" dolls whose bodies he
fragmented and supplemented and posed for photographs, wrote, in a
1934 text, *Die Puppe,* on his first *Doll,* of his childhood wish to be one
of the young girls with whom he played and to explore the inside of
their bodies as he could explore his other playthings. The exclusion
from the mysterious realm of young girls filled him with rage and the
desire to take revenge (Bellmer 1934, 60–64). In a 1936 text entitled
"Le père" (The Father), the artist goes on to tell of his and his brother's

use of masquerade, ruse, and girlishness to stage revolts against their authoritarian father (1958, 71, 73). These elements of matric fetishism—the aggressive curiosity about the inside of the body, along with matric envy, rivalry, masquerade, and contestations of maleness—all come together in the construction of Bellmer's 1934 *Doll*. The disarticulated *Doll* is in part a vengeful simulacrum of the little girls he desired, with the inside of the body visible through the peephole of the navel and, in certain photographs, the girlish-womanly body eclipsed by a fetish supplement of legs and other part-objects. But, more significantly, *Doll* is the imaginary self-portrait of the artist, the artist in drag as the phallic woman fetish, disguising his maleness by a masquerade of girlishness. Bellmer's resistance in the 1930s to the phallic authoritarianism of the Nazi regime, with which he identified his father, took the shape of the feminized *Doll* masquerade. Nevertheless, his matric fetishism, shadowed by the phallic woman fantasy, like all fetishism, ultimately debases both genders by obsessive and cruel fantasies as a defense against forbidden oedipal wishes and fearful anxieties of loss. Unable to reestablish the wished for mother-father wholeness by unifying both genders in one body, or by sexual union with the (m)other, the artist produces a myriad of fantastic fetish-images that obsessively repeat and punish his matric masquerade.

Paul Klee (1879–1940), too, writes in his reminiscences that he recalls wanting to be a girl and "grieved over not being a girl" (1979, 16; my translation). Like so many artists, he compares artistic process to human reproduction, at times favoring matric generativity, at other times stressing phallic energy and superiority (206–7, 320). Although Klee ultimately sought to remove artistic process from matric and phallic rivalries, in 1933 he scribbled a telling drawing of a pregnant man, *ein Dichter geht schwanger* (Pregnant Poet), depicting a full-bodied poet carrying an adult female embryo. Although partly a witty takeoff on the German idiom for grandiose artistic conceptions, the image (and the idiom) nevertheless point to the male wish for female as well as male generativity and to the underlying matric father fantasy.

Before going on to the example of female matric fetishism, I would like to explore briefly a number of startling appearances of the matric father fantasy in the work of Samuel Beckett. In the 1980 text *Company*, into which the author embedded a number of autobiographical fictions, there is a scene in a summerhouse where, as a young man, the personage (referred to in the text in the second person) learns of his lover's pregnancy: "Your gaze descends to the breasts. You do not remember them so big. To the abdomen. Same impression. Dissolve to your father's straining against the unbuttoned waistband. Can it be she is with child" (42). In this flashback within a flashback the son recalls his own father, whose chuckle he loved to imitate when, as a child, he sat opposite him in the summerhouse. And yet the father-identification is doubled by identification with the pregnant woman now before him, the two becoming condensed into the astonishing dissolve to the matric father fantasy.

A more extensive illustration of the matric male fantasy in relation to artistic process is Beckett's *Molloy*. This 1951 novel features a writer who has split himself in two, the mother-identified Molloy narrating the first part, and the father-identified Moran narrating the second. The two-in-one gendered text, a mother-father palimpsest, posits a matric male persona seeking in vain to give birth (and death) to a self through words. The writing persona's womb-tomb fantasy expands into ferocious travesties of matric and phallic gender myths, which the text ultimately seeks to undo. *Molloy* thus illustrates both the perennial artistic rivalry with mother-father generativity and Beckett's determination to free writing from fetishistic fantasies.[9]

There are other instances of the pregnant male in Beckett's work, such as in *Rough for Radio II*, written in the early 1960s, in which a figure called Fox imagines himself pregnant with his own twin refusing to be born. Paul Lawley has perceptively linked the blocked birth in the play as well as another male birth fantasy in *All That Fall* (1957) to Beckett's preoccupations with "imperfect being, utterance and the process of creation" (1989, 10).

Many more examples of male artistic identification and rivalry with matric power come to mind, such as Jean Genet's musings on Giacometti's metamorphosis into the goddesses he is sculpting (1979, 72); Picasso's surrealist drama *Les quatre petites filles* (1968), in which the artist's destructive and constructive impulses are identified with four little girls at play; and Arman's fascination with the inside of his fractured Venus statues, such as his *Vénus des Arts* (1988), recently erected in Paris on rue Jacques Callot. Indeed, the Pygmalion legend and its subsequent elaborations can be rethought in terms of male rivalry with female generativity, since Pygmalion, the male artist, like Klee's "pregnant poet," engenders a fetish-woman.[10]

Again, it is not that there was no awareness of the actual manifestations of male matric fetishism, especially male womb fantasies, female masquerades, and rivalry with women, but that they were consistently subsumed under the reigning phallic orthodoxy.[11]

Female Matric Fetishism

It is through the work of H.D. (Hilda Doolittle [1886–1961]) that I first became aware of a woman fetishizing what the father lacks.[12] Yet, as one would expect from the phallic fantasies that continue to inform theories of gender, critics have largely read her gender scenarios in terms of phallic envy, rivalry, and the wish to be a man, or, in reaction, have celebrated her claims to a "perfect" bisexuality, ascribing to women matric and phallic completeness. One way or another gender is defined in relation to the phallus.[13] In the poem "The Master," which H.D. wrote while in analysis with Freud in 1933, the poet does indeed draw attention to a phallicized fantasy of perfection, or wholeness:

> O God, what is it,
> this flower
> that in itself had power over the whole earth?
> for she needs no man,
> herself
> is that dart and pulse of the male,
> hands, feet, thighs,
> herself perfect.

It has been suggested that the poem's "herself perfect" is to be understood in relation to Freud's emphasis on female loss in his words to H.D. describing a statuette of Athena, "She is perfect . . . *only she has lost her spear*" (H.D. 1984, 69; Buck 1991, 99). There is no doubt that, among the "magnificent charades" played during her analysis with Freud, there is no lack of phallic masquerade, both hers and his (H.D. 1984, 120). But, more often than not, H.D. turns the tables on Freud: in interpreting one of her dreams, for instance, Freud tells her she wants to be a male hero and founder of a new religion (Moses); H.D., shifting from phallic to matric power, maintains instead that she is the princess/mother who will not only save him (Moses-Freud) but also through whom he will be born again (36–39, 120). And then, too, H.D. counters phallic fetishism's fixation on female lack and the phallic woman with matric fetishism's emphasis on male lack and the matric man fantasy. If women need the phallus to be complete, then men need the matrix to be whole again.

In the "Advent" section of *Tribute to Freud*, which H.D. put together in 1948 from her March 1933 notes on the analysis, she recounts and interprets her "cathedral" dream. In a series of associations the cathedral becomes Freud's consultation room, a house that is home, and, finally, the mother-father of regeneration, all of which become further condensed into "the Cathedral of my dream was Sigmund Freud" (H.D. 1984, 147). Although her tendency was to make of Freud the mother in transference, in consonance with the fantasy of mother-father integrity, she preferred to make of him a matric father: "The house in some indescribable way depends on father-mother. At the point of integration or regeneration, there is no conflict over rival loyalties. The Professor's surroundings and interests seem to derive from my mother rather than from my father, and yet to say the "transference" is to Freud as mother does not altogether satisfy me" (146). She continues the passage by quoting Freud's dislike and shock at being the mother in transference, because, as he put it, "I feel so very masculine" (147). Here we have a good example of a display of virility (male homeovestism) in defense partly against anxieties of loss but also against identification with femaleness as a culturally devalued position.

In the poem "The Master," which was written the year of the cathedral dream identifying Freud with the mother-father, the stanzas immediately following the poet's phallic depiction of "herself perfect" identify Freud as an earth father, Uranus, and as the "old man / who will bring a new world to birth." The fantasy of a pregnant father who first devours or destroys and then gives birth to the poet's reborn self reappears in H.D.'s poetic "Trilogy," written between 1942 and 1944 in London, under the bombs. She points out the existence of the name of Isis (the Great Mother) within the name of Osiris (the nocturnal sun god), so that together they fuse into one mother-father figure of death and regeneration (1986, 540–42). In another linguistic and mythic blend H.D. joins the name of the Egyptian sun god, Ra, with Amen, the god of fecundity, to form the Ram/Aries, the sign of cosmic death and rebirth. This figure she addresses as "Father"—"let your teeth devour me / let me be warm in your belly"—and implores him to take her home, to mother her again (526–29).

In drawing attention to the matric dimension of the male Kronus/ Uranus, Osiris, Ra-Amen, and the Ram, H.D. suggests the possible origin of these rebirth myths in early fantasies of the mother-father. The devouring motif, present both in the myth of Kronus/Uranus, who swallowed his own children, and in H.D.'s use of the figure of the Ram, brings to mind Freud's contention that the imaginary devouring father (often in the shape of an animal, although Freud also mentions Kronus) is activated by male phallic castration anxiety and derives from the oral (preoedipal) fear of devourment (S.E. 20: 101–8; 23: 277–78). In the Kleinian sense, though, it would be the aggressive fantasies against the pregnant father containing children in his belly that would be at the origin of the devouring father/animal phobia, which, moreover, is countered by the rebirth fantasy. For Freud's phallic explanation H.D. once again substitutes a matric variant.

In the "Trilogy," continuing her anagrammatic /cryptogrammic use of language, H.D. transforms the word *ram* into its anagram *mar* (*mer, mère*), which, in its association to a long line of maternal figures, again reveals the maternal submerged within the paternal. Yet, H.D. would seem to tire of these masquerades, pointing to the encrypted phantasm:

> what is this mother-father
> to tear at our entrails?
> what is this unsatisfied duality
> which you can not satisfy?

she queries, before, not unlike Klee and Beckett, she opts for a sublimation of matric and phallic figurations into an unnameable indeterminacy outside of representations tied to mother-father identifications (1986, 552–55).

Among other matric anxieties that find their expression in artistic production, one might mention the dread of emptiness and the obsessive fear of the death of a child, the compulsive exteriorization of the interior of the body, and the depictions of wounded skin and torn fabric which one finds in such artists as H.D., Käthe Kollwitz, Eva Hesse, and contemporary artists Thérèse Oulton (mostly the earlier paintings) and Kiki Smith. There is, for example, a striking 1988 painting by Oulton entitled *Second Skin* in which she combines Vanitas motifs (empty vessels, broken string of beads) with repetitive patterns of honeycomb cells suggesting a curtain veiling emptiness or skin molting in cycles of degeneration and regeneration.

Of the many other illustrations of female matric fetishism, I would like to privilege Hélène Cixous's concept of *écriture féminine* (feminine writing), which she associates with a cosmic female libido (sea, earth, sounds, rhythms, odors, body, matter) and pregnancy (1975, 162–80). *Matric writing* might be a more accurate term, since women giving voice to their bodies through writing is set against a long tradition of writing as essentially phallic in nature. And the matric male, the man who dares to become a woman, who explores his unconscious where his femaleness has taken refuge in order to write like a woman— Cixous mentions Kleist, Shakespeare, and Genet—is not excluded from feminine writing (181–84). Is feminine writing, then, not the equivalent in language of female homeovestism and male transvestism fetishizing the matrix? But Cixous is not blind to the cultural categories overlaying the female (and male) body, realizing that there is no return to a body outside of gender masquerades. Her matric reaction against phallic tyranny and constraints is perhaps only that, a reaction that she would ultimately void because it derives from that tyranny:

> Men and women are caught up in a network of millennial cultural determinations of a complexity that is practically unanalyzable: we can no more talk about "woman" than about "man" without getting caught up in an ideological theater where the multiplication of representations, images, reflections, myths, identifications constantly transforms, deforms, alters each person's imaginary order and in advance, renders all conceptualizations null and void. (Cixous 1975, 152; translation from Marks and de Courtivron 1980, 96)

Beyond Fetishism

Is there a "beyond fetishism"? Many of the writers and artists I have mentioned aim for a shift outside of gender, for removing writing and artistic production from the mother-father metaphor. One way of undoing gender identities linked to our imaginary incorporations is to block identification with a stable gendered object, or fetish, a practice particularly in evidence in the works of Beckett and H.D. and the more recent paintings of Oulton. "It comes down to the right of sexlessness, the non-fetish" writes Peter Gidal about Beckett's maneuvers to obstruct viewer identification with a gendered object onstage: "The anti-identification mechanisms . . . disallow any male being held to 'the male,' any female being held to 'the female,' whether in the audience or onstage" (1986, 144, 142). Taking anti-identification to the extreme, Gidal in his own writing and experimental films, such as *Denials* (1985), *Guilt* (1988), and *Flare Out* (1992), aims for a desubjectification obliterating gender and metaphorical mythifications.[14]

The radical feminist critique of gender dichotomies similarly concentrates on unraveling phallic and matric identifications. It is the enclosure of subjects into one or the other sex, gender, or masquerade that precipitates fetishistic fantasies screening the loss of half of an imaginary mother-father unity. If one were not limited to identifying with one or the other, with being one or the other, or with shuttling between one and the other gender, but were able to shift along a gender continuum, what would happen to fetishistic excesses? "Sex, in nature, is not a bipolarity; it is a continuum. In society it is made into a bipolarity," maintains MacKinnon (1987, 44). Or, as Judith Butler's argument runs in *Gender Trouble* (1990), if anatomical sex, gender identity, and gender performance (i.e., masquerade) are all constituted as binary by cultural discourse, then there is no reason why any of these categories should be limited to two. For it is this binary conception that gives rise, as we know, to unending fantasies of loss, rivalries, and hierarchical inequities. (And history has all too amply shown that there is little tolerance for difference or equality, especially sexual or gender difference and equality, except as a myth.) The call for new definitions and discursive practices is based on the appraisal of what gender dichotomies and fetishisms have made us suffer. A new personal definition is possible only "beyond the categories of sex (woman and man)" (Wittig 1981, 53). Fetishism will exist as long as people are culturally required to channel into univocal gender manifestations, one of two, driving them to fetishize what they fantasize as lost.

Notes

1. In these opening sentences I am generally following Freud's pages on fetishism in the 1905 *Three Essays on the Theory of Sexuality* (*S.E.* 7: 153–55) and the 1927 essay on "Fetishism" (*S.E.* 21: 152–57). In accordance with general usage the word *phallus* alludes to a fantasized construct, whereas *penis* refers to an anatomical part. On the question of the constitution of the fetish, I find Wilhelm Stekel's explanation that a fetish is a "symbol"—we would say "a sign"—which results from unconscious material undergoing the transformative processes of displacement, condensation, and reversal (1971, 2: 323) more convincing than Freud's conclusion in 1927 that the fetish refers to the last impression retained before the traumatic moment registering the missing female phallus (*S.E.* 21: 155). The *Three Essays*, on the other hand, show Freud wavering in 1905 and in footnotes added over the years on the question, asserting that a fetish may be determined by "a symbolic connection of thought," which is perhaps related to sexual experiences in childhood (Alfred Binet's derivation of the fetish in the 1880s) or to repressed coprophilic pleasures or to the phallic mother fantasy (*S.E.* 7: 154–55). In a footnote added in 1920 Freud is closer to Stekel's conception in maintaining that the fetish is a "screen" for an occulted phase of sexual development: "The fetish, like a 'screen-memory,' represents this phase and is thus a remnant and precipitate of it" (*S.E.* 7: 154 n. 2). Finally, in the 1938 "Splitting of the Ego in the Process of Defence," Freud came to see the constitution of a fetish as an example of displacement (*S.E.* 23: 277). For the influence that the religious associations of the word *fetishism* have had on the psychoanalytic understanding of the term, see Iacono (1992, 101–16).

2. The term *homeovestism* was coined by the Canadian psychoanalyst George Zavitzianos, on the model of *transvestism*, to refer to the perverse "dressing up in the clothes of the same-sex person" (Kaplan 1991, 249).

3. See Emily Apter's discussion of female fetishism in Maupassant's 1883 *Une Vie* and in Mary Kelly's 1985 *Post-Partum Document* (1991, 113–19). In these pages Apter works at going beyond phallic explanations of female fetishism.

4. Roy Schafer (1978, 153–64) cautions that the role of the preoedipal and oedipal mother must not be underestimated if one is to contest our society's phallocentrism and misogyny and go beyond the mutual envy between the sexes. On the symbolic mother, see also Smith (1989, 1050, 1063). For dis-

cussions of literary examples of the law of the mother, see Moorjani (1992, 162–72, 181–95).

5. In "The Signification of the Phallus" (1958), Lacan realizes that his privileging the phallic signifier cannot be removed from phallic fetishism's depreciation of matric power: "It can be said that this signifier is chosen because it is the most tangible element in the real of sexual copulation, and . . . the image of the vital flow as it is transmitted in generation" (1977, 287). Lacan's later speculations on female sexuality fail to do away with the basic phallic partiality of his views (Lacan 1985, 137–71; Rose 1985, 27–57). Also, psychoanalysts who have theorized a (partially) matric *infantile* fetish based on separation anxiety continue to hold to an adult phallic fetishism. See, for example, Bak.

6. In her famous 1929 essay "Womanliness as a Masquerade," Joan Riviere postulates that there is no difference between "genuine womanliness" and masquerade. Riviere, however, finds that women put on the womanly mask in order to hide their masculine strivings, that is, their phallic masquerade (35–44). As I discuss below, this would make homeovestism a screen for transvestism and vice versa.

7. In his discussion of transsexuality in relation to Marcel Proust's *A la recherche du temps perdu*, Gilles Deleuze defines transsexuality as the presence within one person of male and female part-objects, which, although adjacent, are noncommunicating, as in the original hermaphrodite. Between the male and female partitioned parts communication can be established only obliquely, all relations taking place between male and female partial objects (Deleuze 1970, 146–50). As is true for the fetishist, a totally male gendered or female gendered person is out of the question: women are phallic, men are matric, and relations can as easily be established between the phallic in the woman and the matric in the man as between the matric in the woman and the phallic in the man.

8. For an excellent discussion of the implications of female masquerade, see Heath (1986, 45–61).

9. In addition to Klein, Ehrenzweig points out that artists in fantasy appropriate the generative powers of both parents to give birth to themselves: "Ultimately the divine child himself absorbs the creative powers of both parents. He incorporates the mother's womb. He bears, expels and buries himself in a single act" (1971, 187). For an extensive discussion of the undoing of gender duality in Beckett's *Molloy*, see Moorjani (1982, 96–120; 1992, 181–94).

10. On the Pygmalion legend in relation to matric power and rivalry and for further discussion of the artists and writers mentioned in this essay, see Moorjani (1992).

11. As a recent example of phallic orthodoxy, let me mention George Steiner, who sees only male rivalry at work in artistic process and would explain the lack of female artistic creativity—to which, despite endless examples to the contrary, he still clings—by a woman's capacity for procreation. The experience of giving birth, as Steiner would have it, precludes rivalry with the male creator-god, a sine qua non of artistic production (1989, 203–8). Could there be a clearer illustration of phallic fetishism's rivalry with men screening matric

fetishism's rivalry with women? (I am indebted to Paul Lawley for bringing this passage to my attention.)

12. At a time when I had begun working on this essay, my husband and I encountered three little girls one day playing on a Paris street. One of the three took one look at my husband's slim body with round belly and exclaimed, "Voilà un monsieur qui attend un enfant" (There's a man who's expecting a baby). The other two ran ahead to get a better look at this phenomenon and agreed with the first by affirmative nods of the head.

13. For an overview of psychoanalytic readings of H.D.'s work, see Buck (1991, 1–12, 98–100). H.D. holds a particular fascination for psychoanalytic critics because of her own grasp and poetic interpretations of psychoanalytic theory and her analyses with Mary Chadwick and Hans Sachs (1931–32), Freud (1933, 1934), and Walter Schmideberg, Melanie Klein's son-in-law (1935–38). That she was as conversant with Kleinian as with Freudian categories is clear from the unpublished correspondence with her companion, Bryher. For quotes on bisexuality and the Kleinian mother-father fantasy taken from the correspondence, see Buck (1991, 87) and Edmunds (1991).

14. "Subjectivity is constructed in struggle, resistance, within and against the objective historical social-sexual positions given," writes Gidal, and "asexuality's radicalism is the effect of a lack of identity in the sexual role" (1989, 41, 53).

References

Abraham, Nicolas, and Torok, Maria. *The Wolf Man's Magic Word: A Cryptonymy*. Translated by Nicholas Rand. Minneapolis: University of Minnesota Press, 1986.

Apter, Emily. *Feminizing the Fetish: Psychoanalysis and Narrative Obsession in Turn-of-the-Century France*. Ithaca: Cornell University Press, 1991.

Bak, Robert C. "Fetishism." *Journal of the American Psychoanalytic Association* 1 (1953):285–98.

Beckett, Samuel. *Molloy*. Paris: Minuit, 1951.

———. *All That Fall* (1957). *"Krapp's Last Tape" and other Dramatic Pieces*. New York: Grove Press, 1960.

———. *Company*. New York: Grove Press, 1980.

———. *Rough for Radio II. Collected Shorter Plays*. New York: Grove Press, 1984.

Bellmer, Hans. *Die Puppe*. Karlsruhe: Eckstein, 1934. Reprinted in *Obliques*, special Bellmer issue (1979): 58–69, 80.

———. "Le père." Translated by Robert Valançay. *Le surréalisme même* (Spring 1958). Reprinted in *Obliques* (1979): 71, 73.

Binet, Alfred. "Le fétichisme dans l'amour: etude de psychologie morbide." *Revue Philosophique* 24 (1887): 143–67, 252–74.

Buck, Claire. *H.D. and Freud: Bisexuality and a Feminine Discourse*. New York: St. Martin's, 1991.

Butler, Judith. *Gender Trouble: Feminism and the Subversion of Identity*. New York: Routledge, 1990.

Cixous, Hélène. "Sorties." In *La jeune née*, by Hélène Cixous and Catherine Clément. Paris: Union Générale d'Editions, 1975.

Deleuze, Gilles. *Proust et les signes*. 2d ed. Paris: Presses Universitaires de France, 1970.

Edmunds, Susan. " 'Stealing from "Muddies Body" ': H.D. and Melanie Klein." *H.D. Newsletter* 4 (1991): 17–30.

Ehrenzweig, Anton. *The Hidden Order of Art: A Study in the Psychology of Artistic Imagination*. Berkeley: University of California Press, 1971.

Freud, Sigmund. *The Standard Edition of the Complete Psychological Works of Sigmund Freud*. Edited and translated by James Strachey. 24 vols. London: Hogarth, 1953–74.
Three Essays on the Theory of Sexuality (1905), vol. 7.
"Leonardo da Vinci and a Memory of His Childhood" (1910), vol. 11.
"Mourning and Melancholia" (1917), vol. 14.
The Ego and the Id (1923), vol. 19.
Inhibitions, Symptoms and Anxiety (1926), vol. 20.
"Fetishism" (1927), vol. 21.
"Splitting of the Ego in the Process of Defence" (1938), vol. 23.

Genet, Jean. *L'atelier d'Alberto Giacometti* (1958). *Oeuvres complètes*, vol. 5. Paris: Gallimard, 1979.

Gidal, Peter. *Understanding Beckett: A Study of Monologue and Gesture in the Works of Samuel Beckett*. Language, Discourse, Society. London: Macmillan; New York: St. Martin's, 1986.

———. *Materialist Film*. New York: Routledge, 1989.

———. *Andy Warhol: Films and Paintings: The Factory Years* (1971). Reprint with new preface by the author. New York: Da Capo Press, 1991.

H.D. *Tribute to Freud: Writing on the Wall. Advent* 1956, 1974. Reprint. New York: New Directions, 1984.

———. "The Master." *Collected Poems, 1912–1944*. Edited by Louis L. Martz. New York: New Directions, 1986.

———. "Trilogy" (1944–46). *Collected Poems, 1912–1944*.

Heath, Stephen. "Joan Riviere and the Masquerade." In *Formations of Fantasy*, edited by Victor Burgin, James Donald, and Cora Kaplan. New York: Methuen, 1986.

Iacono, Alfonso M. *Le fétichisme: histoire d'un concept*. Paris: Presses Universitaires de France, 1992.

Kaplan, Louise J. *Female Perversions: The Temptations of Emma Bovary*. New York: Doubleday-Anchor, 1991.

Klee, Paul. *Tagebücher, 1898–1918*. Edited by Felix Klee. Cologne: DuMont, 1979.

Klein, Melanie. "Early Stages of the Oedipus Conflict" (1928). "Infantile Anxiety Situations Reflected in a Work of Art and in the Creative Impulse" (1929). *Love, Guilt and Reparation and Other Works, 1921–1945*. London: Hogarth, 1975.

————. "Some Theoretical Conclusions Regarding the Emotional Life of the Infant" (1952). *Envy and Gratitude and Other Works, 1946–1963.* New York: Delacorte, 1975.

Kofman, Sarah. "Ça cloche." In *Les fins de l'homme: à partir du travail de Jacques Derrida*, edited by Philippe Lacoue-Labarthe and Jean-Luc Nancy. Paris: Galilée, 1981.

Lacan, Jacques. *Ecrits.* Paris: Seuil, 1966.

————. *Ecrits: A Selection.* Translated by Alan Sheridan. New York: Norton, 1977.

————. "God and the *Jouissance* of The Woman. A Love Letter" (1975). "Seminar of 21 January 1975." *Feminine Sexuality: Jacques Lacan and the Ecole Freudienne*, edited by Juliet Mitchell and Jacqueline Rose, translated by Jacqueline Rose. New York: Norton, 1985.

Lawley, Paul. "The Difficult Birth: An Image of Utterance in Beckett." In *'Make Sense Who May': Essays on Samuel Beckett's Later Works*, edited by Robin J. Davis and Lance St. J. Butler. Totowa, N.J.: Barnes & Noble Books, 1989.

MacKinnon, Catharine A. *Feminism Unmodified: Discourses on Life and Law.* Cambridge: Harvard University Press, 1987.

Marks, Elaine, and de Courtivron, Isabelle, eds. *New French Feminisms: An Anthology.* Amherst: University of Massachusetts Press, 1980.

Moorjani, Angela. *Abysmal Games in the Novels of Samuel Beckett.* North Carolina Studies in the Romance Languages and Literatures. Chapel Hill: University of North Carolina Press, 1982.

————. *The Aesthetics of Loss and Lessness.* Language, Discourse, Society. London: Macmillan; New York: St. Martin's, 1992.

Picasso, Pablo. *Les quatre petites filles.* Paris: Gallimard, 1968.

Riviere, Joan. "Womanliness as a Masquerade." In *Formations of Fantasy*, edited by Victor Burgin, James Donald, and Cora Kaplan. New York: Methuen, 1986. Reprinted from *International Journal of Psycho-Analysis* 10 (1929).

Rose, Jacqueline. "Introduction—II." *Feminine Sexuality: Jacques Lacan and the Ecole Freudienne*, edited by Juliet Mitchell and Jacqueline Rose, translated by Jacqueline Rose. New York: Norton, 1985.

Schafer, Roy. *Language and Insight: The Sigmund Freud Memorial Lectures, 1975–76.* New Haven, Conn.: Yale University Press, 1978.

Smith, Joseph H. "Evening the Score." *Modern Language Notes* 104 (1989): 1050–65.

Steiner, George. *Real Presences: Is There Anything in What We Say?* Chicago: University of Chicago Press, 1989.

Stekel, Wilhelm. *Sexual Aberrations: The Phenomena of Fetishism in Relation to Sex.* Translated by Samuel Parker. 2 vols. (1923). Reprint. New York: Liveright, 1971.

Warhol, Andy. *The Philosophy of Andy Warhol: (From A to B and Back Again).* New York: Harcourt Brace Jovanovich, 1975.

Wittig, Monique. "One Is Not Born a Woman." *Feminist Issues* 1, no. 2 (1981): 47–54.

3   Feminism and Pragmatism

Richard Rorty

W hen two women ascended to the Supreme Court of Minnesota
Catharine MacKinnon asked, "Will they use the tools of law as women,
for all women?" She continued as follows:

> I think that the real feminist issue is not whether biological males or bio-
> logical females hold positions of power, although it is utterly essential that
> women be there. And I am not saying that viewpoints have genitals. My
> issue is what our identifications are, what our loyalties are, who our com-
> munity is, to whom we are accountable. If it seems as if this is not very
> concrete, I think it is because we have no idea what women as women
> would have to say. I'm evoking for women a role that we have yet to make,
> in the name of a voice that, unsilenced, might say something that has never
> been heard. (1987, 77)

Urging judges to "use the tools of law as women, for all women,"
alarms universalist philosophers. These are the philosophers who think
that moral theory should come up with principles that mention no
group smaller than "persons" or "human beings" or "rational agents."
Such philosophers would be happier if MacKinnon talked less about
accountability to women *as* women and more about an ideal Minnesota, or an ideal America, one in which all human beings would be
treated impartially. Universalists would prefer to think of feminism as
Mary Wollstonecraft and Olympe de Gouges did, as a matter of rights
that are already recognizable and describable, although not yet granted.
This describability, they feel, makes MacKinnon's hope for a voice
saying something never heard before unnecessary, overly dramatic,
hyperbolic.

Universalist philosophers assume, with Kant, that all the logical space
necessary for moral deliberation is now available—that all important
truths about right and wrong can not only be stated but also be made
plausible, in language already at hand. I take MacKinnon to be siding

with historicists such as G. W. F. Hegel and John Dewey and to be saying that moral progress depends upon expanding this space. She illustrates the need for such expansion when she notes that present sex-discrimination law assumes that women "have to meet either the male standard for males or the male standard for females. . . . For purposes of sex discrimination law, to be a woman means either to be like a man or to be like a lady" (1987, 71).[1] In my terms MacKinnon is saying that unless women fit into the logical space prepared for them by current linguistic and other practices, the law does not know how to deal with them. MacKinnon cites the example of a judicial decision that permitted women to be excluded from employment as prison guards, because they are so susceptible to rape. The court, she continues, "took the viewpoint of the reasonable rapist on women's employment opportunities" (38). "The conditions that create women's rapeability as the definition of womanhood were not even seen as susceptible to change" (73).

MacKinnon thinks that such assumptions of unchangeability will only be overcome once we can hear "what women as women would have to say." I take her point to be that assumptions become visible *as* assumptions only if we can make the contradictories of those assumptions sound plausible. So injustices may not be perceived as injustices, even by those who suffer them, until somebody invents a previously unplayed role. Only if somebody has a dream, and a voice to describe that dream, does what looked like nature begin to look like culture, what looked like fate begin to look like a moral abomination. For until then only the language of the oppressor is available, and most oppressors have had the wit to teach the oppressed a language in which the oppressed will sound crazy—even to themselves—if they describe themselves *as* oppressed.[2]

MacKinnon's point that logical space may need to be expanded before justice can be envisaged, much less done, can be restated in terms of John Rawls's claim that moral theorizing is a matter of attaining reflective equilibrium between general principles and particular intuitions—particular reactions of revulsion, horror, satisfaction, or delight to real or imagined situations or actions. MacKinnon sees moral and legal principles, particularly those phrased in terms of equal rights, as impotent to change those reactions.[3] So she sees feminists as needing to alter the data of moral theory rather than needing to formulate principles that fit preexistent data better. Feminists are trying to get people to feel indifference or satisfaction where they once recoiled and revulsion and rage where they once felt indifference or resignation.

One way to change instinctive emotional reactions is to provide new language that will facilitate new reactions. By "new language" I mean not just new words but also creative misuses of language—familiar words used in ways that initially sound crazy. Something traditionally regarded as a moral abomination can become an object of general satisfaction, or conversely, as a result of the increased popularity of an alternative description of what is happening. Such popularity extends logical space by making descriptions of situations that used to seem crazy seem sane. Once, for example, it would have sounded crazy to describe homosexual sodomy as a touching expression of devotion or to describe a woman manipulating the elements of the Eucharist as a figuration of the relation of the Virgin to her Son. But such descriptions are now acquiring popularity. At most times it sounds crazy to describe the degradation and extirpation of helpless minorities as a purification of the moral and spiritual life of Europe. But at certain periods and places—under the Inquisition, during the Wars of Religion, under the Nazis—it did not.

Universalistic moral philosophers think that the notion of "violation of human rights" provides sufficient conceptual resources to explain why some traditional occasions of revulsion really are moral abominations and others only appear to be. They think of moral progress as an increasing ability to see the reality behind the illusions created by superstition, prejudice, and unreflective custom. The typical universalist is a moral realist, someone who thinks that true moral judgments are *made* true by something out there in the world. Universalists typically take this truth maker to be the intrinsic features of human beings qua human. They think you can sort out the real from the illusory abominations by figuring out which those intrinsic features are, and that all that is required to figure this out is hard, clear thought.

Historicists, by contrast, think that if *intrinsic* means "ahistorical, untouched by historical change," then the only intrinsic features of human beings are those they share with the brutes—for example, the ability to suffer and inflict pain. Every other feature is up for grabs. Historicists agree with the Wittgensteinian view Susan Hurley summarizes as: "the existence of certain shared practices, any of which might not have existed, is all that our having determinate reasons . . . to do anything rests on" (1989,32).[4] So, they think we are not yet in a position to know what human beings are, since we do not yet know what practices human beings may start sharing.[5] Universalists talk as if any rational agent, at any epoch, could somehow have envisaged all the possible morally relevant differences, all the possible moral identities, brought into existence by such shared practices. But for MacKinnon, as for Hegel and Dewey, we know, at most, only those possibilities that history has actualized so far. MacKinnon's central point, as I read her, is that "a woman" is not yet the name of a way of being human, not yet the name of a moral identity, but, at most, the name of a disability.[6]

Taking seriously the ideas of as yet unrealized possibilities and of as yet unrecognized moral abominations resulting from failure to envisage those possibilities requires one to take seriously the suggestion that we do not at present have the logical space necessary for adequate moral deliberation. Only if such suggestions are taken seriously can passages like the one I quoted from MacKinnon be read as prophecy rather than empty hyperbole. But this means revising our conception of moral progress. We have to stop talking about the need to go from distorted to undistorted perception of moral reality and, instead, to begin talking about the need to modify our practices so as to take account of new descriptions of what has been going on.

Here is where pragmatist philosophy might be useful to feminist politics. For pragmatism redescribes both intellectual and moral progress by substituting metaphors of evolutionary development for metaphors of progressively less distorted perception. By dropping a representationalist account of knowledge, we pragmatists drop the appearance-reality distinction in favor of a distinction between beliefs that serve some purposes and beliefs that serve other purposes—for example, the purposes of one group and those of another group. We drop the notion of beliefs being made true by reality as well as the distinction between intrinsic and accidental features of things. So we drop questions about (in Nelson Goodman's phrase) the Way the World Is. We thereby drop the ideas of the Nature of Humanity and of the Moral Law, considered as objects that inquiry is trying to represent accurately or as objects that make true moral judgments true. So, we have to give up the comforting belief that competing groups will always be able to reason together on the basis of plausible and neutral premises.

From a pragmatist angle neither Christianity nor the Enlightenment nor contemporary feminism are cases of cognitive clarity overcoming cognitive distortion. They are, instead, examples of evolutionary struggle—struggle that is Mendelian rather than Darwinian in character, in that it is guided by no immanent teleology. The history of human social practices is continuous with the history of biological evolution, the only difference being that what Richard Dawkins and Daniel Dennett call *memes* gradually take over the role of Mendel's genes. Memes are things like turns of speech, terms of aesthetic or moral praise, political slogans, proverbs, musical phrases, stereotypical icons, and the like. Memes compete with one another for the available cultural space as genes compete for the available lebensraum.[7] Different batches of both genes and memes are carried by different human social groups, and so the triumph of one such group amounts to the triumph of those genes or memes. But no gene or meme is closer to the purpose of evolution or to the nature of humanity than any other, for evolution has no purpose and humanity no nature. So the moral world does not divide into the intrinsically decent and the intrinsically abominable but, rather, into the goods of different groups and different epochs. As Dewey put it: "The worse or evil is a rejected good. In deliberation and before choice no evil presents itself as evil. Until it is rejected, it is a competing good. After rejection, it figures not as a lesser good, but as the bad of that situation" (1983, 14: 193).[8] On a Deweyan view the replacement of one species by another in a given ecological niche or the enslavement of one human tribe or race by another, or of the human females by the human males, is not an intrinsic evil. The latter is a rejected good, rejected on the basis of the greater good that feminism is at present making imaginable. The claim that this good is greater is like the claim that mammals are preferable to reptiles, or Aryans to Jews; it is an ethnocentric claim made from the point of view of a given cluster of genes or memes. There is no larger entity that stands behind that cluster and makes its claim true (or makes some contradictory claim true).

Pragmatists like myself think that this Deweyan account of moral truth and moral progress comports better with the prophetic tone in contemporary feminism than do universalism and realism. Prophecy, as we see it, is all that nonviolent political movements can fall back on when argument fails. Argument for the rights of the oppressed *will* fail just insofar as the only language in which to state relevant premises is one in which the relevant emancipatory premises sound crazy. We pragmatists see universalism and realism as committed to the ideas of a reality-tracking faculty called reason and an unchanging moral reality to be tracked and, thus, unable to make sense of the claim that a new voice is needed. So we commend ourselves to feminists on the ground that we can fit that claim into *our* view of moral progress with relative ease.

We see it as unfortunate that many feminists intermingle pragmatist and realist rhetoric. For example, MacKinnon at one point defines feminism as the belief "that women are human beings in truth but not in social reality" (1987, 126). The phrase "in truth" here can only mean "in a reality that is distinct from social reality," one that is as it is whether or not women ever succeed in saying what has never been heard. Such invocations of an ahistoricist realism leave it unclear whether MacKinnon sees women as appealing from a bad social practice to something that transcends social practice, appealing from appearance to reality, or, instead, sees them as doing the same sort of thing as the early Christians, the early socialists, the Albigensians, and the Nazis did: trying to actualize hitherto undreamt-of possibilities by putting new linguistic and other practices into play and erecting new social constructs.[9]

Some contemporary feminist philosophers are sympathetic to the latter alternative, because they explicitly reject universalism and realism. They do so because they see both as symptoms of what Jacques Derrida has called *phallogocentrism*—what MacKinnon calls "the epistemological stance . . . of which male dominance is the politics" (1987, 50). Other such philosophers, however, warn against accepting the criticisms of universalism and realism common to Friedrich Nietzsche, Martin Heidegger, and Derrida—against finding an ally in what is sometimes called "postmodernism." Sabina Lovibond, for example, cautions against throwing Enlightenment universalism and realism overboard. "How can anyone ask me to say goodbye to 'emancipatory metanarratives,'" she asks, "when my own emancipation is still such a patchy, hit-or-miss affair?" (1989, 12).[10] Lovibond's universalism comes out when she says, "It would be arbitrary to work for sexual equality unless one believed that human society was disfigured by inequality *as such*." Her realism comes out in her claim that feminism has a "background commitment . . . to the elimination of (self-interested) cognitive distortion" (1989, 28).[11]

I share Lovibond's doubts about the apocalyptic tone and the rhetoric of unmasking, prevalent among people who believe that we are living in a "postmodern" period.[12] But, on all the crucial philosophical issues, I am on the side of Lovibond's postmodern opponents.[13] I hope that feminists will continue to consider the possibility of dropping realism and universalism, dropping the notion that the subordination of women is *intrinsically* abominable, dropping the claim that there is something called "right" or "justice" or "humanity" which has always been on their side, making their claims true. I agree with those whom Lovibond paraphrases as saying "the Enlightenment rhetoric of 'emancipation,' 'autonomy' and the like is complicit in a fantasy of escape from the embodied condition" (1989, 12). In particular, it is complicit in the fantasy of escape from a historical situation into an ahistoricist empyrean—one in which moral theory can be pursued, like Euclidean geometry, within an unalterable, unextendable, logical space. Although practical politics will doubtless often require feminists to speak with the universalist vulgar, I think they might profit from thinking with the pragmatists.

One of the best things about contemporary feminism, it seems to me, is its ability to eschew such Enlightenment fantasies of escape. My favorite passages in MacKinnon are ones in which she says things like "we

are not attempting to be objective about it, we're attempting to represent the point of view of women" (1987, 86).[14] Feminists are much less
inclined than Marxists were to fall back on a comfortable doctrine of
immanent teleology. There is a lot of feminist writing that can be read as
saying: we are *not* appealing from phallist appearance to nonphallist
reality. We are *not* saying that the voice in which women will someday
speak will be better at representing reality than present-day masculist
discourse. We are not attempting the impossible task of developing a
nonhegemonic discourse, one in which truth is no longer connected
with power. We are not trying to do away with social constructs in
order to find something that is not a social construct. We are just trying
to help women out of the traps men have constructed for them, help
them get the power they do not presently have, and help them create a
moral identity as women.

I have argued in the past that Deweyan pragmatism, when linguis-
tified along the lines suggested by Hilary Putnam and Donald Davidson, gives you all that is politically useful in the Nietzsche-Heidegger-
Derrida-Foucault tradition. Pragmatism, I claim, offers all the dialectical advantages of postmodernism while avoiding the self-contradictory
postmodernist rhetoric of unmasking. I admit that insofar as feminists
adopt a Deweyan rhetoric of the sort I have just described, they commit
themselves to a lot of apparent paradoxes and incur the usual charges of
relativism, irrationalism, and power worship.[15] But these disadvantages
are, I think, outweighed by the advantages. By describing themselves in
Deweyan terms, feminists would free themselves from Lovibond's demand for a general theory of oppression—a way of seeing oppression
on the basis of race, class, sexual preference, and gender as so many
instances of a general failure to treat equals equally.[16] They would
thereby avoid the embarrassments of the universalist claim that the
term *human being*—or even the term *woman*—names an unchanging essence, an ahistorical natural kind with a permanent set of intrinsic
features. Further, they would no longer need to raise what seem to me
unanswerable questions about the accuracy of their representations of
"woman's experience." They would, instead, see themselves as *creating*
such an experience by creating a language, a tradition, and an identity.

In the remainder of this chapter I want to develop this distinction
between expression and creation in more detail. But first I want to in-
sert a cautionary remark about the relative insignificance of philosophical movements as compared with social-political movements. Yoking
feminism with pragmatism is like yoking Christianity with Platonism or
socialism with dialectical materialism. In each case something big and
important, a vast social hope, is being yoked with something small and

unimportant, a set of answers to philosophical questions—questions that arise only for people who find philosophical topics intriguing rather than silly. Universalists, of both the bourgeois liberal and the Marxist sort, often claim that such questions are in fact urgent, for political movements *need* philosophical foundations. But we pragmatists cannot say this. We are not in the foundations business. *All* we can do is to offer feminists a few pieces of special-purpose ammunition—for example, some additional replies to charges that their aims are unnatural, their demands irrational, or their claims hyperbolic.

So much for an overview of my reasons for trying to bring feminism and pragmatism together. I want now to enlarge on my claim that a pragmatist feminist will see herself as helping to create women rather than attempting to describe them more accurately. I shall do so by taking up two objections that might be made to what I have been saying. The first is the familiar charge that pragmatism is inherently conservative, biased in favor of the status quo.[17] The second objection arises from the fact that if you say that women need to be created rather than simply freed, you seem to be saying that in some sense women do not now fully exist. But then there seems no basis for saying that men have done women wrong, since you cannot wrong the nonexistent.

Hilary Putnam, the most important contemporary philosopher to call himself a pragmatist, has said that "a statement is true of a situation just in case it would be correct to use the words of which the statement consists in that way in describing the situation." Putting the matter this way immediately suggests the question: Correct by whose standards? Putnam's position that "truth and rational acceptability are interdependent notions" makes it hard to see how we might ever appeal from the oppressive conventions of our community to something nonconventional, and thus hard to see how we could ever engage in anything like "radical critique" (1988, 114–15).[18] So it may seem that we pragmatists, in our frenzied efforts to undercut epistemological skepticism by doing away with what Davidson calls "the scheme-content distinction," have also undercut political radicalism.

Pragmatists should reply to this charge by saying that they cannot make sense of an appeal from our community's practices to anything except the practice of a real or imagined alternative community. So when prophetic feminists say that it is not enough to make the practices of our community coherent, that the very *language* of our community must be subjected to radical critique, pragmatists add that such critique can only take the form of imagining a community whose linguistic and other practices are different from our own. Once one grants MacKinnon's point that one can only get so far with an appeal to make present beliefs more coherent by treating women on a par with men, once one sees the need for something more than an appeal to rational acceptability by the standards of the existing community, then such an act of imagination is the only recourse.

This means that one will praise movements of liberation not for the accuracy of their diagnoses but for the imagination and courage of their proposals. The difference between pragmatism and positions such as Marxism, which retain the rhetoric of scientism and realism, can be thought of as the difference between radicalism and utopianism. Radicals think that there is a basic mistake being made, a mistake deep down at the roots. They think that deep thinking is required to get down to this deep level and that only there, when all the superstructural appearances have been undercut, can things be seen as they really are. Utopians, however, do not think in terms of mistakes or of depth. They abandon the contrast between superficial appearance and deep reality in favor of the contrast between a painful present and a possibly less painful, dimly seen future. Pragmatists cannot be radicals, in this sense, but they can be utopians. They do not see philosophy as providing instruments for radical surgery or as microscopes that make precise diagnosis possible.[19] Philosophy's function is, rather, to clear the road for prophets and poets, to make intellectual life a bit simpler and safer for those who have visions of new communities.[20]

So far I have taken MacKinnon as my example of a feminist with such a vision. But, of course, she is only one of many. Another is Marilyn Frye, who says, in her powerful book *The Politics of Reality* that "there probably is really no distinction, in the end, between imagination and courage." For, she continues, it takes courage to overcome "a mortal dread of being outside the field of vision of the arrogant eye." This is the eye of a person who prides him- or herself on spotting the rational unacceptability of what is being said—that is, its incoherence with the rest of the beliefs of those who currently control life chances and logical space. So feminists must, Frye goes on to say, "dare to rely on ourselves to make meaning and we have to imagine ourselves capable of . . . weaving the web of meaning which will hold us in some kind of intelligibility" (1983, 80). Such courage is indistinguishable from the imagination it takes to hear oneself as the spokesperson of a merely possible community, rather than as a lonely, and perhaps crazed, outcast from an actual one.

MacKinnon and many other feminists use liberalism as a name for an inability to have this sort of courage and imagination. "In the liberal mind," MacKinnon says, "the worse and more systematic one's mistreatment, the more it seems justified. Liberalism . . . never sees power as power, yet can see as significant only that which power does" (1987, 221; cf. 137). The phenomenon she is pointing to certainly exists, but liberalism seems to me the wrong name for it. So, of course, does pragmatism. I think the main reason—apart from some reflexes left over from early Marxist conditioning—why pejorative uses of the terms *liberal* and *pragmatist* are still common among political radicals is that, if you say, with Putnam, that "truth does not transcend use," you may easily be taken as referring to actual, present use. Again, if you deny that truth is a matter of correspondence to reality, you may easily be taken as holding that a true belief is one that coheres with what most people currently believe. If you think that emancipatory moral or social thought requires penetrating to a presently unglimpsed reality beneath the current appearances, and find pragmatists telling you that there is no such reality, you may easily conclude that a pragmatist cannot help the cause of emancipation.

When, however, we remember that John Dewey—a paradigmatic liberal as well as a paradigmatic pragmatist—spent a great deal of time celebrating the sort of courage and imagination Frye describes, we may be willing to grant that the relation between pragmatism and emancipation is more complex. Dewey said remarkably little about the situation of women, but one of the few things he did say is worth quoting:

> Women have as yet made little contribution to philosophy, but when women who are not mere students of other persons' philosophy set out to write it, we cannot conceive that it will be the same in viewpoint or tenor as that composed from the standpoint of the different masculine experience of things. Institutions, customs of life, breed certain systematized predilections and aversions. The wise man reads historic philosophies to detect in them intellectual formulations of men's habitual purposes and cultivated wants, not to gain insight into the ultimate nature of things or information about the make-up of reality. As far as what is loosely called reality figures in philosophies, we may be sure that it signifies those selected aspects of the world which are chosen because they lend themselves to the support of men's judgment of the worth-while life, and hence are most highly prized. In philosophy, "reality" is a term of value or choice. (1983, 11: 145)

Suppose we think, as feminists often do, of "men's habitual purposes and cultivated wants" as "the habitual purposes and cultivated wants of the males, the half of the species which long ago enslaved the other half." This permits us to read Dewey as saying: if you find that you are a slave, do not accept your masters' descriptions of the real; do not work within the boundaries of their moral universe; instead, try to invent a reality of your own by selecting aspects of the world which lend themselves to the support of *your* judgment of the worthwhile life.[21]

Dewey's doctrine of the means-end continuum might have led him to add: do not expect to know what sort of life is worthwhile right off the bat, for that is one of the things you will constantly change your mind about in the process of selecting a reality. You can neither pick your goals on the basis of a clear and explicit claim about the nature of moral reality nor derive such a claim from clear and explicit goals. There is no method or procedure to be followed except courageous and imaginative experimentation. Dewey would, I think, have been quick to see the point of Frye's description of her own writing as "a sort of flirtation with meaninglessness—dancing about a region of cognitive gaps and negative semantic spaces, kept aloft only by the rhythm and momentum of my own motion, trying to plumb abysses which are generally agreed not to exist" (1983, 154). For meaninglessness is exactly what you have to flirt with when you are in between social and, in particular, linguistic practices—unwilling to take part in an old one but not yet having succeeded in creating a new one.

The import of Dewey's pragmatism for movements such as feminism can be seen if we paraphrase Dewey as follows: do not charge a current social practice or a currently spoken language with being unfaithful to reality, with getting things wrong. Do not criticize it as a result of ideology or prejudice, where these are tacitly contrasted with your own employment of a truth-tracking faculty called reason or a neutral method called disinterested observation. Do not even criticize it as "unjust" if *unjust* is supposed to mean more than "sometimes incoherent even on its own terms." Instead of appealing from the transitory current appearances to the permanent reality, appeal to a still only dimly imagined future practice. Drop the appeal to neutral criteria and the claim that something large like Nature or Reason or History or the Moral Law is on the side of the oppressed. Instead, just make invidious comparisons between the actual present and a possible, if inchoate, future.[22]

So much for the relations between pragmatism and political radicalism. I have been arguing that the two are compatible and mutually supporting. This is because pragmatism allows for the possibility of expanding logical space, and thereby for an appeal to courage and imagination rather than to putatively neutral criteria. What pragmatism loses when it gives up the claim to have right or reality on its side it gains in ability to acknowledge the presence of what Frye calls "abysses which are generally agreed not to exist." These are situations that give the universalist and the realist trouble, ones in which plenty of assent-commanding descriptions are available but such that none of these descriptions do what is needed.

I turn now to the paradox I noted earlier: the suggestion that women are only now coming into existence, rather than having been deprived of the ability to express what was deep within them all the time. I take MacKinnon's evocation of a "role that women have yet to make" as a way of suggesting that women are only now beginning to put together a moral identity *as* women. To find one's moral identity in being an *X* means being able to do the following sort of thing: make your *X*-ness salient in your justification of important uncoerced choices, make your *X*-ness an important part of the story you tell yourself when you need to recover your self-confidence, make your relations with other *X*'s central to your claim to be a responsible person. These are all things men have usually been able to do by reminding themselves that they are, come what may, *men*. They are things that men have made it hard for women to do by reminding themselves that they are women. As Frye puts it, men have assigned themselves the status of "full persons"—people who enjoy what she calls "unqualified participation in the radical 'superiority' of the species"—and withheld this status from women (1983, 48–49). The result of men constantly, fervently, and publicly thanking God that they are *not* women is that it is hard for women to thank God that they are. For a woman to say that she finds her moral identity in being a woman would have sounded, until relatively recently, as weird as for a slave to say that he or she finds his or her moral identity in being a slave.

Most feminists might agree that it was only with the beginnings of the feminist movement that it began to become possible for women to find their moral identities in being women.[23] But most feminists are probably still realist and universalist enough to insist that there is a difference between the claim that one cannot find one's moral identity in being an *X* and the claim that an *X* is not yet a full-fledged person, a person to whom injustice has been done by forbidding her to find her moral identity in her *X*-hood. For the great advantage of realism and universalism over pragmatism is that it permits one to say that women were everything they are now and, *therefore*, were entitled to everything they are now trying to get—even when they did not know, and might even have explicitly denied, that they were entitled to it.

For us pragmatists, however, it is not so easy to say that. For we see personhood as a matter of degree, not as an all-or-nothing affair, something evenly distributed around the species. We see it as something that slaves typically have less of than their masters. This is not because there are such things as "natural slaves" but because of the masters' control over the language spoken by the slaves—their ability to make the slave think of his or her pain as fated and even somehow deserved, something to be borne rather than resisted. We cannot countenance the notion of a deep reality that reposes unrecognized beneath the superficial appearances. So, we have to take seriously the idea, made familiar by such writers as Charles Taylor, that interpretation goes all the way down: that what a human being is, for moral purposes, is largely a matter of how he or she describes himself or herself. We have to take seriously the idea that what you experience yourself to be is largely a function of what it makes sense to describe yourself as in the languages you are able to use. We have to say that the Deltas and Epsilons of Aldous Huxley's *Brave New World* and the proles of George Orwell's *1984* were persons only in the sense in which fertilized human ova or human infants are persons —in the sense, namely, that they are capable of being made into persons. So we pragmatists have to identify most of the wrongness of past male oppression with its suppression of past potentiality, rather than its injustice to past actuality.

In order to say that women are only now in the process of achieving a moral identity as women, I do not need to deny that some women have, in every epoch, had doubts about, and offered alternatives to, the standard, androcentric, descriptions of women. All I need to deny is that women have been able to *forget* the latter descriptions—the ones that make them seem incapable of being full persons. I am denying that women in previous epochs have been able to avoid being torn, split, between the men's description of them and whatever alternative descriptions they have given to themselves. As an example of the sort of thing I have in mind—of the need to name, and thus to begin to bridge, what Frye calls "abysses generally agreed not to exist"—consider Adrienne Rich's description of her situation when young. She was, she says, "split between the girl who wrote poems, who defined herself as writing poems, and the girl who was to define herself by her relationships with men" (1979, 40). I want to interpret Rich's individual situation as an allegory of the more general situation in which women found themselves before feminism achieved lift-off—of their inability to stop defining themselves in terms of their relationships with men. To envisage this inability, consider how Rich's situation differed from that of a young man in a similar situation.

Since Byron and Goethe men have thought of writing poems as one of the best ways to create an autonomous self, to avoid having to define oneself in the terms used by one's parents, teachers, employers, and rulers. Since 1820, or thereabouts, a young man has had the option of defining himself as a poet, of finding his moral identity in writing verse. But, Rich tells us, this is not easy for a young woman.

What is the difficulty? It is not that there is any dearth of true descriptions that Rich might have applied to herself. There were no well-formed—that is, generally intelligible—questions to which Rich could not have given true, well-formed answers. But, nevertheless, there was, she tells us, a split. The various true descriptions that she applied did not fit together into a whole. But, she is implicitly suggesting, a young male poet's descriptions would have fit together easily. Rich was, in her youth, unable to attain the kind of coherence, the kind of integrity, which we think of as characteristic of full persons. For persons who are capable of the full glory of humanity are capable of seeing themselves steadily and whole. Rather than feel that splits are tearing them apart, they can see tensions between their alternative self-descriptions as, at worst, necessary elements in a harmonious variety-in-unity.

Rich's account of herself as being split rings true, for, as she shows in her essay on Emily Dickinson and elsewhere, the language games men have arranged that young women should play forces them to treat the men in their lives (or the absence of men in their lives) as the independent variable and everything else—even their poems—as dependent variables. So insofar as Rich could not tie her poems in with her relationships with men, she had a problem. She was split. She could not be, so to speak, a full-time poet, because a language she could not forget did not let one be both a full-time poet and a full-time female. By contrast, since Byron the language has let one be a full-time poet and a full-time hero (just as since Socrates it has been possible to be a full-time intellectual and a full-time hero).

What might solve Rich's problem? Well, perhaps nowadays it is a little easier for a young woman to define herself by and in her poems than when Rich was young—simply because she may have read books by Rich, Frye, and others. But only a little easier. What would make it *really* easy? Only, I would suggest, the sort of circumstances which made it easy for a young man in the generation after Byron to make his poetic activity the independent variable in the story he told himself about himself. In the previous generation there had been what now looks to us like a band of brothers—Hölderlin and Keats, Byron and Goethe, Shelley and Chamisso. Bliss was it in that dawn to be alive, and to be a young male with poetic gifts was to be able to describe oneself in heroic terms, terms that one could not have used earlier without sounding crazy. That band of brothers founded an invisible club, a very good club, one that is still giving new members a warm welcome.[24] Thus, young male poets do not face abysses when they attempt self-definition. But, as Rich points out, Emily Dickinson was not allowed into that club.[25] So, to make things *really* easy for future Dickinsons and Riches, there would have to be a good, well-established club that they could join.

Here, I take it, is where feminist separatism comes in. Rich asks that we understand lesbian/feminism in the deepest, most radical sense: as that love for ourselves and other women, that commitment to the freedom of all of us, which transcends the category of "sexual preference" and the issue of civil rights, to become a politics of *asking women's questions*, demanding a world in which the integrity of all women—not a chosen few—shall be honored and validated in every aspect of culture. (1979, 17)

Someone who tries to fit what Rich is saying into a map drawn on a universalist and realist grid will have trouble locating any space separate from that covered by "the category of 'sexual preference'" or by "the issue of civil rights." For justice, in this universalist view, is a matter of our providing each other with equal advantages. Nothing, in this vision, *could* transcend civil rights and the realization of those rights by institutional change. So, for example, lesbian separatism is likely to be seen simply as an arrangement by which those with a certain sexual preference can escape stigma until such time as the laws have been extended to protect lesbians' rights and the mores have caught up with the laws.

Frye offers a contrasting view of the function of separatism when she writes:

Re the new being and meaning which are being created now by lesbian-feminists, we *do* have semantic authority, and, collectively, can and do define with effect. I think it is only by maintaining our boundaries through controlling concrete access to us that we can enforce on those who are not-us our definitions of ourselves, hence force on them *the fact of our existence* and thence open up the *possibility* of our having semantic authority with them. (1983, 106n)

I take Frye's point to be, in part, that individuals—even individuals of great courage and imagination—cannot achieve semantic authority, *even semantic authority over themselves*, on their own. To get such authority you have to hear your own statements as part of a shared practice. Otherwise, you yourself will never know whether they are more than ravings, never know whether you are a heroine or a maniac. People in search of such authority need to band together and form clubs, exclusive clubs. For, if you want to work out a story about who you are— put together a moral identity—which decreases the importance of your relationships to one set of people and increases the importance of your relationships to another set, the physical absence of the first set of people may be just what you need. So, feminist separatism may indeed, as Rich says, have little to do with sexual preference or with civil rights and a lot to do with making things easier for women of the future to define themselves in terms not presently available. These would be terms that made it easy for "women as women" to have what Dewey calls "habitual purposes and cultivated wants"—purposes and wants that, as Rich says, only a chosen few women have at present.

To sum up: I am suggesting that we see the contemporary feminist movement as playing the same role in intellectual and moral progress as was played by, for example, Plato's academy, the early Christians meeting in the catacombs, the invisible Copernican colleges of the seventeenth century, groups of workingmen gathering to discuss Tom Paine's pamphlets, and lots of other clubs that were formed to try out new ways of speaking and to gather the moral strength to go out and change the world. For groups build their moral strength by achieving increasing semantic authority over their members, thereby increasing the ability of those members to find their moral identities in their membership in such groups.

When a group forms itself in conscious opposition to those who control the life chances of its members, and succeeds in achieving semantic authority over its members, the result may be its ruthless suppression—the sort of thing that happened to the Albigensians and which Margaret Atwood has imagined happening to the feminists. But it may also happen that, as the generations succeed one another, the masters, those in control, gradually find their conceptions of the possibilities open to human beings changing. For example, they may gradually begin to think of the options open to their own children as including membership in the group in question. The new language spoken by the separatist group may gradually get woven into the language taught in the schools.

Insofar as this sort of thing happens, eyes become less arrogant and the members of the group cease to be treated as wayward children or as a bit crazy (the ways in which Emily Dickinson was treated). Instead, they gradually achieve what Frye calls "full personhood" in the eyes of everybody, having first achieved it only in the eyes of members of their own club. They begin to be treated as full-fledged human beings, rather than being seen, like children or the insane, as degenerate cases—as beings entitled to love and protection but not to participation in deliberation on serious matters. For to be a full-fledged person in a given society is a matter of double negation: it is *not* to think of oneself as belonging to a group that powerful people in that society thank God they do *not* belong to.

In our society straight white males of my generation, even earnestly egalitarian straight white males, cannot easily stop themselves from feeling guilty relief that they were not born women or gay or black, any more than they can stop themselves from being glad that they were not born mentally retarded or schizophrenic. This is in part because of a calculation of the obvious socioeconomic disadvantages of being so born, but not entirely. It is also the sort of instinctive and ineffable horror that noble children used to feel at the thought of having been born to non-noble parents, even very rich non-noble parents.[26]

At some future point in the development of our society guilty relief over not having been born a woman may not cross the minds of males, any more than the question "noble or base-born?" now crosses their minds.[27] That would be the point at which both males and females had *forgotten* the traditional androcentric language, just as we have all forgotten about the distinction between base and noble ancestry. But, if this future comes to pass, we pragmatists think, it will not be because the females have been revealed to possess something—namely, full human dignity—which everybody, even they themselves, once mistakenly thought they lacked. It will be because the linguistic and other practices of the common culture have come to incorporate some of the practices characteristic of imaginative and courageous outcasts.

The new language that, with luck, will get woven into the language taught to children will not, however, be the language that the outcasts spoke in the old days, before the formation of separatist groups. For that was infected by the language of the masters. It will be, instead, a language gradually put together in separatist groups in the course of a long series of flirtations with meaninglessness. Had there been no stage of separation, there would have been no subsequent stage of assimilation. No prior antithesis, no new synthesis. No carefully nurtured pride in membership in a group that might not have attained self-consciousness were it not for its oppression, no expansion of the range of possible moral identities, and so no evolution of the species. This is what Hegel called the cunning of reason and what Dewey thought of as the irony of evolution.

Those who take the passages I quote from Dewey seriously will not think of oppressed groups as learning to *recognize* their own full personhood and then gradually, by stripping away veils of prejudice, leading their oppressors to confront reality. For they will not see full personhood as an intrinsic attribute of the oppressed, any more than they see human beings as having a central and inviolable core surrounded by culturally conditioned beliefs and desires, a core for which neither biology nor history can account. To be a pragmatist rather than a realist in one's description of the acquisition of full personhood requires thinking of its acquisition by blacks, gays, and women in the same terms as we think of its acquisition by Galilean scientists and Romantic poets.

We say that the latter groups invented new moral identities for them-selves by getting semantic authority over themselves. As time went by, they succeeded in having the language they had developed become part of the language everybody spoke. Similarly, we have to think of gays, blacks, and women inventing themselves rather than discovering themselves and, thus, of the larger society as coming to terms with something new.

This means taking Frye's phrase "new *being*" literally, and saying that there were very few female full persons around before feminism got started, in the same sense in which there were very few full-fledged Galilean scientists before the seventeenth century. It was, of course, *true* in earlier times that women should not have been oppressed, just as it was *true* before Newton said so that gravitational attraction ac-counted for the movements of the planets.[28] But, despite what Scripture says, truth will not necessarily prevail. "Truth" is not the name of a power that eventually wins through but, rather, is just the nominaliza-tion of an approbative adjective. So, just as a pragmatist in the philoso-phy of science cannot use the truth of Galileo's views as an explanation either of his success at prediction or of his gradually increasing fame, a pragmatist in moral philosophy cannot use the rightness of the feminist cause as an explanation either of its attraction for contemporary women or of its possible future triumph.[29] For such explanations re-quire the notion of a truth-tracking faculty, one that latches onto ante-cedently existing truth makers. Truth is ahistorical, but that is not be-cause truths are made true by ahistorical entities.

Frye's term *new being* may seem even more unnecessarily hyper-bolic than MacKinnon's *new voice*, but we pragmatists can take it at face value, and realists cannot. As I read Frye, the point is that before femi-nism began to gather women together into a kind of club, there were female eccentrics such as Wollstonecraft and de Gouges, but there were not women who existed *as* women, in MacKinnon's sense of *as*. They were eccentric because they failed to fit into roles that men had contrived for them to fill and because there were as yet no other roles. For roles require a community, a web of social expectations and habits that define the role in question. The community may be small, but, like a club as opposed to a convocation, or a new species as opposed to a few atypical mutant members of an old species, it only exists insofar as it is self-sustaining and self-reproducing.[30]

To sum up for the last time: prophetic feminists such as MacKinnon and Frye foresee a new being not only for women but also for society. They foresee a society in which the male-female distinction is no longer of much interest. Feminists who are also pragmatists will not see the formation of such a society as the removal of social constructs and the restoration of the way things were always meant to be. They will see it as the production of a better set of social constructs than the ones presently available and, thus, as the creation of a new and better sort of human being.

Notes

This chapter was originally delivered as the Tanner Lectures on Human Values, University of Michigan, December 7, 1990.

1. See also Carolyn Whitbeck's point that "the category, lesbian, both in the minds of its male inventors and as used in male-dominated culture, is that of a physiological female who is in other respects a stereotypical male" (1990, 220). Compare Marilyn Frye's reference to "that other fine and enduring patriarchal institution, Sex Equality" (1983, 108).

2. Frye remarks that, "for subordination to be permanent and cost effective, it is necessary to create conditions such that the subordinated group acquiesces to some extent in the subordination" (1983, 33). Ideally, these will be conditions such that a member of the subordinate group who does not acquiesce will sound crazy. Later, Frye suggests that a person's sounding crazy is a good indicator that you are oppressing that person (112). See also MacKinnon: "Especially when you are a part of a subordinated group, your own definition of your injuries is powerfully shaped by your assessment of whether you could get anyone to do anything about it, including anything official" (1987, 105). Example given, a noncrazy claim to have been raped is one acceptable to those (usually males) in a position to offer support or reprisal. Only where there is a socially accepted remedy can there have been a real (rather than crazily imagined) injury.

3. When Olympe de Gouges appealed in the name of women to the Declaration of the Rights of Men and Citizens, even the most revolution-minded of her male contemporaries thought she was crazy. When Canadian feminists argued, in the 1920s, that the word *persons* in an act specifying the conditions for being a senator covered women as well as men, the Supreme Court of Canada decided that the word should not be so construed, because it never had been. (The Judicial Committee of the Privy Council, be it said, later ruled in the feminists' favor.)

4. Hurley is here offering the implications of Wittgenstein's views, rather than stating her own.

5. In a recent article on Rawls, Susan Moller Okin points out that thinking in Rawls's original position is not a matter of thinking like a "disembodied nobody" but, rather, of thinking like lots of different people in turn—thinking from the point of view of "every 'concrete other' whom one might turn out to be" (1989, 248). Hurley makes the same point (1989, 381). The historicity of justice, a historicity that Rawls has acknowledged in his papers of the 1980s,

amounts to the fact that history keeps producing new sorts of "concrete others" whom one might turn out to be.

6. See the theme of "woman as partial man" in Whitbeck (1986, 34–50). This theme is developed in fascinating detail in Laqueur (1990).

7. Michael Gross and Mary Beth Averill suggest that the term *struggle* is a specifically masculist way of describing evolution and ask, "Why not see nature as bounteous, rather than parsimonious, and admit that opportunity and coop-eration are more likely to abet novelty, innovation and creation than are strug-gle and competition?" (1983, 85). The question gives me pause, and I have no clear answer to it. All I have is the hunch that, with memes as with genes, toler-ant pluralism will sooner or later, in the absence of interstellar travel, have to come to terms with shortage of space for self-expression. There is a more gen-eral point involved here, the one raised by Jo-Ann Pilardi's claim that Hegel, Freud, and others "were burdened with a notion of identity which defines it as oppositional, one which was derived from the psychosocial development of male children" (1990, 12). Just such a notion of identity is central to my claims in this chapter, and particularly to the claims about the possible benefits of fem-inist separatism I make later. So I am employing what many feminist writers would consider specifically male assumptions. All I can say in reply is that the notion of identity as oppositional seems to me hard to eliminate from such books as Frye's *Politics of Reality*, and especially from her discussion of femi-nist anger. Anger and opposition seem to me the root of most moral prophecy, and it is the prophetic aspect of feminism which I am emphasizing here.

8. "Goodness is not remoteness from badness. In one sense, goodness is based upon badness; that is, good action is always based upon action good once, but bad if persisted in under changing circumstances" (Dewey 1969, 3: 379).

9. Suppose we define a moral abomination, with Jeffrey Stout, as something that goes against our sense of "the seams of our moral universe," one that crosses the lines between, as he puts it, "the categories of our cosmology and our social structure" (1988, 159). Then the choice between a realist and a prag-matist rhetoric is the choice between saying that moral progress gradually aligns these seams with the *real* seams and saying that it is a matter of simul-taneously reweaving and enlarging a fabric that is not intended to be congruent with an antecedent reality. Giving an example of such a seam, Stout says, "The sharper the line between masculine and feminine roles and the greater the im-portance of that line in determining matters such as the division of labor and the rules of inheritance, the more likely it is that sodomy will be abominated" (153). Later he says, "The question is not whether homosexuality is intrin-sically abominable but rather what, all things considered, we should do with the relevant categories of our cosmology and social structure" (158). As with the abominableness of homosexual sodomy, so, we pragmatists think, with the abominableness of the absence or presence of patriarchy. In all such cases, up to and including the abominableness of torturing people for the sheer pleasure of watching them writhe, pragmatists think that the question is not about intrinsic properties but about what we should do with the relevant categories—a ques-tion that boils down to what descriptions we should use of what is going on.

10. For a somewhat more tempered account of the relation of postmodernism to feminism, see Soper (1990). In their "Social Criticism without Philosophy: An Encounter between Feminism and Postmodernism," Nancy Fraser and Linda Nicholson argue that "a robust postmodern-feminist paradigm of social criticism without philosophy is possible" (1988, 100). I, of course, agree, but I am less sure about the need for, and utility of, "social-theoretical analysis of large-scale inequalities" (90) than are Fraser and Nicholson. This is because I am less sure than Fraser about the possibility that "the basic institutional framework of [our] society could be unjust" (Fraser 1990, 318) and, hence, about "the utility of a theory that could specify links among apparently discrete social problems via the basic institutional structure" (319). I suspect my differences with Fraser are concrete and political, rather than abstract and philosophical. She sees, and I do not see, attractive alternatives (more or less Marxist in shape) to such institutions as private ownership of the means of production and constitutional democracy, attractive alternatives to the traditional social-democratic project of constructing an egalitarian welfare state within the context of these two basic institutions. I am not sure whether our differences are due to Fraser's antifoundationalist theory hope (see n. 12) or to my own lack of imagination.

11. See Lovibond's reference to "remaking society along rational, egalitarian lines." (12). The idea that egalitarianism is more rational than elitism, rational in a sense that provides reasons for action *not* based on contingent shared practices, is central to the thinking of most liberals who are also moral realists.

12. A rhetoric of "unmasking hegemony" presupposes the reality-appearance distinction that opponents of phallogocentrism claim to have set aside. Many self-consciously "postmodern" writers seem to me to be trying to have it both ways—to view masks as going all the way down while still making invidious comparisons between other people's masks and the way things will look when all the masks have been stripped off. These postmodernists continue to indulge the bad habits characteristic of those Marxists who insist that morality is a matter of class interest and then add that everybody has a moral obligation to identify with the interests of a particular class. Just as *ideology* came to mean little more than "other people's ideas," so *product of hegemonic discourse* has come to mean little more than "product of other people's way of talking." I agree with Stanley Fish that much of what goes under the heading of "postmodernism" exemplifies internally inconsistent "antifoundationalist theory hope." See Fish (1989, 346, 437–38).

13. I am not fond of the term *postmodernism* and was a bit startled (as presumably was MacIntyre) to find Lovibond saying that Jean-François Lyotard, Alasdair MacIntyre, and I are "among the most forceful exponents of the arguments and values which constitute postmodernism within academic philosophy" (1989, 5). Still, I recognize the similarities among our positions that lead Lovibond to group the three of us together. Some of these similarities are outlined by Fraser and Nicholson (1988, 85ff.).

14. See also pp. 50, 54, for the "postmodernist" suggestion that the quest for objectivity is a specifically masculist one.

15. We pragmatists are often told that we reduce moral disagreement to a

mere struggle for power by denying the existence of reason, or human nature, conceived as something that provides a neutral court of appeal. We often rejoin that the need for such a court, the need for something ahistorical that will ratify one's claims, is itself a symptom of power worship—of the conviction that unless something large and powerful is on one's side, one shouldn't bother trying.

16. Were more time and space available, I should argue that trying to integrate feminism into a general theory of oppression—a frequent reaction to the charge that feminists are oblivious to racial and economic injustice—is like trying to integrate Galilean physics into a general theory of scientific error. The latter attempt is as familiar as it is fruitless. The conviction that there is an interesting general theory about human beings or their oppression seems to me like the conviction that there is an interesting general theory about truth and our failure to achieve it. For the same reasons that transcendental terms such as *true* and *good* are not susceptible of definition, neither error nor oppression has a single neck that a single critical slash might sever. Maria Lugones is an example of a feminist theorist who sees a need for a general philosophical theory of oppression and liberation; she says, for example, that "the ontological or metaphysical possibility of liberation remains to be argued, explained, uncovered" (1990, 502). I should prefer to stick to merely empirical possibilities of liberation. Although I entirely agree with Lugones about the need to "give up the unified self" (503), I do not see this as a matter of ontology but merely as a way of putting the familiar point that the same human being can contain different coherent sets of belief and desire—different roles, different personalities, and so forth—correlated with the different groups to which he or she belongs or whose power he or she must acknowledge. A more important disagreement between us, perhaps, concerns the desirability of harmonizing one's various roles, self-images, etc., in a single unifying story about oneself. Such unification, the sort of thing that I describe below as overcoming splits, seems to me desirable. Lugones, on the other hand, urges the desirability of "experiencing onself in the limen" (506).

17. For a good example, see Culler (1988):

> The humanities must make their way between, on the one hand, a traditional, foundationalist conception of their task and, on the other, the socalled "new pragmatism" to which some critics of foundationalism have retreated. If philosophy is not a foundationalist discipline, argues Richard Rorty, then it is simply engaged in a conversation; it tells stories, which succeed simply by their success. Since there is no standard or reference point outside the system of one's beliefs to appeal to, critical arguments and theoretical reflections can have no purchase on these beliefs or the practices informed by them. Ironically, then, the claim that philosophers and theoreticians tell stories, which originates as a critique of ideology, . . . becomes a way of protecting a dominant ideology and its professionally successful practitioners from the scrutiny of argument, by deeming that critique can have no leverage against ordinary beliefs, and that theoretical arguments have no consequences. This pragmatism, whose complacency

seems altogether appropriate to the Age of Reagan, subsists only by a theoretical argument of the kind it in principle opposes, as an ahistorical "pre-
formism": what one does must be based on one's beliefs, but since there
are no foundations outside the system of one's beliefs, the only thing that
could logically make one change a belief is something one already believes. (55)

Culler is right in saying that we pragmatists hold the latter view, but wrong in
suggesting that we think that logical changes in belief are the only respectable
ones. What I have called "creative misuses" of language are causes to change
one's belief, even if not reasons to change them. See the discussion of Davidson
on metaphor in various essays in my book *Objectivity, Relativism, and Truth*
(1991) for more on this cause-reason distinction and for the claim that most
moral and intellectual progress is achieved by non-"logical" changes in belief.
Culler is one of the people I had in mind in n. 11, the people who want to hang
onto the primacy of logic (and thus of "theoretical reflection" and "critique")
while abandoning logocentrism. I do not think this can be done. Culler's charge
can be found in many other authors, example given, Singer (1989): "Rorty . . .
has marginalized the enterprise of philosophy, thereby depriving pragmatism of
any critical bite" (1752). On my view pragmatism bites other philosophies, but
not social problems as such, and so is as useful to fascists such as Mussolini and
conservatives such as Michael Oakeshott as it is to liberals such as Dewey.
Singer thinks that I have "identified reason with the status quo" and defined
"truth as coextensive with the prevailing values in a society" (1763). These
claims are, I think, the result of the same inference as Culler draws in the previous passage. Both Singer and Culler want philosophy to be capable of setting
goals and not to be confined to the merely ancillary role I describe in n.20.

18. See also Robert Brandom's formulation of "phenomenalism about truth"
as the view that "being true is to be understood as being *properly* taken-true
(believed)." Brandom says that what is of most interest about the classical pragmatist stories (C. S. Peirce, William James) is "the dual commitment to a normative account of claiming or believing [Alexander Bain's and Peirce's account of
belief as a rule for action] that does not lean on a supposedly explanatory antecedent notion of truth, and the suggestion that truth can then be understood
phenomenalistically, in terms of features of these independently characterized
takings-true" (1988, 80). Brandom (as well as Davidson and I) would agree
with Putnam that "truth does not transcend use," but I think all three of us
might be puzzled by Putnam's further claim that "whether an epistemic situation is any good or not depends on whether many different statements are true"
(1988, 115). This seems to me like saying that whether a person is wealthy or
not depends on how much money she has.

19. Joseph Singer praises Elizabeth Spelman for "using the tools of philosophy
to promote justice" and suggests that one such use is to show that "the categories and forms of discourse we use . . . have important consequences in chan-
neling our attention in particular directions" (1989). Surely it is no disrespect
to Spelman's achievement, nor to philosophy, to insist that it takes no special

tools, no special philosophical expertise, to make and develop the latter point. The use of notions such as "powerful methods" and "precise analytical instruments" in the rhetorics of analytic philosophy and of Marxism constitutes, to my mind, misleading advertising. An unfortunate result of such mystification is that whenever philosophy professors such as Spelman or I do something useful, it is assumed that they are doing something distinctively philosophical, something philosophers are specially trained to do. If they then fail to go on to do something else that needs to be done, they will usually be charged with using an obsolete and inadequate set of philosophical tools.

20. See Dewey (1984): "Meantime a chief task of those who call themselves philosophers is to help get rid of the useless lumber that blocks our highways of thought, and strive to make straight and open the paths that lead to the future" (5: 160). There is a lot of this road-clearing rhetoric in Dewey, rhetoric that is continuous with John Locke's description of himself as an underlaborer to those who seemed to him the prophetic spirits of his time, corpuscularian scientists such as Newton and Boyle. Both metaphors suggest that the philosophers' job is to drag outdated philosophy out of the way of those who are displaying unusual courage and imagination. Singer says that "Dewey, unlike Rorty, saw the problems of philosophy as inseparable from the problems of collective life" and that, "by separating philosophy from justice, Rorty's vision reinforces existing power relations" (1989, 1759). It is true that Dewey often speaks as if social problems and philosophical problems were interlocked, but I should argue that all these passages can best be interpreted in the road-clearing sense I have just suggested. Dewey never, I think, saw pragmatism in the way in which Marxists saw dialectical materialism—as a philosophical key that unlocks the secrets of history or of society.

21. To use an analogy suggested by Charlotte Perkins Gilman's poem "Similar Cases," it is as if one said to the creatures that were eventually to become the mammals: "Do not try to imitate the ways in which those larger and more powerful fish cope with their environment. Rather, find ways of doing things that will help you find a new environment" (1990, 363–64). The point of the poem is that if it were true that, as feminists were often told, "you can't change your nature," we should have had neither biological nor cultural evolution.

22. As I suggested earlier, it is easy to reconcile Dewey's claim that, in philosophy, *real* is as evaluative a term as *good* with postmodernist views, for example, those found in Weedon (1987). Pretty much the only difference between Weedon's criticism of the philosophical tradition and Dewey's is one that also separates contemporary pragmatists such as Putnam and Davidson from Dewey—the use of *language* instead of Dewey's word *experience* as the name of what it is important for the oppressed to reshape.

Weedon, like Putnam and Davidson and unlike Dewey, is what Wilfrid Sellars called a "psychological nominalist," someone who believes that all awareness is a linguistic affair; she says, "Like Althusserian Marxism, feminist poststructuralism makes the primary assumption that it is language which enables us to think, speak and give meaning to the world around us. Meaning and consciousness do not exist outside language" (1987, 32). The difference with Dewey has few consequences, however, since Dewey would have heartily agreed with Weedon that one should not view language "as a transparent tool for expressing facts" but, rather, as "the material in which particular, often conflicting versions of facts are constructed" (131).

The only real advantage to psychological nominalism for feminists, perhaps, is that it replaces hard-to-discuss (I am tempted to say "metaphysical") questions about whether women have an *experience* different from that of men, or Africans an experience different from that of Europeans, or about whether the experience of upper-class African women is more like that of lower-class European men than that of upper-class European women, with easier-to-discuss (more evidently empirical) questions about what *language* these various groups of people use to justify their actions, exhibit their deepest hopes and fears, and so on. Answers to the latter questions are jumping-off places for practical suggestions about different languages that they might use or might have used. I share MacKinnon's skepticism about the idea that "viewpoints have genitals" and Sandra Harding's skepticism about the utility of notions such as "woman's morality," "woman's experience," and "woman's standpoint." (See Harding [1987].)

Although most of the doctrines (e.g., essentialism, Cartesian individualism, moral universalism) which Weedon attributes to "liberal humanism" are doctrines Dewey, a notorious liberal humanist, also targeted, Weedon does not seem able to eschew a longing for what Mary Hawkesworth calls "a successor science which can refute once and for all the distortions of androcentrism" (1989, 331). But, once you put aside universalism, you should neither hope for knock-down refutations nor talk about "distortion." Hawkesworth goes on to criticize Harding for saying that "feminist analytical categories *should* be unstable at this moment in history" (Harding 1987, 19). But prophecy and unstable categories go together, and Harding's claim chimes with many of the passages I have been quoting from Frye. Harding's further claim that "we [feminists] should learn how to regard the instabilities themselves as valuable resources" is one that Dewey would have cheered.

23. I am too ignorant about the history of feminism—about how long and how continuous the feminist tradition has been—to speculate about when things began to change.

24. The continued attractions of this club in our own cynical century are evidenced by the fact that, even as Bernard Shaw was having Candida make fun of Marchbanks, Joyce had Stephen Dedalus write that he would "forge in the smithy of my soul the uncreated conscience of my race." Joyce was not making fun of Stephen, and even Shaw admitted that Candida "does not know the secret in the poet's heart."

25. "What might, in a male writer—a Thoreau, let us say, or a Christopher Smart or a William Blake—seem a legitimate strangeness, a unique intention, has been in one of our two major poets [Dickinson] devalued into a kind of naïvete, girlish ignorance, feminine lack of professionalism, just as the poet herself has been made into a sentimental object. ('Most of us are half in love with

this dead girl,' confesses Archibald MacLeish. Dickinson was fifty-five when she died.)" (Rich 1979, 167).

26. This is the sort of ineffable horror which creates a sense of moral abomination (at, e.g., intercaste marriage), and thus furnishes the intuitions that one tries to bring into reflective equilibrium with one's principles. To view moral abominableness as capable of being produced or erased by changing the language taught to the young is the first step toward a nonuniversalist conception of moral progress.

27. To realize how far away such a future is, consider Eve Kossofsky Sedgwick's point (an informal comment in a recent lecture) that we shall only do justice to gays when we become as indifferent to whether our children turn out gay or straight as we are to whether they become doctors or lawyers. Surely she is right, and yet how many parents at present can even imagine such indifference? For the reasons suggested by Jeffrey Stout, in *Ethics after Babel*, I suspect that neither sexism nor homophobia can vanish while the other persists.

28. Pragmatists need not deny that true sentences are always true (as I have, unhappily, suggested in the past that they might be—notably in my "*Waren die Gesetze Newtons schon vor Newton wahr?*" [1987]). Stout rightly rebukes me for these suggestions and says that pragmatists should agree with everybody else that the statement "Slavery is absolutely wrong" has always been true, even in periods when this sentence would have sounded crazy to everybody concerned, even the slaves (who hoped that their tribespeople would return in force and enslave their present masters) (1988, chap. 11). All that pragmatists need is the claim that this sentence is not *made* true by something other than the beliefs that we would use to support it—and, in particular, not by something like the Nature of Human Beings.

29. I have criticized realists' claims to explain predictive success by truth in part 1 of my *Objectivity, Relativism, and Truth* (1991). A related point—that the success of a true theory needs just as much historicosociological explanation as the success of a false one—is made by Barry Barnes (1974) and other members of the so-called Edinburgh School of sociology of science.

30. It may seem that the view I am offering is the one that Frye rejects under the name of "the institutional theory of personhood"—the theory that, as she puts it, "'person' denotes a social and institutional role and . . . one may be allowed or forbidden to adopt that role" (1983, 49). She says that this view "must be attractive to the phallist, who would fancy the power to create persons." But I do not want to say that men have the power to make full persons out of women by an act of grace, in the way in which sovereigns have the power to make nobles out of commoners. On the contrary, I would insist that men could not do this if they tried, for they are as much caught as are women in the linguistic practices that make it hard for women to be full persons. The utopia I foresee, in which these practices are simply forgotten, is not one that could be attained by an act of condescension on the part of men, any more than an absolute monarch could produce an egalitarian utopia by simultaneously ennobling all her subjects.

References

al-Hibri, Azizah Y., and Simons, Margaret A., eds. *Hypatia Reborn*. Bloomington: Indiana University Press, 1990.

Barnes, Barry. *Scientific Knowledge and Sociological Theory*. London: Routledge, 1974.

Brandom, Robert. "Pragmatism, Phenomenalism, Truth Talk." *Midwest Studies in Philosophy* 12 (1988).

Culler, Jonathan. *Framing the Sign: Criticism and Its Institutions*. Oklahoma City: University of Oklahoma Press, 1988.

Dewey, John. "Outline of a Critical Theory of Ethics." *The Early Works of John Dewey*, vol. 3. Carbondale: Southern Illinois University Press, 1969.

————. *The Middle Works of John Dewey*. Carbondale: Southern Illinois University Press, 1983.

"Philosophy and Democracy," vol. 11.

Human Nature and Conduct, vol. 14.

————. "From Absolutism to Experimentalism." *The Later Works of John Dewey*, vol. 5. Carbondale: Southern Illinois University Press, 1984.

Fish, Stanley. *Doing What Comes Naturally: Change, Rhetoric, and the Practice of Theory in Literary and Legal Studies*. Durham, N.C.: Duke University Press, 1989.

Fraser, Nancy. "Solidarity or Singularity?" In *Reading Rorty*, edited by Alan Malachowski. Oxford: Blackwell, 1990.

Fraser, Nancy, and Nicholson, Linda. "Social Criticism without Philosophy: An Encounter between Feminism and Postmodernism." In *Universal Abandon?* edited by Andrew Ross. Minneapolis: University of Minnesota Press, 1988.

Frye, Marilyn. *The Politics of Reality*. Trumansburg, N.Y.: Crossing Press, 1983.

Gilman, Charlotte Perkins. "Similar Cases." In *To Herland and Beyond: The Life and Works of Charlotte Perkins Gilman*, by Ann Lane. New York: Pantheon, 1990.

Gross, Michael, and Averill, Mary Beth. "Evolution and Patriarchal Myths." In *Discovering Reality*, edited by Sandra Harding and Merill B. Hintikka. Dordrecht: Reidel, 1983.

Harding, Sandra. "The Instability of the Analytical Categories of Feminist Theory." "The Curious Coincidence of Feminine and African Moralities: Challenges for Feminist Theory." In *Women and Moral Theory*, edited by Eva Kittay and Diana Meyers. Totowa, N.J.: Rowman & Littlefield, 1987.

Hawkesworth, Mary. "Knowers, Knowing, Known: Feminist Theory and the Claims of Truth." In *Feminist Theory in Practice and Process*, edited by Micheline R. Malson et al. Chicago: University of Chicago Press, 1989.

Hurley, Susan. *Natural Reasons*. New York: Oxford University Press, 1989.

Laqueur, Thomas. *Making Sex: Body and Gender from the Greeks to Freud*. Cambridge: Harvard University Press, 1990.

Lovibond, Sabina. "Feminism and Postmodernism." *New Left Review* (Winter 1989).

Lugones, Maria. "Structure/Antistructure and Agency under Oppression." *Journal of Philosophy* 87 (October 1990).

MacKinnon, Catharine. *Feminism Unmodified: Discourses on Life and Law*. Cambridge: Harvard University Press, 1987.

Okin, Susan Moller. "Reason and Feeling in Thinking about Justice." *Ethics* 99 (1989).

Pilardi, Jo-Ann. "On the War Path and Beyond." In al-Hibri and Simons (1990).

Putnam, Hilary. *Representation and Reality*. Cambridge: MIT Press, 1988.

Rich, Adrienne. *On Lies, Secrets, and Silence: Selected Prose, 1966–1978*. New York: Norton, 1979.

Rorty, Richard. "Waren die Gesetze Newtons schon vor Newton Wahr?" *Jahrbuch des Wissenschaftskollegs zu Berlin*. Berlin: Wissenschaftskolleg zu Berlin, 1987.

———. *Objectivity, Relativism, and Truth*. Cambridge: Cambridge University Press, 1991.

Singer, Joseph. "Should Lawyers Care about Philosophy?" *Duke Law Journal* (1989).

Soper, Kate. "Feminism, Humanism, and Postmodernism." *Radical Philosophy* 55 (Summer 1990): 11–17.

Stout, Jeffrey. *Ethics after Babel*. Boston: Beacon Press, 1988.

Weedon, Chris. *Feminist Practice and Poststructuralist Theory*. Oxford: Blackwell, 1987.

Whitbeck, Carolyn. "Theories of Sex Difference." In *Women and Values*, edited by Marilyn Pearsall. Belmont, Calif.: Wadsworth, 1986.

———. "Love, Knowledge, and Transformation." In al-Hibri and Simons (1990).

4   Feminism, Body, Self: Third-Generation Feminism

Wendy Harcourt

> *Having started with the idea of difference, feminism will be able to break free of its belief in Woman, Her power, Her writing, so as to channel this demand for difference into each and every element of the female whole, and, finally, to bring out the singularity of each woman, and beyond this, her multiplicities, her plural languages, beyond the horizon, beyond sight, beyond faith itself.* — Julia Kristeva, "Women's Time"

From Identity to Affinities

The explicitly and politically feminist post-1968 generations have been flirting with psychoanalysis in the transformation from linear, hierarchical, and binary ways of theorizing to problematizing concepts of the feminine, self, gender, and knowledge. We feminist women, constrained to transport the discourse of men and the body of women, are in a special strategic position as new kinds of subjects to think through the potential offered by a major historical, archaeological, epistemological mutation of women and psychoanalysis, entering and disrupting the scene of patriarchal institutions together (Jardine 1990, 77). It is a logical move, since women are the reason for the existence of psychoanalysis, its histories, and its stories: we are its cases.

The common project is the fracturing of our identities, the writing of a new kind of knowledge. Women's history-making move from the private to the public is shaking up the pedagogue in all of us (Jardine 1990, 78). We are rejecting the exclusionary category of woman and recognizing the heterogeneity of the positions and differences among women. A new generation of feminists has taken up the task of emphasizing the multiplicity of female expressions and preoccupations by problematizing the category of woman itself.

What does it mean to be a woman in the newly emerging third generation? Is there a group identity, a specific set of values, which exists outside the various histories and descriptions of woman that are distorted in the histories of culture, in literature, and in the texts of medical and biological science? Does the category of woman maintain a meaning separate from the conditions of oppression? Do we have a subject woman? Or is there another normative point of departure for feminist theory that does not require the reconstruction or rendering visible of a female subject who fails to represent, much less emancipate, the array of embodied beings culturally positioned as women (Butler 1990, 325)?

For Julia Kristeva the category of woman is a political tool: a blank term, a formula for a locus of resistance to symbolization. She rejects the two phases, or two generations, of women, the first wave of egalitarian feminists, which demanded equality with men, and the second generation, which stressed women's radical difference from men. Kristeva sees in this second position a distrust of the entire political dimension. And she invites women instead "to try and understand their sexual and symbolic difference in the framework of social, cultural and professional realization, in order to try . . . to go further and call into question the very apparatus itself" (1986, 198). This feminist subversion is to be brought about by the new generation of women, the third generation, situated on the terrain of the inseparable conjunction of the sexual and the symbolic, in order to try to discover the specificity, first, of the female and, in the end, of each individual woman. The third generation is to attempt a revolt of epochal significance.

> A *third* generation is now forming. . . . [in] this third attitude . . . the very dichotomy man/woman as an opposition between two rival entities may be understood as belonging to *metaphysics*. What can "identity," even "sexual identity," mean in a new theoretical and scientific space where the very notion of identity is challenged? . . . as related to the question of women, I see arising . . . [a] retreat from sexism . . . an *interiorization of the founding separation of the socio-symbolic contract*, as an introduction of its cutting edge into the very interior of every identity whether subjective, sexual, ideological . . . to demystify the identity of the symbolic bond itself, to demystify, therefore, the *community* of language as a universal and unifying tool . . . in order to bring out—along with the *singularity* of each person and, even more, along with the multiplicity of every person's possible identifications—the *relativity of his/her symbolic as well as biological existence*. (209–10)

How do we, who call ourselves *feminist women*, enter the monumental epoch of the third generation? Is the air to remain heavy with our writings? Do we have something new to say? Or are we to be condemned as priestesses/terrorists (fire-eaters) of a W-religion in this epoch of no religion? Do we in our anger and suffering step aside to give birth/voice/space to "avant-garde" feminists? How do we make our move from private to public? From searching for the one to celebrating gender dissonance?

Let me, as a young woman, as a *feminist woman*, share my particular history of the gendered subject. Let me think through the potential of the two projects, feminism and psychoanalysis, in the disruption/mutation of the category woman.

My text is one of the many nonauthoritative voices of women now being heard in the psychoanalytic and feminist projects, which offer the her—and not his—story of their bodies. It looks toward the new feminist/woman/psychoanalytic affinity.

The Hope of the Inward Journey

Kristeva poses a split between psychoanalysis and feminism in her text "Women's Time" (1986). Her distancing from "second generation" feminists and dismissal of the "veritable exploration of the *dynamic of signs*, an exploration which relates this tendency at least at the level of its aspirations, to all major projects of aesthetic and religious upheaval" (194) has attracted critical responses. Why does she not instead seek connections? In this Kristeva has placed herself in a position of "major disagreement" to that held by other feminists. Some go so far as to see Kristeva's political disengagement from feminist struggles as an "anti-feminism" (Grosz 1990, 93). She looks to the avant-garde movement rather than to feminists as spokespersons (spokesmen) for the liberation of the subject, which will restore our repressed femininity and lost maternity. Her division of the masculine/symbolic and feminine/semiotic element within each subject ignores, to the point of annihilation, women's struggles for their sexual specificity and autonomy. Her discrediting of the feminist project is disquieting and offers little for women working in the real world of sexual inequality.

We feminist women in the 1980s and 1990s, in our aim to destabilize norms, expectations, and inequalities, cannot be relegated, as Kristeva attempts, to a politically simplistic movement that aims to make women indistinguishable from men. Feminism in its theory and practice has more to offer than a form of secular humanism or a naive, uncritical acceptance or rejection of patriarchal representations of maternity. The modern feminist project to understand woman as a discursive, constructed identity is based on a critique of subjectivity and sexuality and common assumptions of power, ideology, and representations. The feminist project aims to transform the prevailing models of sexual valuation and women's oppressed social positions. The apparent "block" of feminism "on the horizon of the discursive and scientific adventure" of psychoanalysis (Kristeva, quoted in Grosz 1990, 97) can be resolved by recognizing the similarity of the projects of psychoanalysis and feminism rather than by setting them up as two opposing camps. The practice and theory of psychoanalysis, as Kristeva shows, has important insights to offer on the concepts of sexuality and the unconscious, but so too do feminist theory and practices that aim to move "beyond gender." Kristeva's insights, especially in her critique of the subject Woman, are inspiring, but I propose that we go beyond her disowning of female sexual identity and the need for women's political space and, in a strategic move, expose the connections between her analysis and the feminist project.

My generation (should I equate it with Kristeva's third generation?) grew out of the recognition that despite the sexual revolution of the 1960s and 1970s patriarchy is deeply embedded in women's and men's psyches and social relations. Seeing psychoanalysis as the understanding of gender identity and its relation to desire and power is necessary if we are to influence social change. Feminism has turned to, indeed evolved with, psychoanalytic theory in order to further our knowledge of patriarchy and gender, to understand how our fantasies and social relations interact. Psychoanalytic theory, practice, and methodology constitute an important tool directed toward the investigation and understanding of how we develop and experience ourselves and others. By feminism entering into a dialogue with psychoanalysis, one that has its historical and political context, we broaden and deepen our understanding of patriarchy in our project to change male domination and the masculine defense and to redefine women's relationships to their own bodies, culture, and psyches.

Psychoanalysis and feminism have converged in taking childhood and sexuality as central subjects in the formation of our identity and using the spoken word as a way to explore and heal. The feminist consciousness-raising groups and women's ability to network and to "talk through" problems all mirror the task of analysis. A generation of feminists has come to understand the world through basic psychoanalytic tenets. We work with the existence of the unconscious and the importance of childhood in our adult desires and behaviors. Our shared premises are that gender is a social construct and that women would benefit if men feared them less and if culture regarded women as more than mothers or sexual partners. We are comfortable with the ideas that psychoanalysis changes individuals and that feminists can bring about

broader social transformations with the knowledge these changes produce (see Gardiner 1992, 440–41). Our feminism embraces psychoanalysis as a means of comprehending the unconscious structure of
patriarchy, while seeing feminist practice as the means for providing a
strategy for change.

Despite the rhetoric of opposition, psychoanalysis is basically addressing the same issues as feminism: the respective role of mothers
and fathers, redefining gender identity and the relation to the body, the
construction of gender identity, the relation between biological and
cultural facts. In this chapter I wish to take up some of the most important aspects of this joint project: to undo the definition of women with
the body and to recognize the (m)other in ourselves in our search to
find a more political definition of the female body. I do this not from an
authoritative position as the possessor of truth but, rather, as part of the
radical questioning of subject-object relations that explores the fragmented identity of gender in the late twentieth century—a time that
has no place for polarized gender. My text sets out to explore the
boundaries between the psychoanalytical and the social, the psychoanalytical and the medical, in order to deepen our political understanding
of human embodiment.

As a third-generation feminist / feminist woman, I look in this text at
the concept of self and body in order to tell my story of a female gendered identity in relation to the real of biological reproduction. I explore the constitution of the anatomical body in shaping the current
conditions of femininity by exploring how biological givens are orga-
nized by complex unconscious forces that contribute to our current
gender relations. In doing so, I embrace the psychoanalytical gift to feminism: that of acknowledging self-discovery, of the hope of the inward
journey, of the freedom to explore one's inner space, where one's own
desire can emerge.

My text begins with the question: What difference does it make
in the constitution of my social experience that I have a specifically female body? What are my personal histories, identities, and desires in the
answering of this question? How do I bring the private to the public?
From where can such a question be posed? What are the grounds of its
possibility?

My story of the inner journey of self, of body, of my desire for understanding and knowledge/power of identity, begins with three scenarios
in which I am situated as both the subject and object of the text. My
scenarios offer a history of a third-generation feminist. They chart a
voyage for self-identity and map out the deconstruction of the concept
of the female body. They belong to my search for a politics that de-

mands that I move beyond embodiment, beyond the polarization of gender, to gender dissonance. My project is not a psychoanalytic one, but my scenarios illustrate how psychoanalytic concepts and assumptions inform and are demanded by my third-generation feminist gaze.

Scenario 1: Giving Voice to Body, Self

Scenario 1 is a story from my childhood: the struggle with my early consciousness of sexual difference as I discovered the meaning of transporting a female body in the post-Freudian age and the struggle to find identity as a feminist.

I grew up in the shadow of the household Freud. The *oedipal complex* was a childhood term. My feminist mother (then training as a therapist) was careful to protect me from the unkindness of the Freudian denial. While we watched my little brother pee, she assured me that we women did not need such an appendage, so vulnerable, so uncontrollable in its liability to growth and shrinkage. But despite such reassurances and encouragement from both parents, I could only but note the awkwardness of having a female body. In my liberal family the penis was the subject of many jokes, but we retained an anxious, reverent silence toward any part of the female anatomy. My father's jockstraps were displayed, but my mother's intimate clothes and menstrual pads were secreted in cupboards, hidden below the ironed sheets. Despite our frank discussions about my approaching maturity, unbidden, I hid the fact of my menstruation from my father and brothers. And it was many years after I began an active sexual life that I discovered that sexual intercourse was not the only route to pleasure.

Feminism was also part of my early family history. As an Australian, I was aware that the publication of *The Female Eunuch* (1970), by Germaine Greer, marked the beginning of a public discourse on feminism. I was duly presented with the book by my mother, though she covered it with brown paper, to hide the disturbing cover of a headless, limbless, female torso hanging Dali-like from a rod, before I was allowed to take it to school. I celebrated, at the age of eleven, the coming of my equality with men with the bidding of Germaine Greer to taste my as yet unshed menstrual blood. But despite such calls for liberation, my female body seemed tangibly in the way of entering the male world. I wanted to live my mother's desire, which became my desire, to defy the prominence of the penis and any envy I might have and enter into the male world regardless. I embraced feminism as the tool with which I could change the world and unseat the dominance of men and their penises and the denial of female equality. But the unstated—the mysteries of why it was that because I had a female body I was an outsider, "not to be"—remained unspoken, unanswered. From my childhood the dominance of men and the invisibility of the female body, my body, were intertwined, and that mystery demanded to be untangled, challenged, and understood.

The need to do this was underlined at the onset of menstruation, which suddenly displaced the authority of my mother and father over my bodily aches and pains to that of the doctor, reducing my mother to confidante and banishing my father completely from my bodily experiences. Menstruation, the signal to the world of my maturity, restricted me to the female, "not male" world. And in this world the silent monthly "illness" that marked my femininity was not a thing to joke about but to hide and to be tended by experts.

Choices in my life did not lie with my own desires but were determined by my having a female body. I could not escape the physical reality of my sex, nor escape the authority of others.

Scenario 2: The Search for Power/Knowledge

My second scenario relates how, through feminist theory and history, I sought to understand the ways in which the female body was constituted by social and cultural gender relations and how I sought to deconstruct the links between femininity, illness, and medical authority.

I chose history and feminist theory as a way to explain how I was constituted as an embodied being, socially positioned as "woman"—as a way to explain the lack in my constructed subjective identity. My doctoral dissertation explored the problematic of a gendered body, the link between sex and gender, body and feminine identity, through a deconstruction of the language and practice of medical discourse in the nineteenth century as one of the most powerful discursive practices in the location and articulation of female identity. My desire was to reclaim the female body from "his-story" and to make it "her-story" (my story).

My her(his) stories moved my private search for self to the public. As a feminist writer, I had to defy disciplinary boundaries, to find a language in which I could explore the gendered subject and to break the positivist mold of writing history. In my research I blurred the distinction between the literary and the historical, between the public and private, between theory and politics, between authoritative and marginal knowledge, between fact and text. In my history/her(my)story I sought to challenge medical knowledge/power by disrupting the natural and closed concept of the female body. I chose nineteenth-century medical texts as the historical point at which medical discourse entered the private/public domain of female reproductivity and embodiment.

My dissertation looked at the constitution of the female body in nineteenth-century gynecological and obstetrical discourse. My reading of the gendering of the female body in nineteenth-century medical discourse brought out the particular and multiple meanings of woman embedded in the cultural and historical perception of gender. The theoretical disruption of the unity of the category woman was affected through the interpretation of the female body as a physiological image that contained different philosophical and social meanings of woman. The female body was not an object of truth but, rather, a shifting concept constituted through a specific set of historical and social meanings.

Although the physiological concept of the female body appeared as a natural fact in medical texts, removed from the political and social domain, it held important political implications. The nineteenth-century female medical subject was categorized as having a general individuality based on her physiology, a categorization that collapsed women's individual rights to natural reproductive social duties.

My reading of medical texts sought to deconstruct the notion of women as a transcultural and transhistorical concept by specifying the historically specific characteristics of the female body in nineteenth-century medical discourse. My thesis disrupted a series of assumptions about the medical female body in order to reclaim the individuality of the modern female subject and to challenge the privileging of the natural or the scientific, real and observable world, which gave a dominance to the medical understanding of women over other discourses. In disrupting the notion of the eternal feminine, the natural woman as "the other" in the clinical domain, I explored how medical discourse had no more access to the truth of the female body than other discourses; the concept of the natural body is just as much part of cultural and social perceptions as other meanings of woman.

I also sought to disrupt the concept of the universality of the female body as the reproductive body by showing the historical context of this concept in the nineteenth-century debates on the evolution of the race, the general quest for national efficiency, feminist campaigns, and debates on women's health and social purity.

Metaphor, Gender, Embodiment

My findings were that in nineteenth-century social discourse "woman" was situated as a powerful metaphor that produced a complex set of meanings about femininity in relation to both individuality and the social body. The concept of body operated at these two levels: the physiological identity of the individual body and the metaphor of the social body as the management, measurement, and nurturing of the population.[1] Society was envisaged as a body so that the physical structure of the individual body was linked metaphorically to this "social body."

The meanings that woman signified in nineteenth-century discourse were woman as mother; woman as moral; woman as passive; woman as species being; woman as social body; woman as "the sex";[2] and woman as reproductive economy. These metaphors of woman were contained in the representations of the female body in medical discourse. The major themes signifying femaleness in the nineteenth century were that women's sexuality and identity resided in the uterus; the reproductive function was the meaning, essence, and health of woman and constituted the physiological, anthropological, and social difference between men and women.

Woman as reproducer and as disorder informed the representation of the individual female body as a medical subject. Reproductivity indicated a general level of ill health in women. Women were seen as both defined by and continually weakened by the event of reproductivity. Obversely, the body also became ill if the reproductive potential was not fulfilled and failed to menstruate or to become pregnant. The reproductive periodicity to which women were continually subject also signaled a complexity that marked the female body as different and more liable to disorder. Women were presented as suffering more from diseases such as cancer, a general invalidism and displacement of the internal organs. The female body was read as a visible sign of women's difference, otherness, and abnormality in being not-male.

Integral to the descriptions of the female body as an individual medical subject was the notion of sexuality. Women's desire was equated with maternity as the "natural outlet of her energy and affection" (Harcourt 1987, 92). Women's generative organs were not defined as the seat of women's sensual pleasures but, rather, as the site of sexual difference, the "hallowed receptacle of intercourse" (123). Women's sexuality was represented by the maturity of the reproductive organs so that utility, rather than female pleasure, was emphasized. This was a passive utility; the female body was part of the passive natural order that strived instinctively to reproduce. According to the nineteenth-century medical view, women sought sexual activity not for sensual pleasure but in order to maintain health. As the representation of instinctive propagation, the female body was depicted as the essence of sexuality, the prototypical sexual organism. Women's reproductivity brought her closer to the essential workings of the natural world so that the female body became the sign of functioning human sexuality. The representation of the individual female body's sexuality signified woman as the reproductive, docile, and maternal body. As the representation of the mother, she was also the sex and desired for her reproductive utility.

This concept of the maternal body was important in terms of male fears of the other. Women's sexuality was rendered passive, and women were categorized as all the same and therefore not individually threatening. The nineteenth-century metaphor of "woman as womb" did not signify the sexual mother but women's reproductive role in the natural order, an order that had been scientifically "conquered." Women's potential sexuality/power was rendered a socially useful function that could be medically managed and therefore brought into the sphere of male understanding. The sexual activity of women's social reproductivity (where women's sexual role was seen as the reproduction of the species) was also the point at which the social body could be managed. The richest area of metaphor in the medical texts was the representation of the female body as the social body, in which the female body was seen as the base of generative social progress.

In the nineteenth century the reproductive female body was a powerful sign of human progress and order. It represented the disordering properties of civilized existence and the dangers of race suicide. Women's body paid nature's price for the degenerating activity of civilized living. Women were a metaphor for evolutionary progress, of the progress of civilization, but also of the strain of civilized living, which worked against women's reproductive existence. The female body carried within it the key to social stability, the thwarted potential of the instinctive laws of nature. In this series of representations the female body was a metaphor for the essential feminine, conceptualized as fundamentally closer to the natural order, with a history that could be traced back to biblical, classical, evolutionary, and legal discourses.

In nineteenth-century medical discourse reproduction was a complex series of meanings that appeared to be naturalized in the physiology of the female body and in women's "natural" role as reproducer of the race. The notion of woman as the other and as essentially different from man was translated in the medical gaze as an essential disorder of the female body. Women's physiology was seen as more complicated than the male physiology. The greater social significance of women's reproductive role gave the reproductive function more centrality in the female physiology than in the male body. In the medical gaze this essential female disorder, difference, complexity, and social significance was seen as residing in the reproductive organs—in particular, the uterus, as the central point of physiological difference. In this representation of female physiology reproduction bore the symbolic weight of nineteenth-century meanings of woman as both the identity of the individual woman and as the symbol of the social body. The medical gaze naturalized these social and cultural meanings in the interpretation of the female body as a disordered physiology. To be a healthy female, to have a uterus, to bleed monthly, to reproduce, was simultaneously to signify disorder, a closeness to the natural order, maternity, and the growth of the species.

The explicit denial of women's sexual desire in the description of reproduction was important in the constitution of women's modern individuality and in the utilizing of the female body for social reproduction. In nineteenth-century medical discourse women's sexuality was constituted as reproduction. The medical gaze separated out sexuality from reproduction in such a way as to constitute women's sexuality as a potential power that could not find sexual expression precisely because women were not male. True sexuality was denied and yet invested in the female body as the source of feminine identity because of that denial. It defined the modern female body's true sexual expression safely within the clinical gaze. Women's reproductivity was defined by her physiology, and gynecology and obstetrics, as the science of women's physical space, managed women's potential sexuality and utilized it for social reproduction. The saturation of the female body with sexuality positioned woman as a reproductive being enmeshed in a network of power that rendered the reproductive body best interpreted by the clinical domain. The common reference to women as the sex indicates how closely women were identified with their reproductivity and physical being. Notions of woman as the other, as the sex, as reproductive, were naturalized in the medical gaze, which at once defined women's power and identity as reproductive and simultaneously desired this power in order to maintain the reproduction of the social body.

The relevance of this history to the current feminist project is that to argue for the liberation of women's reproductive potential as the essential political and sexual freedom of women would be to adopt the same medical and social framework that the feminist project seeks to challenge. By placing the concept of the female body in its historical context, we can disrupt the apparently natural or closed concept of the female body; that is, we can show how the reproductive body is not the essential representation of femaleness. Rather, the female body is a historically and culturally specific concept that enmeshes women in a set of historically bound contradictions and social relations.

Feminists need to open out the concept of the female body to other interpretations. This does not mean that we replace medical interpretations of the female body by liberationist ones—positive assertions about women's reproductivity rather than repressive ones—or that we must create a new feminist language based on the experiences of living within the female body which "the (m)other speaks." In relation to the power/knowledge of the female body, medical and social practices need to evolve that produce different identities for women identities that do not reduce the complexities of gender relations and women's individuality to reproduction as the essence of female expression in modern society. The female body is enmeshed in a series of relationships, one of which is as an object of social and medical thought, knowledge, and practice, the subject of special concern, to be controlled and regulated. Women's physical identity is just one expression of women's identity— a part of, rather than the defining aspect of, an identity that includes other social and political identities. The female body, like any other concept, has a history and place in social relations that can be disrupted by the feminist project.

For the psychoanalytic project my reading of the body and sexuality in medical discourse as opposed to unconscious desire suggests some need for caution in treating gender as a transhistorical/transcultural concept. The assumed links between femaleness and disorder, the understanding of maternity and sexuality, expert and patient, were part of the historic moment when Freud began his psychoanalytic disjuncture. We need to be aware that this historically and culturally determined sexualized position is carried forward in psychoanalytic practice and theory.

Scenario 3: The Promise of Female Desire

My third and last scenario is the story that runs parallel to my writing of the history of the female body in nineteenth-century medical discourse: my political activities as a feminist.[3] In my feminist practice I explored meanings of the body in feminist campaigns against rape, pornography, and war. I fought the academe as one of the upcoming generation of feminist scholars refusing the conditions under which the earlier pioneer generation had to live, working to disrupt the institution in which I worked, mixing theory with practice, political with personal. In the feminist movement I challenged current attitudes and practices related to the female body. In my feminist living I explored my political identity, my desires, and my fantasies.

My political activism both on and outside the campus protested against the abuse of the female body and sought, by doing so, to reinstate women's position in sexual politics. This involved a multilevel strategy on diverse issues such as women's right to walk safely at night and women's need for safe spaces and legal protection against violence. But perhaps the most interesting was the campaign against women raped in war.

For several years on November 11, the day when Australians commemorate soldiers fallen in war, we marched behind the returned soldiers to remember the women who were raped in past wars and in the present "war of the sexes." We disturbed the conservative public with our claims that rape was a strategy of all wars and of every day and by bringing the abuse of the female body to the public domain. The response was to ban women from marching "against rape," but we fought the order and won the removal of the ban by using television and print media to demand our right to march. November 11 became a time when we could annually break the silence around the abuse and violence against women's bodies. One year we staged an exhibition that demonstrated the use of women's bodies in media, revealing their pornographic stance in contrast to advertisements using male models. We played with the reversal of the norms by stating that only accompanied men could gain entrance. We wanted to unsettle assumptions about everyday images of women in advertising by revealing how the image of the appealing woman is of the watched, the desired, but that, ultimately, the woman who appeals is a passive subject, often placed in physically uncomfortable (sometimes impossible) positions and not in control.

We played on the edge of desire and fantasy, political activism and gender identity. In our public protest campaigns we were often aware that social construction did not explain fully the treatment of women as sexual objects nor our own complex feelings about violence and sexuality, being the desired of our own desires. Some of our group chose to go more deeply into the puzzles of feminism and sexual desires. We held a "women-only" fancy dress ball, attended by many women who came dressed as their fantasy. Our aim was to release our inner fantasies away from the restrictions of politically sound feminism but within a safe space for women. We continued these explorations with group discussions in which we spoke frankly about our feminist politics in relation to our sexual identity and desires. We ran a workshop on sexual desire at the annual socialist feminist conference, which overflowed with participants, comments, and criticisms. From the interest in such events it seemed that there was much that was often denied in the feminist political discourse which drew us beyond the givens of feminist perception of male oppression and cultural discrimination toward the unraveling of our sexual fantasies and desires.

In a series of discussions on pornography we spoke out our hidden desire to be watched or to be watching and our response to violence and sexuality. We pushed our statements further by experimenting in the making of a pseudo-porn film. But, interestingly, in this project we reached the line of transgression. Our group was perceived by the feminist community as going beyond the boundaries of the politically acceptable, of what was safe in terms of the real world and what was permissible to play with in our exploration of body/desire/self. We were called to order by the women's movement to justify such nonfeminist activity. Such contradictions, such speaking of secrets, were dangerous to the solidarity of the women's movement, which fought against child abuse and rape and wife battering. We were aligning ourselves with men, and the group was told to disband.

These activities thus had a number of consequences that indicated that I was pushing the boundaries between the public and the private, and I was forced to look at the meaning of my private and public identities within the feminist movement, in the academe, and in the public world. It seemed that in all three areas I had transgressed boundaries by questioning the apparent givens of female identity. In my public feminist activity we were challenging the myth of the fallen hero by bringing to public attention the inglorious side of soldiers' behavior in war—rape and sexual abuse of women—highlighting the experience of women who, along with men, suffer from war. We blurred the public vision of the hero by placing alongside him the vanquished: reducing heroism to the male conqueror and the sexual conquest. As young women, in extending the image of war and rape to everyday life, we were refusing our feminine role publicly and bringing private sorrows to public display.

In academe I pursued a topic that refused to be defined within traditional disciplines. The tools of history had to be bolstered with those of social philosophy, textual analysis, literary criticism. I demanded that my thesis have political relevance to my own life and feminist practice. I pursued feminist concerns alongside academic study, mixing private/public boundaries as I questioned university policy on sexual harassment and spoke publicly off campus on war and rape, working across disciplines, with women from both in and outside academe. I refused the notion of expert, of truth, of objectivity, of hierarchy. My (male) head of department no longer addressed me by name when we served on the same committees. And my (female) supervisor, unsure if I was doing history, feminist polemic, or some unintelligible fantasy of my own, suggested that I should find others to supervise my work.

In my feminist world I refused absolutes of sexual politics: of women as absolutely good and men as always the enemy; of women as pure, doomed to be victims, and men as wicked, never able to avoid the destiny of their nature. Moreover, I wanted to look at how my desire and my identity as a woman were formed in the modern world in which I lived, to break free from the musts of a good feminist along with the musts of a good woman. I wanted to play with my desire and identity in what I saw as a safe environment. But there, too, I transgressed boundaries and shifted "me" as an identity from one of "us" to one of "them."

I learned from these political experiences that if I was strong enough to refuse the comfort of absolutes, I could embrace many identities and meanings, many strategies and potential affinities. In recognizing pluralities by continuing to transgress boundaries, I could uncover a much more empowering feminist strategy and move beyond us and them, right and wrong, private and public, men and women, fact and fantasy.

Myth or Fantasy: World without Gender

In my first scenario I identify the contradictions and hidden meanings I felt in recognizing my embodied femininity. My second scenario describes the project of deconstructing texts and medical practice in order to reclaim other meanings of woman away from the dominance of the medical gaze. My third illustrates the fluidity in which private/public identities were played out by young feminist women. In my speaking of my self, my self-identity, theoretically and politically, I have sought to illustrate that feminism, like psychoanalysis, offers a strategic position to women as new subjects to think through and act upon problems in new ways. My histories of child/woman, feminist/scholar, feminist/activist, belong to the search to challenge concepts of nature, science, technology, and gender polarities in order to move beyond the relations of domination. Feminist theory in its fluidity moves between the self, the political, subject/object, wholes and parts, and transgresses the boundaries of gender and identity. In a revision of narrative strategies for locating and articulating gender identity, we can allow for gender dissonance and multiple affinities.

In this project I find Kristeva's refusal of feminism too limiting, as it does not provide a strategy for social change in the real world of gender oppression and male dominance. Instead, jumping off from Kristeva's psychoanalytic and theoretical insights on identity and difference, Donna Haraway and Luce Irigaray provide strategic theorizing that is more viable in explaining my strategic moves as described in the three scenarios.

In her fantasy/manifesto for cyborgs feminist subversive Haraway, working on twentieth-century science and technology, resists the myth of the natural world in a decoding of the interests and power relations that establish the nonidentity of gender in a cyborg "world without gender." Her political fiction takes forward the decoding of the category woman in an analysis of the confusion of boundaries in the postmodern, high-tech world. She explores the blurring of boundaries: of Western science and politics, of reproduction of self and others, of patriarchy, of progress, of the appropriation of nature as a resource for the production of culture, of organism and machine. She proposes that in our cyborg world dominations no longer work by medicalization and normalization, but, rather, normalization gives way to automation and the discourse of biopolitics to technobabble. She sees the monstrosities of the cyborg myth both as a Star Wars apocalypse, a masculinist orgy of war and appropriation, and as the potential to transgress traditional boundaries to a political resistance that moves beyond dualism— beyond the search for unity to a politics that embraces partially contradictory and permanently unclosed construction of personal and collective selves (Haraway 1990, 199). Our postmodernist realities, lived socially and bodily, are such that people are not afraid of permanently partial identities and contradictory standpoints, so that the potential for myths of resistance could hardly be greater (197).

In a cyborg world the feminist subversion is the struggle for a continuous cultural reinvention in which identities are contradictory, partial, and strategic. The feminist theoretical and practical struggle against unity through domination has shown the limits to identification. In our recognition of the social and historical constitution of gender, race, and class there is nothing in being female that naturally binds women. Painful fragmentation among feminists along every possible fault line has made the concept of woman elusive. In the endless splitting and searches for a new unity we find, instead, coalition and affinity (Haraway, 1990, 197).

In our feminist project of affinity none of us any longer has the symbolic or material capability for dictating the shape of reality to any others. The consciousness of the noninnocence of the category woman changes the configuration of all previous categories—it denatures them. In the dissolving of identities and in the reflexive strategies for constructing them, the possibility opens up for weaving more than a "shroud for the day after the apocalypse" (Haraway 1990, 199).

Haraway acknowledges Kristeva's dissolution of woman into women in our time (Haraway 1990, 202). But she argues that it is no accident that the symbolic system of the family of man—and so the essence of woman—breaks up at the same moment that networks of connection among people on the planet are unprecedentedly multiple, pregnant, and complex. We have no excuse for participating unreflectively in the logics, languages, and practices of white humanism in a search for a single ground of domination. Nor in acknowledging our failures can we lapse into endless difference and give up on making real connections in our coalitions and affinities. Unlike Kristeva, Haraway argues that it remains to be seen whether all the epistemologies as Western political people have known them fail us in the task of building effective affinities.

Discussing the "informatics" of domination, Haraway points to the strategies feminists and progressive peoples can move to in her vision of a world without gender. The high-tech world of communications technologies and biotechnologies offers crucial tools to embody and enforce new social relations. In a world not divided into us and them the boundary is permeable between tool and myth, instrument and concept, historical systems of social relations and historical anatomies of possible bodies. The rearrangements of race, sex, and class made possible in high-tech social relations can make feminism more relevant to progressive political change. In the modern communications sciences and biology the worldwide material organization for the production and reproduction of daily life and the symbolic organization for the production and reproduction of culture and imagination are equally important and implicated in the potential for change. The boundary maintaining the public and private has been transgressed. The cyborg world of science and technology provides fresh sources of power, and we need fresh sources of analysis and political action (Haraway 1990, 205–7).

Haraway's vision of a world without gender provides an analysis that allows us to better contest for meanings and other forms of power and pleasure in our technologically mediated society. Her analysis opens up new possibilities for strategies, for a holistic politics that moves beyond the production of universal, totalizing theory and argues that we have to take responsibility for the social relations of science and technology; we must embrace the skillful task of reconstructing the boundaries of daily life, in partial connection with others, in communication with all of our parts, and this means both building and destroying machines, identities, categories, relationships, spaces, stories.

Haraway's "political fiction" offers a potent strategy for a new social order that reaches beyond the norms of representations and the structures of sexual identity. The strategic response to my original question, "What difference does it make in the constitution of my social experience that I have a specifically female body?" is that in deconstructing the myth of the female body in medical discourse, we can begin to build new strategies that take on the monstrosities of high tech and find in the apparent abstractions of science the power of resistance.

To Haraway's political fiction we can also join the subversion of Luce

Irigaray. Irigaray offers another strategic position that enables feminism to join with psychoanalysis toward new identities and new ways of working with embodiment. Irigaray rejects gender polarity and the corresponding oppositions between subject and object, self and other, insider and outsider, by moving beyond patriarchal logic. She takes the tactic of acknowledging the autonomy of women in relation to a space beyond women as understood in our present language and cultural discourse. Irigaray's project is to recreate women in a new "female genealogy" in order to bring about a complete reorganization of the social order. She reveals the fluidity of female sexuality as opposed to patriarchal knowledge, the solidity and stability of male sexual identity. In her metaphor of "the two lips" she represents a positive female sexuality that moves beyond the confining representations of women in the dominant patriarchal discourse.[4] She reconceptualizes woman by reclaiming the history and context of the woman of every mother and daughter, which have been covered and destroyed in patriarchal representations of maternity. She moves beyond "the dark continent of the dark continent" to ask that both mother and daughter reject their role, their lack, which culture has prescribed for them, and enter into active subject-subject relations.[5]

This strategy has far more positive implications for women as they become their own subjects, able to change their own conditions by acknowledging what they have, not what they lack. This subversion requires, no less than Kristeva's project, a new mode of language that represents both mother and daughter as self-referential subjects. Further, it means a reorganization of desire so that women are no longer the lost object, and mother and daughter together can defy the binary polarities that the oppositions of patriarchy require. Irigaray invites the woman in both the mother and daughter to take up a discursive and sexual space without the mediation of men, a space that women can inhabit without giving up a part of themselves but, rather, one in which they can recognize the possibilities in the fluidity of all parts (see Grosz 1990, 126–27).

Like Haraway, Irigaray poses a strategic space for women that demands a thorough reworking of sexual identity, seeing and developing new forms of discourse, different forms of evaluation, and new procedures for everyday life (including antisexist revisions for equal pay, abortion, contraception, etc.). They both show how femininity cannot simply be added to existing discursive frameworks but, instead, must be found in new ways of knowing, different methods and aspirations, if women are to overcome their restrictive containment in patriarchal representations and discursive practices.

Irigaray asks that we subvert the functioning of dominant representations and knowledge by challenging their single claims to universal truth, by exposing the sexualized positions from which they are produced. In a parallel move to Kristeva she challenges the apparent neutrality of knowledge, but, differently from Kristeva, she argues that this neutrality is only possible by ignoring the specificity of particular groups (such as women). She raises the important and strategic question for political action of "who speaks for whom." Women and femininity are the other, they are spoken of and on behalf of by men. She indirectly refutes Kristeva's call for the avant-garde as the leaders of the subversion of dominant knowledge by stating that social change cannot happen if women continue to be the objects of metaphors and images in a language that is in fact produced by men only. It is this very objectification of women that maintains the alienation and exploitation of women in and by society (Irigaray 1977, 62).

In our search for a self-determined position from which to write and speak as feminist women, we aim to create new representational systems, new pleasures, new knowledge, new constructions of women's identities, new differences, new spaces in which to speak and to desire. In order to change radically the social order we need to become familiar with patriarchal discourses, knowledge, and social practices. Our strategy, however, is not to use the old rules to win but, rather, to disrupt the old game and initiate new rules, to create new tools to make intervention possible.

Haraway and Irigaray, in their interruption of the game of patriarchy, build from feminism and psychoanalysis new strategies, or tools, for feminist ways of knowing. They rupture the apparent self-evidence of the prevailing model in order to create a space for women to produce alternative frameworks of knowledge and representation. They help to untie women from the series of concepts and values that oppress them. Their strategies are multidirectional and multidimensional in order to deconstruct the many facets of male-dominated knowledge. In recognizing the oppression of women, they play with the concept of female embodiment in language and practice. By calling modern masculine oppression by its name and refusing its self-proclaimed status as universal, unlike Kristeva, they open up ways for women to find strategic positions in which to move beyond gender in the real world.

My text is an experiment with different voices, styles, and levels of meaning, an exploration of new myths and new strategies. We find in the breaking of the subject woman the power of resistance for a feminist theory and practice that is based not on the essential whole but on pluralities and the partial. My experiment began with Kristeva's invitation to move beyond gender, but my experience as a third-generation woman, my feminist activism and theorizing, resonates more with Haraway's and Irigaray's call to create new connections and new politics in the world systems of domination. In their political fiction, poetics, and play with meanings they map ways "to break free of . . . belief in Woman" (Kristeva 1986, 208), but not by denying women's experience and political oppression. They, too, move beyond a religion of Woman and contribute to the project of deconstructing patriarchal systems of thought and knowledge, but, in doing so, they do not relegate women again to the dark continent. Their writings disrupt the old game and open up ways for feminist women to find new creativities and the potential to forge new affinities and coalitions with others toward a new social order based on gender dissonance.

Notes

1. Michel Foucault uses the term *biopolitics* in the first volume of *History of Sexuality* (1981) to explain the interest of public administration in the management of the population in the late eighteenth century. In my doctoral dissertation (1987) I explore in more detail the practices of biopolitics in the late nineteenth century. In these practices women's role in the social body was constituted as the nurturer of the family's hygiene and health and the social agent most able to provide the efficient management of a healthy population. Their "grand function" in the "national economy" was reproducing the species.

2. *The sex* was a common term for women in both popular and medical texts in the nineteenth century, somewhat equivalent to Simone de Beauvoir's use of the term *the second sex*.

3. The works cited in this essay reflect my engagement in a particular feminist theoretical discussion. In addition to these authors, I have been especially attentive to the work of Barret (1992), Benjamin (1988), Berg (1991), Mitchell (1978), and Rose (1986).

4. "The two lips" is Irigaray's symbol for female sexuality and pleasure, which challenges the phallocentric image of the Freudian understanding of masculine clitoral activity and feminine vaginal passivity. Female sexuality is positively represented by two lips, which are both one and two simultaneously—both genital and oral. The image does not represent female anatomy as such but contests dominant phallomorphic representations of the body. The phrase challenges the assumed sexual positions in the imagery of the body: that dominant male sexuality is symbolized by the phallic image of the erect penis, whereas passive female sexuality is symbolized by either the clitoris as a poor imitation of a penis or by the vaginal passage, which is always in need of the male penis to be complete.

5. The phrase "the dark continent of the dark continent" is Irigaray's refer-

ence to preoedipal relations with the mother, described by Freudian psychoanalysis as the dark continent. According to Irigaray, mother-daughter relations
are even more obscured in our social order, hence her play on the term *dark
continent*. In her focus on the mother-daughter relationship Irigaray tries to
throw some light on this dark cultural space in order to help our culture acknowledge its debt to the maternal.

References

Barret, Michèle. "Psychoanalysis and Feminism: A British Sociologist's View."
    Signs 17, no. 2 (Winter 1992): 455–66.
Benjamin, Jessica. "A Desire of One's Own: Psychoanalytic Feminism and Inter-
    subjective Space." In *Feminist Studies / Critical Studies*, edited by Teresa de
    Lauretis. London: Macmillan, 1988.
Berg, Maggie. "Luce Irigaray's Contradictions, Poststructuralism, and Femi-
    nism." *Signs* 17, no. 1 (Autumn 1991): 50–70.
Butler, Judith. "Gender Trouble, Feminist Theory, and Psychoanalytic Dis-
    course." In *Feminism and Postmodernism*, edited by Linda J. Nicholson.
    New York: Routledge, 1990.
Foucault, Michel. *A History of Sexuality*. Vol. 1. New York: Penguin Books, 1981.
Gardiner, Judith Kegan. "Psychoanalysis and Feminism: An American Human-
    ist's View." *Signs* 17, no. 2 (Winter 1992): 437–54.
Greer, Germaine. *The Female Eunuch*. New York: McGraw-Hill, 1970.
Grosz, Elizabeth. *Feminist Subversion*. Sydney: George Allen & Unwin, 1990.
Haraway, Donna. "A Manifesto for Cyborgs: Science, Technology, and Socialist
    Feminism in the 1980s." In *Feminism and Postmodernism*, edited by Linda J.
    Nicholson. New York: Routledge, 1990.
Harcourt, Wendy. "Medical Discourse Relating to the Female Body." Ph.D. diss.,
    Australian National University, 1987.
Irigaray, Luce. "Women's Exile." *Ideology and Consciousness* 1, no. 1 (1977).
———. "That Sex Which Is Not One." In *Language, Sexuality and Subversion*,
    edited by P. Foss and M. Morris. Sydney: Feral, 1978.
Jardine, Alice. "Notes for an Analysis." In *Feminism and Psychoanalysis*, edited
    by Teresa Brennan. New York: Routledge, 1990.
Kristeva, Julia. "Women's Time." In *The Kristeva Reader*, edited by Toril Moi.
    New York: Columbia University Press, 1986.
Mitchell, Juliet. *Psychoanalysis and Feminism*. New York: Penguin Books,
    1978.
Rose, Jacqueline. *Sexuality in the Field of Vision*. London: Verso, 1986.

5 Tribute to the Older Woman: Psychoanalytic Geometry, Gender, and the Emotions

Kathleen Woodward

I begin with a scene drawn out of memory from my childhood, remembered as I was reading psychoanalysis and feminism in preparation for writing this essay. I like to think that this memory of a long afternoon surfaced in response to thought and theory and that, in its way, it corroborates the affective tone and theoretical trajectory my words take in the following pages.

I was ten and on vacation with my father's parents. My grandfather stayed behind (he always did), while my grandmother and I went down to the beach. It was too cold to swim, it was our first day, and so we walked along the water's edge to the rocks at the far end of the shore. I remember climbing those rocks for hours. What we had forgotten, of course, was the deceptive coolness of the sun. We returned to the hotel, our skin painfully, desperately burned. We could put nothing against our bodies. Not a single sheet. We lay still and naked on the twin beds, complaining, laughing, talking. Two twinned, different, sunburned bodies—the body of a ten-year-old girl and the body of a sixty-two-year-old woman.

To my mind's retrospective eye it is important that this scene is not a story of the mother and the daughter, a story whose psychoanalytic plot revolves around identification and separation, intimacy and distance, and engages what I call the strong emotions of psychoanalysis (whether in the writing of Freud, Klein, or Lacan); I am thinking of the potentially explosive emotions of envy, fear, hostility, desire, guilt, and jealousy. Instead, it is a story of an older woman (surely a missing person in psychoanalysis) and a young girl who are separated by some fifty years. Yet I do not want to say that the two of them are *divided* by generations. Rather, they are somehow *connected* by them. What would I say of the affect associated with this memory? I will return to this question, but first I want to take a brief detour to insist on the subject of affect.

In *Le discours vivant* (1973), an excellent if unfortunately little known book on the emotions and psychoanalysis, André Green shows how Freud moved from an emphasis on the role of *representation* in psychic life in his earlier work (notably in *The Interpretation of Dreams* [1900]) to an emphasis on *affect* itself in his later work ("Mourning and Melancholia" [1917] and *Inhibitions, Symptoms and Anxiety* [1926] are two prime examples). This shift in emphasis parallels Freud's concern with castration and the figure of the father in his earlier work and with separation anxiety and the figure of the mother in his later work. The later work of Freud prefigures object relations theory and attachment theory, which inform my thinking here. In particular I welcome the later Freud's explicit analysis of the emotions, which all too often are implicitly associated with the feminine and thus denigrated.[1]

I turn first to a short text by Freud written late in his life, which does privilege the analysis of affect but which nonetheless returns us to the figure of the father and oedipal anxiety. When he was eighty years old Freud mulled over the complex of negative feelings associated with a vacation he had taken to Greece with his brother a little over thirty years before (a coincidence of seaside vacations that has only now occurred to me). I am referring to his letter to Romain Rolland, published under the title of "A Disturbance of Memory on the Acropolis" (1936). Freud tells us that what prompted him to write this text was the recurrence in recent years of a similar "disturbance of memory" and, we are given to assume, a disturbance of similar feelings. These he describes as depression and gloom, as discontent and irresolution, as, in short—and in a wonderful if morose phrase—"the expression of a pessimism" (*S.E.* 22: 242). What does it mean for feelings to cause a disturbance? I take it Freud means that they interrupted a false composure, or broke an illusion of peace, or interfered with a *mood* (I will come back to this in a moment). In the final analysis Freud attributes these disturbing feelings to filial guilt. An ambitious man, he concluded he had gone further than had his father (both literally, in terms of travel some thirty years before, and symbolically, in terms of intellectual accomplishment over his long life) and that he was to be punished for it. His feelings of foreboding, his "pessimism," are *themselves* that punishment, exacted by the superego. I have commented elsewhere on the place of this text in the context of Freud's work and the discontents of the aging body (Woodward 1991). Here I want only to remark that in "Disturbance of Memory" we find ourselves thick in the Freudian world of two generations with the eighty-year-old son still bound tragically after all these years to his long dead father by the cord of the Oedipus complex, with its dynamic of desire and prohibition, guilt and punishment. Thus, this version of the Oedipus drama is not played out between two people but in the solitary mise-en-scène of the psyche.

What interests me also in Freud's "Disturbance of Memory" is the notion of the repetition not of an event but of a complex of emotions, particular emotions that Freud took as his task to analyze and that had long been central to the structuring narrative of the Oedipus complex. And yet earlier Freud had remarked that "every affect . . . is only a reminiscence of an event" (1989, quoted in *S.E.* 20: 84). I take him here in his materialist sense. But, actually, I would insist that it is never the event itself that is ultimately important to us—it is the emotion (or complex of emotions) associated with it. Moreover, in the case of Freud's disturbance of affect, his feelings of foreboding are not in fact a reminiscence of an event but, rather, an *expectation* of one, foreboding that arises out of fantasy, the specifically Freudian fear of castration or punishment.

How would I understand the complex of emotions associated with my childhood memory of my grandmother and myself at the beach, of our two sunburned bodies? Not as a disturbance in Freud's sense, not as a foreboding "expression of a pessimism," but as an expression of reassurance. Yet not as *jouissance,* as an expression of woman's libidinal economy, which Hélène Cixous has described in "Sorties" (1981) this way: "Unleashed and raging, she belongs to the race of the waves. She arises, she approaches, she lifts up, she reaches, covers over, washes ashore, flows embracing the cliffs least undulation, already she is another, arising again, throwing the fringed vastness of her body up high, follows herself, and covers over" (91)—I break off here, unwilling to follow Cixous's fluvial prose any longer along this sinuous beach into its realm of intoxication, vertigo, mystery, and effervescence. Instead, I understand the affect associated with my memory of a seaside scene, which is drawn from everyday life, as nothing more perhaps, but certainly nothing less, than a palpable *sociality,* a convivial ease. My affective memory (Stanislavski), now over thirty-five years old, is a reminiscence of an event, not a fantasy that takes place in the private mise-en-scène of the psyche (Freud), not a textual feminist utopia of rhapsodic proportions (Cixous).

John Bowlby (1973) would describe this scene in terms of attachment, Jessica Benjamin (1988) in terms of emotional attunement. Indeed, for me the emotional precipitate that is the reminiscence of this event I understand to be based on what Benjamin calls mutual recognition.[2] But we lack a variegated and rich theoretical vocabulary to describe such emotions. Given the discourse of psychoanalysis with its attention to the "stormy passions," as Freud has put it (*S.E.* 11: 75),[3] we should not be at all surprised by this: psychoanalysis has devoted little attention to the elaboration of what for want of a better term we might call the positive emotions (we certainly *do* need a better term than this), or what I have elsewhere called the "quiet" emotions (1990–91) and Sartre the "subtle" emotions (1948, 22). Furthermore, within the classical parameters of psychoanalysis it might be more accurate to refer to what I have described as a *mood*.

Here I want to draw on the excellent distinction made by Lawrence Grossberg between desire and mood, or, more precisely, between what he identifies as libidinal economies of desire and affective economies of mood. The two economies represent different ways of organizing psychic energy, which Grossberg describes in the following way: "If desire is always focused (as the notion of cathexis suggests), mood is always dispersed. While both may be experienced in terms of needs, only libidinal needs can be, however incompletely, satisfied. Moods are never satisfied, only realized. If desire assumes an economy of depth (e.g., the notion of repression), mood is always on the surface (which is not to be equated with consciousness). It is the coloration or passion within which one's investments in, and commitments to the world are possible" (1988, 285).[4] Desire is focused on an object and is goal oriented; mood arises out of a situation and gives to it a certain tone.

Significantly, Grossberg implicitly (although not exclusively) associates an affective economy of mood with a psychoanalysis of object relations; this is how he can understand the affective economy of mood to yield the possibility of difference. Affective needs, he writes, are "never satisfied by particular relationships but only by a more general attitude or mood within which any particular relationship has its effects" (285). Grossberg's theorization of the affective economy of mood (in its "positive" manifestation) resonates with Benjamin's theorization of emotional attunement in an intersubjective space. How would I describe, then, the mood of my memory of that summer afternoon some thirty-five years ago? It was one of fluent companionship that, important for what I turn to now, stretched across the continuity established by three generations.

Psychoanalysis is a discourse obsessed with making triangles out of the elements of two generations. Its developmental politics is twofold. First, the constitution of male and female sexuality is understood to be achieved simultaneously with the rigid separation of generations, and, second, both the sexes and the generations are ever after to remain unequal in power. This geometry of the nuclear family is established only through force, which enlists the emotions of fear and anxiety. Thus, classically, the father (or the Name of the Father) is cast as the third term that intervenes in the mother-child dyad.

How might we rethink this triangulation? In "Place Names" (1976) and "Motherhood according to Giovanni Bellini" (1975) Julia Kristeva introduces into the equation another term altogether: the mother's mother. As we shall see in a moment, however, for Kristeva it is not the mother's mother who is the third term. In the event of giving birth, Kristeva writes, a woman "replays in reverse the encounter with her own mother" ("Place Names," 279); she "enters into contact with her own mother" ("Motherhood," 239).[5] Kristeva reads this alternative triangle as mother-mother-child, with the child serving as third term, as a kind of go-between who brings a woman into psychic continuity with her mother. The woman, her mother: the two are, Kristeva writes in "Motherhood," "the same continuity differentiating itself" (239). Kristeva is, however, ambivalent about this identification—and well she should be, given the mystical aura with which she endows it. Thus, she also presents the child as the third term, which also breaks this imaginary and revelatory bond between the woman and her mother. As she puts it brilliantly in "Place Names," the child is also an *analyzer* (279), who releases the woman, now a mother, from what Kristeva provocatively calls "the homosexual facet of motherhood" ("Motherhood," 239), and, more clinically, "the daughter-mother symbiosis" and "the undifferentiated community of women" ("Place Names," 279).

I must leave behind many complexities here, but before I do I want to insist on three fundamental features of Kristeva's rewriting of this basic figure of psychoanalytic geometry. It is at the very least two-thirds female. It touches three generations. And the child plays an active if contradictory role.

Who is this child, and what is the child playing with? By asking *who,* I mean, of course, to introduce the question of gender. In his lecture on "Femininity" (1933) Freud rehearses the process by which a woman "comes into being . . . out of a child with a bisexual disposition" (*S.E.* 22: 116). That is, he theorizes the constitution of a specifically female sexual identity where before, he assumes, there was none. In this late text Freud admits that the preoedipal attachment of the little girl to the mother is much more powerful and richer than he had before believed. He comes to this conclusion in part by calling attention to the little girl's practice of playing with dolls. How does he explain her play? It can't be an expression of her "femininity," for that has not yet been established. So he finds himself forced to conclude that it is an expression of her "identification with her mother," with the phallic mother (she is "phallic" because the little girl does not yet recognize her mother as "castrated"). It is, in Freud's eyes, an "affectionate" attachment, although he expresses it in ambiguous terms: the little girl "was playing the part of her mother and the doll was herself: now she could do with the baby everything that her mother used to do with her" (*S.E.* 22: 128).

In the opening pages of his essay Freud cautions his readers not to think of masculinity and femininity—the polarity that dominates sexual life, as he puts it—in terms of activity and passivity. But, in fact, he can find no other way of describing (or theorizing) the little girl's behavior: the little girl, identifying with her mother, substitutes "activity for passivity" (128). Notwithstanding many of Freud's disclaimers, then, the conventional connotations of sexual difference cling to the words *active* and *passive* like a phallic slip, reinscribing themselves retrospectively in the preoedipal period. Similarly, by describing the preoedipal mother as "phallic," Freud continues to read the scene of a little girl's play in terms of a *sexual* economy.[6] Indeed, Freudian psychoanalysis can admit no other economy than a sexual economy. Just as important for my purposes, Freud can only imagine two generations in this scene: the mother and the child.

I want to read this scene differently: for the child the doll represents not her self (as Freud would have it), nor the other, but simply and profoundly an other, a baby. This baby, however, is not a sibling, that is to say, a member of the same generation (in such a case we might predict jealousy of a conventional triangular sort).[7] Rather, this "baby" belongs to the next generation. She is a child to whom the little girl transfers, as Luce Irigaray has put it, "quasi-maternal affects" (1989, 132).[8] We thus have a model of three generations, similar to but different from that sketched by Kristeva, in which the third term, the child, does not separate the mother from the child but is added to the two of them (in fact, we again find several mothers here). We have, in other words, not a *triangle* but the further elaboration of a *line,* a plumb line—one that has specific gravity and weight to it. Furthermore, it is not sexual difference that distinguishes this economy, but generational linkage, or generational continuity.

In "Femininity" Freud is concerned with sexuality and its structuring binary of masculinity and femininity. Within this framework he was bound to conclude the following: "When you meet a human being, the first distinction you make is 'male or female?'" (*S.E.* 22: 113). Sexuality is the content, we can say, of Freudian psychoanalysis,[9] which is itself an instance of the seemingly endless production of the discourse of sexuality in Western culture, a phenomenon to which Foucault has so persuasively drawn attention (1980). Thus, Freud insists that sexual difference (although he does not use this term) is the most distinctive feature of a person. But we are not obliged to agree. What of race, for example? And what of the category of age? For indeed, when we meet someone one of the first distinctions we make, as self-consciously or subliminally as distinctions of sexual or racial difference, is that of *age,* and, more generally, of generation.

Lending support to my hypothetical model of generational continuity is the fascinating research of Ernest A. Abelin (1980) on preoedipal triangulation during the rapprochement subphase (identified by Margaret Mahler as occurring at around eighteen months). Abelin finds not one triangle but two. Both triangles are gender specific: one is for little girls, one for little boys. Significantly, however, only one of them is based on *sexual difference.* The triangle for the little boy is familiarly Freudian to us: it consists of father, mother, and self and establishes gender identity for the little boy based on his perception of sexual difference. For the little girl, by contrast, the triangle is composed of mother, self, and baby and establishes gender identity based on her perception of *generational continuity.* Abelin explains the difference between the two triangles this way: "Generational identity establishes the self 'between' two objects, along one linear dimension. 'I am smaller than mother, but bigger than baby,' or, rather, in terms of wishes: 'I wish to be taken care of by mother and I wish to take care of baby.' By contrast, gender identity classifies the self in relation to the dichotomy male/female" (158).[10] For the little girl, then, core gender identity is not based on sexual difference but, rather, on generational linkage.

Abelin's research provides a critical vantage point from which we can see again just how saturated classical psychoanalysis is with the discourse of sexuality and sexual difference. The provocative conclusion of his research is that there is another gender-specific content to identity, that of generation, which has not been elaborated by psychoanalysis. Why? In part because in Freud's male hands the two founding figures of psychoanalysis—the hysterical Dora and the felonious Oedipus—present an impediment, if not a dead end, to thinking a third generation. The children of Oedipus were born out of incest and thus outside the law (and we know what happened to them). And the generational economy of the hysteric cannot count to three: the sterile hysteric will produce no children.[11]

But Abelin's geometry is complicit with Freudian analysis and is faulty. Where he sees a preoedipal triangle for little girls based on generational identity, he should instead see a line. As Abelin himself says, generational identity is established along a "linear" axis.

I have up to now used the word *identity* without being precise about exactly what I mean by it. *Identity* is often used in the sense of "wholeness," and I do not wish it to carry that meaning here. *Identity* is also often opposed to "difference," and I do not want it to be construed in this sense either. Recent debates have placed a terrible strain on the notions of "identity" and "difference." It will suffice, I hope, to say that in the context of this essay *identity* does not preclude difference. Generational identity entails a difference based on *similarity* that finds its temporal expression in *continuity*.

To summarize, we have, then, this theoretical scene: a mother whose little girl, playing, invents the younger generation. The child is the third term, a term that signifies continuity and not intervention. The tragic binary of Freudian psychoanalysis of two generations can be written in this way.

But in doing so I find that I have reproduced the paradigm of the mother and the infant daughter, and I contend that we have had enough in recent feminist psychoanalytic criticism and theory of this very couple. A child, in my judgment, should not be asked to bear so much meaning. It would be appropriate, however, to ask an older woman to do so. Thus, I propose we look at this plumb line, or lineage, from a different point of view, from the perspective of the older woman. Kaja Silverman has insisted that for the choric fantasy of women's unity to function effectively, it must point forward as well as backward (1988, 153).[12] Turning our attention to the figure of the other woman, the older woman, as the third term is precisely one way of moving forward, of thinking prospectively rather than retrospectively (although it will involve this also). And to up the ante I suggest that we imagine her as a figure of knowledge who represents the difference that history, or time, makes, a difference that she, in fact, literally embodies.

I have already remarked that the older woman is a missing person in Freudian psychoanalysis. The cultural historian Lois Banner has concluded that if Freud had difficulty in general in dealing with women in his writing, he had particular difficulty with aging women (1992). It is therefore not surprising to me that in the one place, to my knowledge, in which Freud does discuss a cultural representation of three generations, only two generations are in effect present. The older woman is absent; she has been painted over. I am referring to Freud's analysis of Leonardo da Vinci's painting of Saint Anne with her daughter Mary and the baby Jesus. Freud comments upon this painting in his study of Leonardo, which focuses on one of Leonardo's memories from childhood (naturally Freud interprets it in sexual terms) (*S.E.* 11: 57–137).[13] Startlingly, Leonardo, with whom Freud clearly identifies, has painted the older woman (the grandmother) as a member of the same generation as her daughter. Saint Anne is described by Freud as "a young woman of unfaded beauty," indeed "a woman of radiant beauty" (113). Why are there two mothers of the same generation for the Christ child, instead of one? Why is the older woman not represented as such? Why is her older body reconstructed in the masquerade of youth?

Freud offers the following analysis based on the peculiarities of Leonardo's birth and upbringing. The illegitimate Leonardo was raised exclusively by his birth mother until he was five and thereafter by his stepmother in his father's home. Thus Leonardo, so strongly attached to mother figures (and not to the father, who was missing from his first five years), has, in Freud's words, "given the boy"—that is, himself—"two mothers" (113). But I would argue that Freud's own fascination with this painting tells us more than this: Freudian psychoanalysis could only figure a child's relation to a woman positively in terms of the paradigm of the younger mother and infant. The relationship portrayed in this scene—it is a doubled-over pietà—is maternally idyllic. The celebrated Leonardo smile is the familiar, almost banal "blissful smile of the joy of motherhood" (113). The affect here is Freudian utopian sublime, one that can only be associated with the pietà of the young mother and infant in the "prehistory" of man.

Although Freud asserts that he dismissed the notion, held by some of Leonardo's biographers, that Leonardo "could not bring himself to paint old age, lines and wrinkles" (113), Freud relegates Saint Anne—an older woman but not necessarily *old*—to the outcast territory of old age. In Freudian psychoanalysis a woman beyond childbearing age is old, dysfunctional in sexual (reproductive) terms, a dysfunction that is written on her body in folds and wrinkles for everyone to see. Such a woman, we might say, cannot even be represented within the discourse of classical psychoanalysis. Within the parameters of psychoanalysis we can imagine a point when increasing age (it is ticking away) intersects with female sexuality at the biological time bomb of menopause, when female sexuality vanishes, leaving only gender behind. The dilemma, however, is this: Freudian psychoanalysis cannot contain the concept of gender as distinct from sexuality. Thus: the older woman cannot exist. If in Freudian terms a female child prior to the Oedipus complex is consigned to a *prehistorical* state, a postmenopausal woman, an older woman, is dismissed from the world as *posthistorical,* finding herself outside of the discourse of history yet again.

In general the older woman, the woman of the third generation (and she, or we, may be older than this), has not found a place in the locus of feminist criticism and psychoanalysis.[14] In much recent feminist psy-

choanalytic criticism in the United States a woman is implicitly theorized or represented as a mother to young children.[15] To be sure, she
may appear in the guise of a woman juggling work of her own with the
demands and pleasures of motherhood, but at her oldest she tends to be
cast as on the young side of middle age (I think here of the surprised,
almost shocked tone with which I have heard some of my only slightly
younger colleagues refer to an older woman as—of all the impossible
things—a *grandmother*). Or, if age is explicitly analyzed, what we find
is the Freudian plot of a struggle for power between two close but emotionally distant "generations": the mother and the daughter have gotten
older, but they don't seem to have learned much—or they have learned
too well how to jockey for power. Thus, literary critic Marianne Hirsch,
writing candidly in her book *The Mother/Daughter Plot* of her experience in a discussion group on the maternal, notes the "painful set of
divisions which emerged between the discourse of mothers and that of
daughters"; "the sympathy we could muster for ourselves and each
other as *mothers*," she confesses, "we could not quite transfer to our
own mothers" (1989, 26). Thus, also, Alice Jardine in a recent essay
(1989) describes the relationship between the two successive post-1968
groups of feminists in the American academy as thoroughly oedipal.
She does not want, she says, to "succumb" to this paradigm, but in fact
she does, and for good reasons: the oedipal paradigm does describe
accurately the struggle between two adjacent generations, a struggle
that I suspect we have all witnessed and in which we have all probably
consciously or unconsciously played at least one part and possibly two.
As Jardine expresses it: "I would like to avoid the mother/daughter
paradigm here (so as not to succumb simply to miming the traditional
father/son, master/disciple model), but it is difficult to avoid being positioned by the institution as mothers and daughters. Structures of debt/
gift (mothers and increasingly daughters control a lot of money and
prestige in the university), structures of our new institutional power
over each other, desires and demands for recognition and love—all of
these are falling into place in rather familiar Freudian ways" (1989, 77).
Yes, I agree. But I would argue that it is not just the patriarchal structure
of the institution that places us in oedipal struggle but also our way of
analyzing that relation between generations, limited as it is to two.

Thus, one of the ways to construct a "theoretical genealogy" of
women[16] is to stretch our attention to include another generation. We
must do so not in order to figure a new notion of a *horizontal* relation
between women, such as Irigaray advises, but in order to give a new
meaning to the notion of *vertical,* which is conceived in classical psychoanalysis in terms of hierarchy and authority. This is precisely what

Nancy Chodorow has done in a recent essay (1989) in which she reports on a series of interviews she had in the early 1980s with female psychoanalysts who had trained in the 1920s, 1930s, and 1940s. I greatly admire this essay. In it Chodorow seeks to understand across time, history, age, and generation why these older women were not feminists in Chodorow's own sense of the word. The title of her essay, "Seventies Questions for Thirties Women: Gender and Generation in a Study of Early Women Psychoanalysts," suggests the answer to her question. It is a simple lesson, one we too often forget: we must remember to respect the differences rooted in history. We have no right to expect to hear the answers we would give to the questions we ask of generational others. It is a vain and immature enterprise to wish either to be mirrored at our age (what is it? how old are you? *tell*) or to enter automatically into struggle.

What Chodorow conveys is precisely a sense of mutual recognition (Benjamin 1988) between two generations widely separated by time but brought together in part by the very wish for understanding, that is, connection. But not symbiosis. We do not find, pace Kristeva, an "undifferentiated community of women" ("Place Names," 1980, 279). Exactly not.

Chodorow had thought these older women, whom she esteemed in so many other ways, were—of all things—gender blind. Through time and conversation she came to conclude that they had a different form of gender consciousness, or gender identity. She came to see, she writes, that "differences in women's interpretations of a situation may be understood not only in terms of structural categories like class and race but also historically, culturally, and generationally" (1989, 200). She came to recognize that "hyper-gender-sensitivity" characterizes women of her—and I will say with Chodorow *our*—generation (218). One of the rare achievements of Chodorow's essay, which I hasten to add is not in any way eloquent (it does not move us emotionally to understanding), is its sense or tone of deep respect. This is achieved in part, I think, through its rhetoric of candor, which disarms the hierarchy associated with positions of truth, a position that Chodorow has given up.

It is the time for many of us to invent ourselves consciously and critically as older women, making the place we want for ourselves to the best of our abilities. If the older woman has been a missing person in psychoanalysis and in feminist criticism in general, this is fortunately not the case in contemporary culture. Older women are making it, if we only know where to look. Women—and not all of them older—are contributing to the representation of older women. I am thinking, for example, of Yvonne Rainer's recent films, of the work of the perfor-mance artists Suzanne Lacey and Rachel Rosenthal, of Margaret Drab-ble's novel *A Natural Curiosity*, of Annie Dillard's *An American Child-hood*, of Amy Tan's *The Joy Luck Club*, of so much of Marguerite Duras's writing, of Alice Noggle's photographs of old women, of Cecilia Condit's videotape *Not a Jealous Bone*. There is much more: rich and varied work for us to investigate and to live into the future with, for identifica-tions do not cease with childhood, nor is fantasy bound only to infancy. As Teresa Brennan suggests, we make not just formative identifications but also identifications that permit different ways of thinking—and, I would add, of living (1989, 10). And the phantasmatic, as Jean Laplanche and J.-B. Pontalis emphasize, is constantly drawing in new materials (1973, 317).

Informing my chapter is a fantasy of a particular kind of older woman, one I confess is narcissistic, although it is a very general one (one you could not guess from my opening anecdote). Chodorow, drawing on the work of Judith Kestenberg, concludes that for female analysts of the 1930s whom she interviewed, three faces of femininity presented themselves: motherhood, sexuality, and intellectual work (1989, 210). In my essay I have been implicitly privileging the latter aspect of the older woman—intellectual work, characterizing a woman who as a teacher and writer is bound through her work to many generations. When I was young this is how I perceived many older women, includ-ing my grandmother. I am not alone in this, of course. I do not think we should dismiss what our experience in everyday life has so often told us. It is common knowledge that struggle can skip a generation, that many of us have formative relationships with women a generation, if not more, older than our mothers. I also think we should attend to Simone de Beauvoir's second great book, an analysis as sweeping and trenchant as *The Second Sex*. I am referring, of course, to *La vieillesse*, published under the title *The Coming of Age* in the United States, a book that has been virtually ignored by feminists.

In closing, then, I want to echo my opening anecdote with words drawn not out of my memory but from my recent reading. They are taken from a collection of essays by bell hooks, a black American who teaches at Yale (1990). "bell hooks" (a.k.a. Gloria Watkins) is in fact the name of her great-grandmother, which Watkins took as her own, a name signifying "talking back" (1986–87). bell hooks (who is she then?). She writes about going to school in the rural South and about the women there. "It was," she tells us in her essay "The Chitlin Circuit," "a world of single older black women schoolteachers, they had taught your mama, her sisters, and her friends. They knew your people in ways that you

never would and shared their insight, keeping us in touch with generations. It was a world where we had history" (1990, 33). To her grandmother Sarah Hooks Oldham, a woman with a "renegade nature" who
instructed bell in the ways of establishing "kinship and connection," a
woman who could not read or write, a long-lived woman who had
taught her so much, to her bell hooks dedicates an essay in this collection. It is a portrait of her grandmother as a maker of quilts, of "history
worked by hand" (115). Entitled "Aesthetic Inheritances," this essay is a
tribute to an older woman, as, in a way, is mine. Here the Freudian
stormy emotions of two-generational, same-sex oedipal violence are
nowhere in evidence, much less privileged. Not at all.

It may be wondered if in my emphasis on the subtle emotions (I will
use Sartre's word), on a quiet and companionable geniality in my case,
on a boisterous conviviality in the case of bell hooks, I have not strayed
too close to that emotion—or, better, mood—held most in contempt
in contemporary cultural studies. I am, of course, referring to nostalgia.[17] Nostalgia is generally associated with a regressive and weak, wistful
longing for the past—with, in short, a retrograde politics. But neither
hooks, if I may speak for her, nor I have a desire to return to the past.

Nor am I arguing that certain emotions are specifically, essentially
female and others male. What I have been concerned to do is to see
where the analysis of an affect—the mood of convivial ease—would
lead me, and it took me to the figure of the older woman, who was, in
fact, present in my past all along and who will be—"she" will be "I"—
present in my future, time willing.

Notes

1. See, for example, Griffiths (1988).

2. Benjamin writes: "What I call *mutual recognition* includes a number of
experiences commonly described in the research on mother-infant interaction:
emotional attunement, mutual influence, affective mutuality, sharing states of
mind" (1988, 16). For Benjamin the analogue in adult life to mother-infant interaction is erotic union. I would disagree and argue that a reciprocal sociality,
in its many modes, is a more appropriate model. I would further disagree with
Benjamin's insistence that we can share feeling states with other people; I do
not think we can ever know that.

3. The complete sentence reads: "The stormy passions of a nature that in-
spires and consumes, passions in which other men have enjoyed their richest
experience, appear not to have touched him" (*S.E.* 11: 75).

4. Grossberg's distinction between libidinal economies of desire and affective economies of mood resonates with Winnicott's distinction between doing

and being (Winnicott associates the former with masculinity, the latter with femininity). See Winnicott (1971).

5. I am indebted to Kaja Silverman's reading of these essays (see n. 12). I am also grateful to Tim Murray for his helpful comments. Elizabeth Grosz calls this identification of the birth mother with her own mother "vertiginous" (1989, 80), which, I would argue, it certainly need not be.

6. Luce Irigaray also makes this point (1985).

7. It is of the utmost importance that we specify *which* generation. Both Freud and Lacan have commented on the explosive emotions of sibling rivalry. Lacan, for example, is fond of quoting Saint Augustine on this point: "I have seen with my own eyes and know very well an infant in the grip of jealousy: he could not yet speak, and already he observed his foster-brother, pale and with an envenomed stare" (1977, 20). Freud links the drive to knowledge, or *epistemophilia*, to the arrival of a new baby, which stimulates the child's sexual curiosity. The question to be asked is: Where do babies come from? Freud develops this idea in *Three Essays on the Theory of Sexuality* (1905) (*S.E.* 7: 194–95). See also his "Notes upon a Case of Obsessional Neurosis" (1909) (*S.E.* 10: 237–49).

For recent work on *epistemophilia* from a feminist point of view, see Moi (1989). Moi concludes, "If reason is always already shot through with the energy of the drives, the body, and desire, to be intellectual can no longer be theorized simply as the 'opposite' of being emotional or passionate" (203). See also the brilliant essay by Gloria-Jean Masciarotte, "The Madonna with Child, and Another Child, and Still Another Child . . . " (1991–92). Masciarotte observes that in a later edition of *Three Essays* Freud "notes that girls never question a new baby." This, she concludes, "suggests a different relation to knowledge, a different ordering of curiosity and expectations based on gender" (124 n. 8).

8. In her 1989 essay Irigaray comments on the difference between the play of little boys and little girls in the absence of the mother. Irigaray contrasts the famous Freudian paradigm of play for little boys (Freud's grandson Ernst and the spool, the solitary game of *fort-da*), which she reads as play with an object (the mother is "reduced" to an object), with the little girl's play with a doll, which she regards as a "quasi-object," because the "mother's identity as a subject is the same as hers" (132). This is convincing enough, although I would argue that the doll could be either a boy doll or a girl doll; it does not matter, as we shall see. More important, it is not at all necessary to hypothesize the *mother's absence*. The daughter's play can, and often does, go on in the presence of the mother. My point is that these two models of play, based on gender, are *not* symmetrical. Finally, Irigaray concludes (not on the basis of this paradigm alone, of course) that the "mother always remains too familiar and too close" (133); this also need not necessarily be the case. I should add that Freud himself saw the little girl's relation to her doll in terms of subject and object. As he puts it in "Female Sexuality" (1931), the child "actually makes its mother into the object and behaves as the active subject towards her" (*S.E.* 21: 236).

9. It is not surprising that many feminists, critiquing Freudian psychoanalysis (and its patriarchal followers), have chosen to do so precisely in terms of sexuality itself, and in terms of same-sex or lesbian practices. For excellent recent

work in this vein, see Adams (1989) and de Lauretis (1990–91).

10. I discuss gender and generational identity with reference to Eva Figes's novel *Waking* in *Aging and Its Discontents* (1991, 92–108).

11. With regard to the hysteric Freud explains the internal exchange between the two generations this way: "an exchange is established between the generations: 1st generation: Perversion. 2nd generation: Hysteria, and consequent sterility" (1954, 180).

12. The word *choric* is, of course, a reference to Kristeva. For a thoughtful discussion of several of the texts by Kristeva and Freud to which I have referred here, see Silverman (1988, 101–86). Silverman argues that the little girl's attachment to the mother in the preoedipal period is one of both identification and object-choice (sexuality enters her analysis here in a way that it does not enter mine), and at one point she suggests, albeit tentatively, that "although there *is* a third term, and it is—as usual—the father," she "cannot help but wonder whether there is not another, more important third term here, one that plays a far more central place within the daughter's early libidinal economy than does the father. I refer, of course, to the child" (153). Thus, Silverman reads Robert Altman's 1977 film *Three Women* in terms of three generations of women. But she does not pursue this analysis.

13. Interestingly enough, Freud identifies one of the conflicts central to Leonardo's character as that between knowledge (reason) and emotion, concluding that Leonardo sublimated passion into the search for knowledge. Could one not say the same of Freud himself?

14. We might note, for example, that Teresa de Lauretis prefaces her essay "The Violence of Rhetoric" with an epigraph from Nietzsche. It is a quotation from *The Gay Science* that begins: "Older women are more skeptical in their heart of hearts than any man." De Lauretis, however, generalizes from "older women" to "woman": the opening line of her essay reads: "Woman's skepticism, Nietzsche suggests, comes from her disregard for truth" (1987, 31). Mary Ann Doane, on the other hand, comments pointedly on the recurrent image of the older woman in Nietzsche. See Doane (1989).

15. The bibliography is too lengthy to be rehearsed here. One of the most influential books, of course, is Nancy Chodorow, *The Reproduction of Mothering: Psychoanalysis and the Sociology of Gender* (1978). See also, for example, *The (M)Other Tongue: Essays in Feminist Psychoanalytic Interpretation*, edited by Shirley Nelson Garner, Claire Kahane, and Madelon Sprengnether (1985); and Luce Irigaray, *Le Corps-à-corps avec la mère* (1981).

16. I am here echoing Rosi Bradotti (who is referring, of course, to Irigaray), "The Politics of Ontological Difference" (1989, 96). Yet, even as Bradotti subscribes to the project of constructing a new female symbolic and reads Irigaray's work as a strategic intervention in patriarchal culture, she nevertheless seems to subscribe to what psychoanalysis has had to say about generational politics. Bradotti:

> The psychoanalytic situation brings about, among other things, the fundamental dissymmetry between self and other, that is constitutive of the sub-

ject; this is related to the non-interchangeability of positions between analyst and patient, to the irrevocable anteriority of the former, that is to say,
ultimately to time. Time, the great master, calling upon each individual to
take his/her place in the game of generations, is the inevitable, the inesca-
pable horizon. One of the ethical aims of the psychoanalytic situation is to
lead the subject to accept this inscription into time, the passing of generations and the dissymmetries it entails, so as to accept the radical otherness
of the self. (98)

Thus, Bradotti can speak elsewhere in the same essay of that old bugaboo, generation gaps.

17. See, for example, Rosaldo (1989).

References

Abelin, Ernest A. "Triangulation, the Role of the Father and the Origins of Core
    Gender Identity during the Rapprochement Subphase." In *Rapprochement:
    The Critical Subphase of Separation-Individuation,* edited by Ruth F. Lax,
    Sheldon Bach, and J. Alexis Burland. New York: Jason Aronson, 1980.
Adams, Parveen. "Of Female Bondage." In Brennan (1989).
Banner, Lois. *In Full Flower: Aging Women, Power, and Sexuality.* New York:
    Alfred A. Knopf, 1992.
Benjamin, Jessica. *The Bonds of Love: Psychoanalysis, Feminism, and the
    Problem of Domination.* New York: Pantheon, 1988.
Bowlby, John. *Separation: Anxiety and Anger.* London: Hogarth Press, 1973.
Bradotti, Rosi. "The Politics of Ontological Difference." In Brennan (1989).
Brennan, Teresa, ed. *Between Feminism and Psychoanalysis.* London: Rout-
    ledge, 1989.
Chodorow, Nancy. *The Reproduction of Mothering: Psychoanalysis and the
    Sociology of Gender.* Berkeley: University of California Press, 1978.
————. "Seventies Questions for Thirties Women: Gender and Generation in a
    Study of Early Women Psychoanalysts." In *Feminism and Psychoanalytic
    Theory.* New Haven, Conn.: Yale University Press, 1989.
Cixous, Hélène. "Sorties." In *The Newly Born Woman,* by Hélène Cixous and
    Catherine Clément. Translated by Betsy Wing. Minneapolis: University of
    Minnesota Press, 1981.
de Beauvoir, Simone. *The Coming of Age (La vieillesse).* Translated by Patrick
    O'Brian. New York: Warner, 1978.
de Lauretis, Teresa. "The Violence of Rhetoric." *Technologies of Gender: Essays
    on Theory, Film, and Fiction.* Bloomington: Indiana University Press, 1987.
————. "Film and the Primal Fantasy—One More Time: On Sheila
    McLaughlin's *She Must Be Seeing Things.*" University of Wisconsin, Mil-
    waukee, Center for Twentieth Century Studies Working Paper 7 (1990–91).
Doane, Mary Ann. "Veiling over Desire: Close-ups of the Woman." In *Feminism

and Psychoanalysis, edited by Richard Feldstein and Judith Roof. Ithaca: Cornell University Press, 1989.

Foucault, Michel. *The History of Sexuality.* Vol. 1: *An Introduction.* Translated by Robert Hurley. New York: Vintage, 1980.

Freud, Sigmund. *The Standard Edition of the Complete Psychological Works of Sigmund Freud.* Edited and translated by James Strachey. 24 vols. London: Hogarth Press, 1953–74.

The Interpretation of Dreams (1900), vols. 4, 5.

Three Essays on the Theory of Sexuality (1905), vol. 7.

"Notes Upon a Case of Obsessional Neurosis" (1909), vol. 10.

Leonardo da Vinci and a Memory of His Childhood (1910), vol. 11.

"Mourning and Melancholia" (1917), vol. 14.

Inhibitions, Symptoms and Anxiety (1926), vol. 20.

"Female Sexuality" (1931), vol. 21.

"Femininity" (1933), vol. 22.

"A Disturbance of Memory on the Acropolis" (1936), vol. 22.

———. *The Origins of Psycho-Analysis: Letters to Wilhelm Fliess, Drafts and Notes: 1887–1902.* Edited by Marie Bonaparte, Anna Freud, and Ernst Kris. Translated by Eric Mosbacher and James Strachey. London: Imago, 1954.

Garner, Shirley Nelson, Kahane, Claire, and Sprengnether, Madelon, eds. *The (M)Other Tongue: Essays in Feminist Psychoanalytic Interpretation.* Ithaca: Cornell University Press, 1985.

Green, André. *Le discours vivant.* Paris: Presses Universitaires de France, 1973.

Griffiths, Morwenna. "Feminism, Feelings and Philosophy." In *Feminist Perspectives in Philosophy,* edited by Morwenna Griffiths and Margaret Whitford. Bloomington: Indiana University Press, 1988.

Grossberg, Lawrence. "Postmodernity and Affect: All Dressed Up with No Place to Go." *Communication* 10 (1988): 271–93.

Grosz, Elizabeth. *Sexual Subversions: Three French Feminists.* Boston: Allen & Unwin, 1989.

Hirsch, Marianne. *The Mother/Daughter Plot: Narrative, Psychoanalysis, Feminism.* Bloomington: Indiana University Press, 1989.

hooks, bell. "Talking Back." *Discourse* 8 (Fall–Winter 1986–87): 123–28.

———. *Yearning: Race, Gender, and Cultural Politics.* Boston: South End Press, 1990.

Irigaray, Luce. *Le Corps-à-corps avec la mère.* Montreal: Editions de la Pleine Lune, 1981.

———. *Speculum of the Other Woman.* Translated by Gillian G. Gill. Ithaca: Cornell University Press, 1985.

———. "The Gesture in Psychoanalysis." Translated by Elizabeth Guild. In Brennan (1989).

Jardine, Alice. "Notes for Analysis." In Brennan (1989).

Kristeva, Julia. "Motherhood according to Giovanni Bellini" (1975). "Place Names" (1976). *Desire in Language: A Semiotic Approach to Literature and Art.* Translated by Thomas Gora, Alice Jardine, and Leon S. Roudiez. New York: Columbia University Press, 1980.

Lacan, Jacques. "Aggressivity in Psychoanalysis." *Ecrits*. Translated by Alan Sheridan. New York: Norton, 1977.

Laplanche, Jean, and Pontalis, J.-B. *The Language of Psychoanalysis*. Translated by Donald Nicholson-Smith. New York: Norton, 1973.

Masciarotte, Gloria-Jean. "The Madonna with Child, and Another Child, and Still Another Child . . . : Sensationalism and the Dysfunction of Emotions." *Discourse* 14, no. 1 (1991–92): 88–125.

Moi, Toril. "Patriarchal Thought and the Drive for Knowledge." In Brennan (1989).

Rosaldo, Renato. "Imperialist Nostalgia." *Culture and Truth: The Remaking of Social Analysis*. Boston: Beacon, 1989.

Sartre, Jean-Paul. *The Emotions: Outline of a Theory*. Translated by Bernard Frechtman. New York: Philosophical Library, 1948.

Silverman, Kaja. *The Acoustic Mirror: The Female Voice in Psychoanalysis and Cinema*. Bloomington: Indiana University Press, 1988.

Winnicott, Donald W. "Creativity and Its Origins." *Playing and Reality*. London: Tavistock, 1971.

Woodward, Kathleen. Introduction to Special Issue on the Emotions. *Discourse* 13, no. 1 (1990–91): 3–11.

———. *Aging and Its Discontents: Freud and Other Fictions*. Bloomington: Indiana University Press, 1991.

6   Equality and Difference

Joseph H. Smith

I shall argue here that a sense of unconditional worth of self and other, beginning in the bonding with initial caretakers but tempered and reclaimed in subsequent eras, is the common element in basic trust, in the capacities for intimacy, love, and mourning and also in the capacity to be dedicated to justice for all.

The forerunner of bonding is what D. W. Winnicott (1958) called the "primary maternal preoccupation" of the mother with her unborn child. This relationship with a not-yet-other requires, as does any form of intimacy, a capacity for nondefensive regression and merger or, in this instance, acceptance of being merged with an other, an other that evokes both love and foreknowledge of inevitable loss and mourning, regardless of the degree of ambivalence that obtains. This other coming to be in and from her, the bearing of such an other, and she who bears such an other are and ought to be, at some level, fully idealized. At such a level the worth of the one, the worth of the two as one, is infinite.

After birth the first major step in psychological separation comes with the infant's achievement of what Freud called the higher unity of primary narcissism. Before the ego can *have* an ideal, the ego *is* ideal. If this state is not tempered through further stages of separation in development, if the ego remains an ideal ego, the consequence will be an extreme of psychopathology. Maintaining (or reclaiming at a higher level) the sense of unconditional worth is essential not only for adult love, however, but also for the owning of one's aggression and for moving from an egocentric position through and beyond gendercentric, familiocentric, and ethnocentric positions (Smith 1992). Here it is not a matter of equality versus difference; the sense of unconditional worth of each individual affirms the uniqueness of each and also is the equality that counts. Any effort to counter injustice not animated by a sense of equality that affirms difference is likely to be motivated by envy and revenge and, if so, often veers toward the impossible aim of obliterating difference.

109

Vive l'égalité

> *Precisely when most strongly entrenched in one's difference, then strongly to apprehend the equality, that is the simple wise man's noble piety.*
> —Kierkegaard, *Concluding Unscientific Postscript*

Even if it were generally true that one difference between the girl and boy is that the girl is less frightened of being like the mother and therefore less driven toward individuation as a defense, and less inclined toward gender stereotyping, the possible pitfalls of her development would be no less complex than those of the boy. The crucial preoedipal issues for both are separateness, preliminary wholeness, and the beginnings of the capacity to mourn and the capacity for object love achieved in what Melanie Klein called the depressive position. Hampered preoedipal development of any kind hampers the achievement of this position. Any other advantage a child might have, such as intellectual endowment, particular talents, potential roles, or benevolent familial or cultural surround, pales into insignificance compared with the achievement of this inaugural wholeness.

Klein dated the depressive position at around age one. It is also the time of the beginnings of speech. Without speech (and the imagery that is the precursor of speech as a way of remembering and anticipating the object) no sense of transience, no intimation of mourning, no putting together of the good and bad mother to be loved and hated as a whole person, no sense of one's own separate and gendered subjecthood, and no sense of the immeasurable worth of a thus liberated self and other could appear. This sense of the unconditional worth of self and other is the insight that is the accompaniment of achieving the depressive position. An unhampered achievement of this insight would leave anyone dedicated to the proposition that all persons are created equal.

Reality and the complexity of development are such, however, that no individual's development is unhampered; each person is always subject to a falling away from that insight, even when it has been achieved. The interplay of need, demand, desire, resentment, rage, and the competitive struggle for advantage occupies center stage—as if some advantage were possible that could obliterate transience and death. The insight into the unconditional worth of each will eventually come to be based on the owning of transience and death, including the owning of one's grief and rage in the face of that destiny. The competitive struggle for advantage, for dominance, is a vain effort to disown transience and death. For that reason the struggle against injustice would ideally be a struggle against the radical disowning of transience and death and the radical denial of the unconditional worth of each that injustice signifies. If, instead, the struggle remains an effort to get "my fair share" of the spoils of injustice, it is to identify with the motives of the enemy—to engage in the same denial.

Since each person's development is hampered, each subject to a falling away from insight achieved, each more or less motivated to deny transience and death, there is, as everyone knows, no easy remedy for injustice. Jacques Lacan believed that even the idea that all persons are created equal, the idea that I here present as the core human insight, is only a defensive delusion of liberty in which "modern man," as Gregory Ulmer paraphrases him, "maintains with himself a sort of permanent discourse on liberty, affirming to himself his independence from any master or god, amounting, for Lacan, to a delusion of one's irreducible autonomy as an individual, couched in phrases concerning 'the rights of man, the right to happiness, and so forth'" (1986, 39).

Well, as election oratory will regularly attest, what Jefferson and Lincoln saw as most nobly human can be pressed into the service of gaining egocentric advantage. But could anyone other than Garry Wills (1979, iv–xx, 368) believe that the cadences and content of Lincoln's words at Gettysburg were so motivated? It is my belief that even though the greatest of ideas often may be defensively deployed—and many of us fall for such ploys—they are still great ideas, genuine insights. I have argued against Lacan that while claims of liberty and equality are often defensive, the nondefensive dimension of the human quest for liberty and equality is not for some total, frozen state of "unity," "wholeness," or "autonomy" (Smith 1991).

Hamilton once accused Jefferson of being a lover of paradoxes (Malone 1951, 459). With Jefferson and against Lacan, I suggest that the crucial paradox that pertains here is that a high degree of nondefensive unity (beginning with the achievement of the depressive position and leading on through the adolescent steps toward the owning of transience and death) is required for owning the absolutely unsurpassable dividedness and *lack* of unity of the speaking subject.

The adult capacities for intimacy, love, and mourning are a product of working through the adolescent fears of closeness. Overcoming these fears, or at least overcoming them, well enough, allows for reclaiming at a higher, nondefensive, nonnarcissistic level the sense of unconditional worth of self and other.

The Fear of Intimacy

How is it that the prospect of intimacy is regularly frightening and actual intimacy often unconsciously avoided? The urgency of this question begins in adolescence. Preadolescent intimacy, assuming fortunate life experience up to that time, is as easy as the turn of the preoedipal child toward the mother or father. Is it just the surge of sexual desire that disturbs even normal adolescence and marks intimacy as a danger? To what extent do the dangers of adolescent intimacy recapitulate those of the oedipal era, and to what extent do they differ from them?

The yearning for and fear of remerger with the mother is the crucial dilemma of preoedipal development. A phrasing of that dilemma which comes closer to clinical discourse is that loving must be avoided if one is unable to risk the regression and suspension of boundaries that occurs in loving. Love must also be avoided if one is unable to mourn. The acknowledgment of transience comes to its fullest in loving. A major aspect of the poignancy and intensity of being in love is the affective awareness of two people that in loving they consciously or unconsciously commit themselves not merely to the risk of loss but also to the inevitability of loss. For that commitment persons must be confident of their capacity to mourn. If mourning is blocked, one dare not risk loving. Analysis tries to help a person mourn in order to love; it also attempts to help persons love in the hope that, by so doing, they will become able to mourn.

The interimplications of love and mourning point away from incest as the danger crucial to adolescent and adult intimacy. When oedipal attachments have been reasonably resolved the adolescent is capable of relating to a new object primarily *as* a new object. The danger of intimacy is, then, not so much the danger of incest (or of remerger with the mother, which fantasies of incest cover [Smith 1991, 10–12, 55]). The danger is, instead, that of a more fundamental separateness to be wrought in the face of a more far-reaching apprehension of finitude and death, incomprehensible to the preadolescent or younger child.

In both the male and female failure of oedipal resolution means a persistent narcissistic attachment to the mother, a compulsively primitive attachment that can be transferred intact as a dual mode of relating to the father or other new objects. But, then, no new object of desire is really new; each *is* my mother, and/or, to the extent I remain merged with my mother, each "new" object is I. This is narcissistic love. No one is or ought to be altogether free of it, since consummation of object love requires the capacity for transient regression into narcissistic merger. The paradox is that the acme of adult intimacy, life at its fullest moment, is at once merger *and* the most vivid experience of separateness, transience, finitude, and the death toward which one lives. The individual whose relationships are dominantly narcissistic is fearful of remerger (incest) but motivated to merge as a denial of separateness. For the individual capable of object relatedness, capable of owning and repeatedly and more deeply reowning separateness and finitude, capable of turning toward rather than away from transience as a danger, love is a mode of mourning, a way of remembering the lost object but also of celebrating the separateness, finitude, and worth of the self and the new object.

In neither the oedipal nor the adolescent period is the parental "no" simply a no to incest. The no to incest covers a more fundamental and individuating no to the tendency of each person to disavow, deny, or defer awareness of separateness and of transience. Awareness of transience, arising from language-based capacities of memory and anticipation, opens a world beyond the wish for and fear of merger and beyond the desire to be the desire of the mother. The meaning of love then shifts from being predominantly a mode of denying transience toward loving more deeply because transience is owned. From the beginning the voice that Freud called that of the father of individual prehistory (a voice that is first of all that of the mother herself [*S.E.* 19: 31n; Smith 1991, 100]) is a call toward this way of being in the world.

If what I have so far outlined is central in structuring what it is to be human, it can be assumed that this is known at some level by every human. Such conscious or unconscious knowledge of merger and separateness, love and mourning, would condition each parent's mode of rearing a child, modified, of course, by the extent and nature of each parent's disavowal or denial of such knowledge. It is not, however, the kind of knowledge that lends itself to explicit transmission. It would be, at first, a matter of the child's sensing some important but enigmatic, owned or disowned parental understanding, which the child would be left to learn on his or her own.

I have no doubt that the achievement of such knowledge would nevertheless be easier for children whose parents were least defended against it. Before moving too quickly to idealize the ideal, however, we can be reminded that persons with the greatest difficulty have at least a chance for achieving the deepest understanding. More precisely, the person whose separateness was most traumatically wrought carries and severely defends against the deepest sense of danger and loss, which is the accompaniment of achieving separateness. If a person can overcome such defenses, he or she is in a position to see more clearly the meaning of less severe, more or less universal defenses that ward off anxiety connected with both the desire for and the fear of intimacy. The actual disadvantage can prove to be an advantage.

To recapitulate, the ultimate desires that structure the human's way of being are the desire for remerger with the mother, on the one hand, and the desire for individuation and separateness, on the other. Neither of these desires should be taken as *only* a defense against the other. The ultimate dangers that structure the human being are precisely the ultimate desires. Whatever goes in the direction of remerger with the mother goes in the direction of regressive loss of subjecthood; whatever goes in the direction of separateness portends finitude and death. This is the fundament of human ambivalence. It is a polarity to be contrasted with defensively imposed binarisms.

Polarities Encountered, Binarisms Imposed

That the human is structured by objects of desire which are also objects of danger is, I believe, a polarity within which the human can negotiate a passage, but not one that lends itself to deconstruction in the sense in which that term is ordinarily taken.

Of course, "Polarities Encountered, Binarisms Imposed" can be taken as a binarism I pose here in a way that attributes value, truth, and reality to the first term and a lack or distortion of such in the second. Let me put it this way: the polarities encountered and handed down from Western onto-logo-theology—such as good and evil, truth and nontruth, presence and absence, man and woman—can congeal into defensively imposed binarisms, which Derrida calls us to deconstruct (not meaning to destroy but meaning to analyze and reassemble or not assemble).

Polarities, to be sure, are not simply out there in the world, "real," to be encountered, as opposed to defensive binarisms, which come purely from within to distort the real world. Nothing out there comes to light except by way of the interpretations by which humans structure their world, and no interpretation could be utterly devoid of defensive elements. Deconstruction is a matter of elucidating the defensive aspects of interpretation. What I here choose to call "binarisms imposed" involves, in the extreme, not only radical oversimplification but also tendentious distortion. In such use of binarisms, positioning one term before the other, valuing one over the other, reimposing on every such arena the infantile illusion of good(mother)/bad(mother), is an effort to ward off the complexity of human ambivalence. But the object of desire discovered also as object of danger is not a simplistic binarism defensively imposed *on* the world but, instead, a dilemma inherent in being human. Each person's story is the story of how that person refuses the either/or of merger/individuation and how variations on the theme of that refusal are repeated in every subsequent instance of conflict, choice, loss, and mourning.

Of course, such polarities as truth and nontruth, presence and absence, good and evil, and man and woman can be (and regularly are) pressed into the service of politically motivated, stereotypical, defensive binarisms. Roy Schafer and Angela Moorjani, among others in this volume, have emphasized the crucially defensive and destructive role of the tendency to stereotype rigidly what it is to be a woman and what it is to be a man. In terms of such narrowly compartmentalized notions no one fits the criteria for being either a man or a woman. In those terms everyone is more both than either. Schafer and Moorjani deconstruct such stereotypy by showing its sources and motivation. The aim is to acknowledge an equality that affirms difference. This would not be difference definitively spelled out and forever to remain the same, as if anyone could fully know or predict who he or she is or will become or who another is or will become. It would, instead, be difference at least in part deferred, difference as yet unknown, or difference that could evolve or change.

A major source of gender stereotyping is, I believe, currently understood to be persisting fears of the early mother. Fear of the primitive mother includes fear of the fantastically elaborated primitive witch mother, intermixed with fear of and guilt about one's own hate and envy projected onto the bad mother. Beyond that nightmare is the less clear fear of the good mother, intermixed with the fear of one's own love and desire to remerge, together with the fear of such love and desire projected onto the good mother.

With these early dilemmas in mind it becomes difficult to ask someone, "Did you have a happy childhood?" The only response one could expect would be "What kind of dumb question is that?" Since most infants, however, seem reasonably content most of the time, there must be effective ways of dealing with such dilemmas. Splitting and primitive processes related to splitting (denial/disavowal, introjection, projection, or the precursors of those defenses) gradually yield to repression and related higher-level defenses. The main power, though, to provide passage through the dilemmas is, of course, with the mother. The defenses are weak, but she is strong.

The beginning of the mother's strength is in her original idealization of the two as one. The strength of the mother, however, depends also on her being beyond the narcissistic position of needing the infant to be only an extension of herself. Such a motive on the part of the mothering person would augment the infant's fear of and desire to merge and its fear of and desire to individuate; the dilemma pertaining to both re-merger and to individuation would be intensified.

On the other hand, the nonnarcissistic mother who knows from the start that she must mourn the loss of her idealized infant and knows herself from the start to be capable of that mourning provides an un-pressured presence in which the child's love and hate, admiration and envy, closeness and distance, can be borne. She intuitively knows, that is, that these positions of the child are not its positive and negative judg-ments of the mother's worth but, rather, necessary way stations in the child's passage through the first stages of the lifelong issue of merger/individuation.

Defensive stereotyping of what it is to be a man and what it is to be a woman is generally more manifest in males than in females. Why should that be? Does being like the mother for the male imply a feared castra-tion? But being castrated or not castrated, at least in the older psycho-analytic literature, is another defensive binarism bearing the literal meaning of having or not having the penis. This would suggest that the fear of being like the mother is not the fear of being castrated but, in-stead, somewhat the reverse of that. Having the penis is proffered as proof against the deeper fear; one is therefore not like one's mother; one is not one's mother. One is, the idea could proceed, completely different from one's mother, from women—so much so that women are utterly incomprehensible. Who could know what they might want, or be?

An irony is that the more persons protest that they are completely different from the mother, the more they reveal a lack of separateness —a secret holding on that betrays the fear of individuation. Thus it is that another meaning, also defensive but opposite to that already de-scribed, can be simultaneously attributed to having a penis. Castration means being cut off. There is no way of limiting the multiple levels of meaning of "cut off" to the literal absence or anticipated absence of the penis. "Cut off" could mean cut off from the mother, the father, or life itself. Having the penis could be unconsciously taken as evidence that one is *not* cut off from one's mother, that one, in fact, *is* one's mother, or even that one is not subject to death.

Although more manifest in the male, defensive stereotyping of what it is to be a woman and what it is to be a man is by no means a rarity among women. Of course, the issue of merger/individuation is there, irrespective of gender. But casting women and men as simplistically opposite would do nothing to alleviate the woman's fear of being like (being) her mother, as it presumably does for the man. Still, since the frightening and frighteningly desirable primitive mother is there at the

beginning for everyone, *some* derivative tendency to distance, dero-
gate, and disempower women might be expected in all men and women.
There are, certainly, women who are overtly hell-bent on not being like
their mothers, but that could be for a variety of reasons.

Although the issue of remerger/individuation is there for both genders, perhaps being like the mother carries a greater threat for the male
over a longer period of early childhood. For the boy the threat of being
like the mother would likely be intensified, not only because his path
toward individuation is a path toward becoming a man but also because
the boy continues to be drawn by love into the mother's orbit through
the oedipal period. His oedipal love, itself frightening at another level,
could be confused with or added to the fearful desire to remerge with
her. His refuge is in being like the father. The girl's oedipal love for her
father is also frightening at a higher level but is directed away from the
more primitive wish/fear for remerger with the mother. This makes it
relatively safer for her to be like the mother. She can be like the mother
in attracting the father without the same danger of being drawn back
toward remerger with the mother. It is thus less dangerous for the girl
to be seductive with the father than the boy with the mother. It is also
safer for her to be like the mother because her path toward individuation, which is to say her path away from remerger, is toward becoming a
woman. Finally, because being like the mother is less dangerous, the girl
is less defensively driven than the boy to see males and females as radical opposites.

It is possible that I here overdraw the difference in the response of
the boy and girl to being like the mother and emphasize the greater
danger for the male in accord with the tendency of each gender to believe the other has it easier. To illustrate a bit of the complexity that the
above sketch does not include, the meaning and manner of the girl's
oedipal turn to her father will vary depending on how things went with
her mother in the preoedipal period. Such a turning, ideally the natural
flowering of the girl's oedipal desire, may instead be motivated by intense fear of and flight from the primitive mother.

Both genders, after all, are subject to narcissistic difficulties. The primal common pathway for all narcissistic difficulty or disorder is that of
a hampered separation from the primitive mother and the persistence
at some level of a dyadic (dual, symbiotic) mode of relating directly
transferred from the early mother to subsequent love objects. In such
flight from the early mother there has been no chance to consolidate a
sense of the mother, good and bad, as one person and of the self, good
and bad, also as one person—an integration in which a sense of the
unconditional worth of each is reclaimed at a higher, more complex

level and no longer confined to the fantastically idealized good mother/ good me position.

Where integration of the good and bad has not been achieved, where separateness from the mother is thus flawed, the subject's fate is to be involved in the quest for reestablishment of good object/good me relationships, which means that he or she will be involved in narcissistic relationships that are inevitably intense and inevitably unstable. The girl's turn to her father, under these conditions, will not be to the father who, as a third term, has played an important role in facilitating separation from the mother. Instead, the girl will turn to the father as a less frightening but still narcissistically loved substitute for the feared primitive mother. The same way of turning to the father can also be the fate of the boy when integration of the good and bad is similarly flawed. Rather than being in the place of the symbolic father in a triadic relationship that fosters separation, the father is, in some measure, similarly substituted for the primitive mother in a repetition of the dyadic, symbiotic, narcissistic mode of relating.

In summary, in fortunate development wherein the depressive position (seeing the good mother/bad mother as one and the good me/bad me as one, having the capacity for ambivalence, and being able to mourn) has been achieved, the girl can more freely turn with her sexual love to the father and the boy to the mother. When preoedipal separateness has been achieved each gender can experience the father as a new object rather than his being simply a substitute for the mother. Even so, the girl's oedipal turn to the father is less fraught with danger than the boy's to the mother because the father is other than the primitive object of desire and fear.

In unfortunate development in which the depressive position, adequate separateness, and the capacity for object love have not been achieved, the girl's turn to her father and the boy's turn to his mother may be affected in a variety of ways. The boy's primitive attachment to and fear of the mother, and his envy, hatred, and guilt in relation to her, may hamper an oedipal attachment, and thereby his future capacity for heterosexual love. This could leave him, in this culture, with a tendency toward exploitation and aggressive subjugation of women. For the girl the same burden of fear and guilt from her preoedipal relationship with the mother may be such that she is unable to turn at all to the father. Or, on the other hand, the fear and guilt may motivate an urgent flight from the mother with an intensified sexual turning to the father and subsequent love objects that parallels male Don Juanism. Whether hampered preoedipal development leads to inhibition or intensified acting out, however, the guilt and fear, combined with cultural pressures, are such that there is a basic difficulty in owning her own sexuality or her own aggression except in projected form.

Conclusion

The prolonged struggle against the unjust treatment of women has culminated in the widespread readiness of women and many men to confront any such injustice. The motives for such confrontation vary, however, from the radically defensive to the reasonably nondefensive. This is part of the reason why no easy solution is at hand. I have attempted here to give some of the background for the complexity of the motivations involved.

There is, as I have stressed, a consensus that core issues involve fear of and anger toward the primitive mother. It is a point implicit in the thought of Melanie Klein, thematized by Karen Horney (1967) and, more recently, by Dorothy Dinnerstein (1977) and Nancy Chodorow (1989). Rigid and homophobic gender stereotyping, especially by men, is generally understood as being at least in part a response to such fear and anger. Schafer and Moorjani, as I have mentioned, advocate countering such stereotyping through analysis of its motives. Dinnerstein has suggested that fear of the early mother and the consequent defensively reactive derogation of women might be alleviated by a strict sharing in the care of infants by the mother and the father.

No one has suggested that it would be easy to put in place or carry through such a project, which is not to say it should not be attempted. Yet, this and other such projects, if attempted, should be undertaken with as full an understanding as possible of the complexity of the defenses and resistance to be encountered. If fear of the primitive mother signifies a hampered preoedipal development, if gender stereotyping is a manifestation of the universal tendency to deny transience and death, would simply substituting the father half-time for the mother in the care of the infant in itself be a cure? If a large portion of the feminist battle against injustice is motivated by the same denials that animate the injustice, what can the result of that battle be? If a man's fear of the early mother hampers his wholeness and motivates sexual exploitation and aggressive subjugation of women, if a woman's fear of the early mother hampers the owning of her own sexuality and aggression in favor of projecting sex and aggression onto men, if a woman as a consequence of such projections does battle largely from a position of defensively accusatory, righteous indignation, then what kind of resolution of gender warfare can be anticipated?

To offer yet another impossibly utopian solution, if the war between the genders could cease in favor of persons taking stock of their own defenses, that in itself could amount to the realization of a kind of equality. From recognizing the universality of defenses against transience and death regardless of gender, perhaps there could arise, based on that recognition, a more profound sense of the infinite worth of each person.

References

Chodorow, Nancy J. *Feminism and Psychoanalytic Theory*. New Haven: Yale University Press, 1989.

Dinnerstein, Dorothy. *The Mermaid and the Minotaur: Sexual Arrangements and Human Malaise*. New York: Harper & Row, 1977.

Freud, Sigmund. *The Ego and the Id* (1923). *The Standard Edition of the Complete Psychological Works of Sigmund Freud*, vol. 19. Edited and translated by James Strachey. London: Hogarth Press, 1961.

Horney, Karen. *Feminine Psychology*. New York: Norton, 1967.

Kierkegaard, Søren. *Concluding Unscientific Postscript* [1846]. Translated by D. F. Swenson with notes by W. Lowrie. Princeton: Princeton University Press, 1968.

Malone, Dumas. *Jefferson and the Rights of Man*. Boston: Little, Brown, 1951.

Smith, Joseph H. *Arguing with Lacan: Ego Psychology and Language*. New Haven: Yale University Press, 1991.

———. "Ambivalence, Instincts, and Mourning." *Common Knowledge* 1, no. 2 (1992): 97–104.

Ulmer, Gregory L. "Sounding the Unconscious." In *Glassary*, by John P. Leavy, Jr., with a foreword by Jacques Derrida. Lincoln: University of Nebraska Press, 1986.

Wills, Garry. *Inventing America: Jefferson's Declaration of Independence*. New York: Vintage Books Edition, 1979.

Winnicott, D. W. "Primary Maternal Preoccupation." In *Collected Papers: Through Paediatrics to Psycho-analysis*. New York: Basic Books, 1958.

7 Gender and Sexuality: Some Unconscious Articulations

Wilfried Ver Eecke

To stress the equality of men and women as a means of obtaining equal rights is essential in the economic and the political domains. It is, for instance, reprehensible to pay systematically a lower wage or a lower honorarium for a same or substantially similar performance solely because the service was rendered by a female. It is unacceptable to make political office and voting rights dependent upon being male. Such differentiation is as reprehensible as discrimination based upon race, religion, or national origin. Efforts to eliminate such discriminatory practices are morally laudable. The question I wish to address, however, is whether or not gender difference makes a difference within the broadly conceived domain of the family. I see that domain as covering the noneconomic and nonpolitical relation between sexes and the role of sexuality in the reproduction and rearing of children.

As a matter of personal taste, I would find the world a duller place if I were in a civilization that tried to make sexual difference irrelevant in all cultural relations. Such a civilization would have to try to erase differences in dress, in grooming, in ways of walking, in character difference (popular view of female = warmth, of male = strength), in moral sensitivity (female = caring, male = rule- or justice-oriented). Wherever I would look I would see only human persons, never a female or a male. I assume that such a civilization would devote energy, ingenuity, and productive capital to inventing means of making bodily differences (beard—no beard, breasts—no breasts, etc.) as invisible as possible.

Clearly, the project of making gender independent of sexuality would require giving much thought to bodily differences in order to make them appear nonexistent. Such a project would solely link gender and sexual differences in order, ultimately, to sever the dependence of gender upon sexual differences. But, in such a project, what would remain of the concept "gender"? Would the ideal not be, in this project, to eliminate the concept altogether?

In this chapter I want to explore the legitimate connection between gender and sexuality. I will restrict my reflection to unconscious motives for that connection and will therefore rely almost exclusively upon psychoanalytic arguments. My exposition will therefore have methodological limitations. Psychoanalysis is a theory and a practice of origins, of archaeology. Psychoanalysis is also a theory that has difficulties addressing satisfactorily the problem of sublimation. Finally, psychoanalysis is a practice that *must* leave the patient the freedom to create his or her own life project. My decision to rely heavily upon psychoanalysis will therefore result in my being restricted to proving the original link between gender and sexuality. It will make it impossible for me to argue how that link has to be worked out, except for the fact that the original link may not be denied or repressed.

A fundamental contribution of twentieth-century thought is its deep awareness of human finitude and of the difficulty human beings have in accepting that finitude. Heidegger connects the idea of finitude with acceptance of "death." Lacan and Derrida connect the idea of finitude with the necessary structures of language. Freud, too, makes us aware that human beings have a hard time renouncing their wishes, even if they are contradictory. Freud stresses that in the unconscious negation is absent. In my opinion, however, the unique contribution of Freud to the twentieth-century theme of human finitude is that he connects the experience of finitude with the subjective experience of sexual difference.

Some early statements of Freud connect the experience of finitude with the *seeing* of the genital difference between boy and girl, more specifically, the presence or absence of the penis.[1] The subjective experience of finitude thus takes the form of fear (of castration) for the boy[2] and (penis) envy for the girl.[3] Freud then tried to speculate how this subjective experience of the genital difference led to a different morality in male and female. In his view the female would have a lesser superego and thus a lower quality of moral life (*S.E.* 19: 256–58). Feminist authors have rightly objected to this kind of gender definition by psychoanalysis (Chodorow 1974; Nicholson 1990; Grosz 1991, 7).

Some feminists, in my opinion, then went too far by rejecting all (psychoanalytic) arguments for gender differentiation.[4] One could easily reread the above Freudian speculation in light of the broader Freudian corpus in order to validate some of the crucial claims of the feminist movement. Thus, the Freudian corpus could easily be used to claim that there is nothing inferior about a female morality that is person oriented. Female care morality is either simply different from or may be frankly superior to male rule-guided morality. In light of Freud's later reflection about the negative consequences of the superego, Freud himself could be invited to reevaluate his condescension toward female morality, without having to give up his speculation about the relation between sexual body and moral "mood." Indeed, Freud later argued that neurotics are often paralyzed because they have too strong a superego. As a consequence, they want to be more moral than they can be. They are therefore moral hypocrites.[5] The solution Freud suggests is to lower the demands of the superego so that the neurotic can accept being only as morally good as he can be.[6] To have a less strong superego, a condition Freud condescendingly attributes to the female, is, in light of Freud's later thought, not to be despised. Whether true or not as a matter of empirical fact, whether true or not as a matter of speculative theory, having a lesser superego is, in the later Freud, not necessarily negative.

Fear of castration itself, another point of contention between feminism and the psychoanalytic tradition, also receives another meaning in the later Freud. Freud doubts that seeing of genital difference can by itself produce *fear* of castration.[7] He also changes the name of the last preoedipal phase from genital to phallic (*S.E.* 7: 199–200 n. 2). But that change in name, although significant in that it moves away from anatomical sexuality, is nevertheless problematic inasmuch as the new name is used by Freud to signal that only male sexuality is entertained by children.[8]

Lacan uses the move away from anatomical sexuality by Freud and stresses that the problem of sexual difference lies in the imaginary.[9] For Lacan the *image* of the phallus serves to cover up the sense of lack that is constitutive of human existence. Acceptance of lack is for Lacan the origin of human desire.[10] That acceptance of lack is, in accordance with Freudian theory, an unconscious acceptance. Furthermore, it is tied to the acceptance of sexual difference and also to language and culture, which Lacan calls the symbolic (Muller and Richardson 1982, 93–94).

Lacan's attempt to connect the emergence of gender with language allows him and his followers to stress that gender, like language, is based upon arbitrary distinctions and that little if anything about gender is necessary. Lacan's theory can thus be seen as a conceptualization of a correction that Freud himself started and that undermines some of the theoretical claims that are most offensive to women. Lacan's conceptualization of that Freudian correction requires a clarification of the three Lacanian master-concepts of the real, the imaginary, and the symbolic (Laplanche and Pontalis 1973, 210, 439–41).

Two psychoanalysts, inspired by Lacan, have provided us with power-ful short vignettes that can illustrate and differentiate these three Laca-nian concepts. Julia Kristeva reports the case of Paul, who came to her after a hospitalization in St. Anne (1987). "He is a man of sober ap-pearance, precise in speech and capable of telling his story in a skillful and charming way." Paul's stories, his words, were a facade to cover up an "'uncommon and almost incommunicable' drama in his life" (13). Tragedy had struck Paul at age four. It involved "his father, a high official in the French colonial administration." He "was brutally tortured and murdered while his family watched" (14). This kind of unspeakable ex-perience Lacan calls the real. I agree with Kristeva's comment that such an event, such an experience of the real, may be sufficient to destroy a life. In the case of Paul, however, there was more.

The torture-murder of the father also functioned as a cover-up of a difficult childhood, which culminated in Paul's discovering his mother with a lover. Paul was then three years old. Paul adored his mother and had, according to Kristeva, an extraordinarily close relationship with her. "It bordered on identification . . . [and] was almost cannibalistic." The mother reacted to being found out by violently threatening Paul: "If you say anything, I'll never speak to you again." Kristeva interprets the mother's reaction as a threat "to withdraw her love if Paul chose a sym-bolic alliance with the father." In giving in to the mother, the son com-mitted, according to Kristeva, "the first explicit murder of the father" (14). It was a murder committed by accepting the mother's interdiction against speaking. But what kind of murder was it? What father was mur-dered here? Not the father of flesh and blood; that occurred only a year later. Not the imaginary father, which would involve the child's per-sonal image. In order to see which father was murdered in the case of Paul, we need to discover still another kind of father. That other father is connected with the fact that human sexuality is conjoined with a compact. Sexual relations outside that fact are called infidelity. Such a morally negative label means that our culture believes that some funda-mental right is violated. The rights violated by infidelity belong to the father as symbolic person, that is, as a being defined by cultural and social relations that involve mutual obligation and commitments.[11] In accepting the prohibition against speaking about his mother's infidelity, Paul "murdered" the *symbolic* father. But what is it in the murder of the symbolic father that is so pathogenic?[12] We will get a glimpse of that if we understand the seductive power of the imaginary.

François Peraldi, in an article about the work of Marguerite Duras, provides us with an autobiographical detail that can illustrate Lacan's concept of the imaginary (1984, 41). That detail, the departure of his father for war, when he himself was only eighteen months old, produced such a deep impact on him that thirty years later even a psychoanalysis could not undo the traumatic effects. Peraldi writes that he had been very seriously ill just prior to his father's departure and that this father had taken care of him and had been very "maternal with his sick boy." When the father left Peraldi recalls being very, very sad. To console him his mother gave him a picture of his father. The author recalls putting the picture carefully next to his bed. About a year later the father returned from the war and appeared in front of the house as a skinny, dirty, and unshaven man. Little François refused to believe that this man was his father. He ran to his room and returned with the picture of his father that he had received from his mother and screamed to his mother with extraordinary vigor: "This is my father." Peraldi further writes that nothing could convince him as a child that the man who had come back to live with his mother was his father. Thirty years later Peraldi relived the pain of his father's departure in his personal psychoanalysis. And in an extraordinary bit of personal confession he writes that even his psychoanalysis could not let him recognize the lost father in the father who had returned and with whom he had spent a good part of his life.

What is the significance of Peraldi's not being able to recognize his father? In other words, what pain was the child trying to avoid by resisting the recognition of his father? We get a hint if we look carefully at how the returning father appears to his young son. He was skinny, dirty, and unshaven. And he came to live with the boy's mother. The father who had left was, in the mind of the son, fused with the father of a picture in which he was well fed, clean, and well dressed. The father who had left was also a father who had cared for his son in a maternal way and was therefore fused with the maternal figure. The illness of the son and the father's caring had given objective validation to a subjective projection of children of about one and a half years: "the united parents." The mother and the father are not experienced as separate figures. They are projected to have the same task, the maternal task of caring. The father is thus seen by the child at that age as an extension of the mother figure. The father is not yet understood as having his own and different function. The father is understood only as the child can imagine him. This is the *imaginary* father. Presumably, two characteristics of the returning father did not fit the picture of Peraldi's imaginary father: that he could be dirty and that he lived with the mother. If the father can be dirty and skinny, he is not perfect. If he lives with the mother, he is an intruder in the cozy relationship the boy imagines he has with the mother. Jointly, these two points bring the threat of finitude to the child. If they do, we can understand why any child might be motivated to stick with an imaginary father rather than move on to a symbolic father.

We are now in a position to articulate *one aspect* of the concept of gender, that is, the unconscious dimension implied by a Lacanian re-reading of Freud. Lacan's concept of the real includes something unspeakable. In the case of Paul the unspeakable concerns the torture-murder of the father in his presence and the prohibition by his mother against telling his father about the mother's love affair. The example of Paul, however, refers to anecdotal, accidental events that happened to someone but which need not have happened and do not happen to most individuals. Still, Lacan maintains that *for every human being* the real includes something unspeakable. Lacan uses different words to point to that unspeakable: relying upon Freud, he calls it castration (Lacan 1977, 198); relying upon Heidegger, he calls it death (103); relying upon his medical training, he calls it the fetalization of the human baby (4). Each of these three ways of characterizing the unspeakable dimension of the real needs to be carefully interpreted. Suffice it to stress that for Lacan the human infant has to deal with an unspeakable dimension. In the language of common sense one could say that an infant needs to face and deal with its total helplessness. Even if that is not identical with Lacan's real, it allows us to have some commonsense referent for it.

Given this threatening dimension of the real, what is it that allows the infant to even face the real? Common sense again has an answer: the love of the mother. Lacan's answer is articulated in his theory of the mirror stage. That theory starts from the observable phenomenon that the human baby from about six months of age on reacts with jubilation to its own images in the mirror. Lacan takes that jubilation to mean that the child experiences a great gain in seeing and recognizing itself in the mirror. The gain consists in the child's discovering itself as a unity and a totality as opposed to its prior experience of itself as body parts: mouth, hand, foot. Furthermore, images of unity remain contradicted by the proprioceptive experience of the body, which at that early age remains chaotic. However precarious, the new self-image allows the child to invest itself libidinally. Self-love and narcissism become possible.

There has been an evolution in how Lacan understands the empowering that results from the mirror image. In his original formulation Lacan attributed to the function of seeing itself the force of empowering the child to face the real, in particular, the experience of its own body as chaotic.[13] In the revisions of his theory of the mirror stage

Lacan explicitly includes the mother's desire.[14] Aulagnier and Mannoni, both students of Lacan, take the desire of the mother as central for the process of empowering the child. Crucial in Lacan's theory remains the idea that the empowering of the child occurs on a nonrealistic basis: it is visual; it is *imaginary*. Typical for the imaginary is that the infant ascribes to itself (and others) a visual fullness, a visual perfection, which it (and others) does not possess.[15] This narcissistic aspect of the imaginary ultimately must be corrected, or the infant will become a mentally ill person.

The question of gender enters in a decisive way when Lacanian authors reflect upon the conditions for properly correcting the imaginary. Both Aulagnier and Mannoni analyze the desire of the mother to answer that question. Aulagnier points to an obvious difference between pregnant mothers. The difference concerns what I want to call "the labor of imagination" (Aulagnier 1964, 49–50, 53–55). Mothers who have given birth to children who later turn out be mentally healthy report that during their pregnancy they were actively concerned with their future children. Sometimes they wondered how the baby would look: for instance, would it have blue or brown eyes? They wondered whether it would be a boy or a girl. They wondered whether it would look more like themselves or like the father. They dreamt about how they would dress the baby, how the baby would behave. They would give a name to the baby and talk to it, even though in some instances they knew that the name might be provisional because they had not yet agreed with their husbands on what to name the baby.

According to Aulagnier, this labor of the imagination has a salutary effect upon the desire of pregnant women. Pregnancy has as one of its effects the reemergence of narcissistic feelings. The labor of the imagination transforms these narcissistic feelings into expectations for the future child (Aulagnier 1964, 50–51).

Mothers who had psychotic children remembered their pregnancies differently. The difference was not physiological; it was not that their pregnancies were more difficult or easier than those of mothers with mentally healthy children. Among both kinds of mothers some had difficult and some had easy pregnancies. The major difference was the way they experienced the pregnancies. Thus, mothers of psychotic children who had had difficult pregnancies surmised, for example, that their babies must have pushed against their bladders or against their stomachs. Mothers of psychotic children who had had easy pregnancies and had not experienced some problems during pregnancy that they had had before pregnancy would surmise that their babies must have pushed their bladders or their stomachs back into their proper places. These mothers thus experienced their babies as organs next to other organs. They *did not imagine* their future babies (Aulagnier 1964, 53).

A big difference between the two kinds of mothers emerges in the psychological reaction toward the event of giving birth. For both mothers giving birth is physiologically losing the child. For the mothers who did the "labor of imagination," giving birth is not just losing the child inside of them; it is *also* participating in the advent of the *expected* child. For mothers who did not do the labor of imagination, giving birth is predominantly experienced as *losing* the child. These mothers are often subject to a more or less severe postpartum depression (Aulagnier 1964, 50, 55). Aulagnier also reports that these mothers had a tendency to deny unconsciously the sexual origin of the baby. In this phenomenon she sees the origin of the foreclosure of the Name of the Father, which Lacan's theory makes responsible for psychosis (54–55).[16]

Aulagnier sees a close connection between the facts reported in the previous paragraph. A pregnant mother who unconsciously denies the sexual origin of the child is able to experience herself unconsciously as the sole maker of the future child. But, if she is the sole maker, the child is hers. There is no reason to acknowledge the father. If the mother feels she is the sole maker of the child, the child is hers in another sense as well: it belongs in her, it belongs to her, it is her possession, just as her other organs are her possessions (Aulagnier 1964, 54). Aulagnier and Mannoni stress that such mothers may have very deep affection for their children but that such affection is narcissistic. Their affection is suffocation.[17] It is not love for the child as *other* than the mother. The unconscious acceptance of the sexual origin of the child is credited with the ability of transforming the narcissistic desire of the mother into love for the child as *other* and *autonomous*.

If these analyses are correct, then we notice that women who become mothers have the very specific unconscious task of what I called the labor of the imagination. That task is critically important because it helps to transform a narcissistic affection into love for the child as a separate person. Presumably, ancient Roman culture sensed something of the importance of the labor of the imagination: it encouraged pregnant women to take walks and to admire beautiful statues.

The imaginary is that which allows the child to deal with the threatening real. But the imaginary needs to be corrected. The correction happens, according to Lacanian theory, by the child's insertion into the symbolic order. That insertion displaces the child from its imaginary fullness and requires the child to create a new self-conception. Lacan himself reflected mainly on the displacement involved in the insertion of the symbolic.[18] Let us try to understand the displacement involved.

The imaginary solution to the threat of the real consists in the child's believing in a sort of symbiotic unity with the mother in which the child simultaneously attributes to the mother fullness and omnipotence *and* believes that it itself is the object that fulfills the mother's desire. If we attribute this subjective position to the child, we can understand that the child is *demanding* and *reacts with anger* to any restriction of its wishes. Indeed, such a child feels that it is worthy of having all its wishes fulfilled and that the mother always has the resources to satisfy them.

How will such a child mature emotionally? Structurally, the Lacanian answer is simple. Because for such a child only it and the mother exist unconsciously, the crucial figure to promote maturation is the mother. The miracle of emotional maturation, the miracle of correcting the narcissistic and imaginary solution to the threat of the real, is called by Lacan *paternal metaphor*. It is Lacan's linguistic reinterpretation of the Oedipus complex.[19]

The correction is invited by a move of the mother. If the mother shows respect for the Name of the Father, then the mother signals to the child that she is different from the one the child created in its imaginary solution. Instead of being omnipotent and self-sufficient, the mother shows that she relates to someone else. Furthermore, that someone else is not the child. Instead of allowing the child to situate itself in a dyad, the mother invites the child to accept a triangle. This invitation carries an enormous burden for the child, because it invites the child to accept the fact that lack is constitutive of personhood. The child becomes aware of this in seeing that the mother relates to and finds fulfillment in the father. The child then realizes that he or she is not the fulfillment of the mother, which it imaginarily thought it was. The child must, therefore, accept that it lacks that which might satisfy the mother's desire (Lacan 1977, 200).

The pain of accepting such a lack might be refused. A simple defensive strategy is to wish that the one who sustains the third angle of the triangle (the father) would disappear. This is the wish to murder the father in Freud's formulation of the Oedipus complex.

I must stress one point. The correction to the imaginary is not the result of conscious thought but, rather, is an unconscious process. To say this is to argue that the process is moved more by images than by thoughts and, more specifically, by bodily inspired images. Freud's and Lacan's claim is that the correction of the imaginary is made by means of the image of the phallus, which, in the correction, the child, girl or boy, experiences as not having (Muller and Richardson 1982, 338–39). Lacan's conceptual formula for the castration complex thus becomes that the child accepts that it lacks the imaginary phallus it originally thought it possessed (or, put more strongly, that it thought it was) (Lacan 1977, chap. 8).

By her respect for the Name of the Father the mother invites the child to accept this lack. By his structural role the father represents the necessity of that lack. In Lacanian terms the father represents the *unconscious law of prohibition of incest*, that is, the prohibition of the imaginary solution to the threat of the real (Lacan 1977, 66–67). Lacan argues that the father representing the law must not have an imaginary and narcissistic self-image either. Otherwise, the child unconsciously misinterprets the law of prohibition of incest. The child then interprets that law as an arbitrary imposition by an omnipotent father, rather than as the law of being a human person, to which the father too submits (Lacan 1977, 218–19; Ver Eecke 1988, 108–14).

Thus, again we see that male and female are invited to play different roles in order to contribute to the correction of the imaginary solution by the child to the threat of the real. The female (the mother figure) is called upon to show respect for the Name of the Father. The male (the father figure) is called upon to have a proper attitude toward the law of prohibition; he must *represent*, rather than *be*, the law.

Until now we have approached the question of gender only from the point of view of the roles the male and female are expected to play for a "happy" evolution of the child's development. We can now add one more step. Let us return to the moment at which either boy or girl has accepted that it is not the phallus it imagined it was. As a consequence, both boy and girl need to establish a new unconscious body image: that new image cannot have the fullness that the imaginary solution had. The new body image must include a *mark of the lack* that the correction of the imaginary solution revealed. In the language of psychoanalysis the new unconscious body image must have the mark of castration. But boys and girls have different bodies by which to *represent* castration. This problem of representation will direct the unconscious self-representation for the boy and the girl in different directions. It is normal to wonder what is meant by the claim that the unconscious self-representation for the boy and the girl will follow different directions. An easy line of argumentation is to point out that boy and girl have different anatomical bodies by which the self-representation as wanting beings, as beings with a lack, is to be done (Montrelay 1990, 261–62). This line of argumentation, however, gives too exclusive a role to the anatomical body. Self-representation, even unconscious self-representation of the body, is a psychological act. As such, it is difficult to see how the task of creating an unconscious body image would not be influenced by purely cultural signals, such as the difference in cultural reaction to masturbation by girls and boys.[20] These cultural signals are, however, not unrelated to the anatomical body. Thus, Montrelay points out that "the girl is less subject than the boy to threats and to the defenses [repression] that penalize masturbation." But within the same paragraph she adds: "The anatomy of the boy . . . exposes him very early to the realization that he . . . experiments, not only with chance but also with the law and with his sexual organs: his body itself" is at stake (261).

My own position is that the unconscious postoedipal body image is an act of representation. As such, it cannot be thought of as rigidly determined. No psychic act is. On the other hand, it is difficult to see how the anatomical difference would not be relevant for the creation of the unconscious body image. Culture has the freedom to create. It does not have the license to disavow.

Conclusion

I have argued that, as parents, males and females have different roles to fulfill in order to promote a happy development of the child. The female, as mother, has two crucial roles to fulfill: during pregnancy she needs to go through a labor of the imagination, allowing her to transform narcissistic libido into love for a future autonomous child, other than herself; she also needs to provide the occasion for the child to correct its imaginary solution to the threat of the real. The male, as father, has the task of representing rather than omnipotently being the law. These different roles are nothing more than an invitation for male and female to accept what is needed for the proper structuring of the unconscious in the child.

I have also argued that male and female can be expected, unconsciously, to represent differently the experience of being a lack, because the unconscious representation works with a different body, and body representations are crucial for unconscious representations.

I have restricted my argument of the desirable or necessary difference between male and female to theoretical reflections. But is there any empirical evidence for the correctness of my theoretical conclusions?

Let me refer to Antoine Vergote's conclusions based on empirical research done by a group under his direction. According to that research both delinquents and schizophrenics have a *different image* of the father than the one I theoretically derived as desirable for the healthy development of the child. In delinquents the image of the father is "essentially characterized by the rational trait of systematic mind, a trait which, in the absence of law, doubtless takes on the sense of efficacious calculation." In schizophrenics the image of the father is not connected with representing the law. Rather, "the primary factor is composed of two opposing dimensions, one expressing the idea of decision, a more concrete term than law-authority, and the other containing the idea of availability" (Vergote and Tamayo 1980, 194).

The conclusions of Vergote invite me to make an important specification. The theory of Lacan does not require for the healthy development of the child that a real father be physically present. An absent father, even a dead father, can be psychologically very present. In order to make this point Lacan refers to the symbolic father as the Name of the Father. It is even the case that somebody other than the biological father can assume the role of the symbolic father. In some primitive tribes it is the brother of the mother or some specific ancestor (Ortigues and Ortigues 1966, 191, 197, 221–23). In Hindu cultures it is to some extent the Hindu God as law giver (Vergote and Tamayo 1980, 194–95, 197, 213). It remains the case that the mother has a special function in promoting the acceptance of the law, however culturally presented to the child.

Let us now turn to one application. Mary Ann Glendon, a Harvard professor specializing in comparative law, points out that recent American family law does not give the father the same legal position as most European law.[21] In European law provisions are made to establish fatherhood effectively in most cases and to demand, equally effectively, child support from absent fathers (1987, 57). Furthermore, we have witnessed the recent refusal by the U.S. Supreme Court to let stand the Pennsylvania requirement that, before an abortion, the father be notified, even though that requirement had a number of exemptions (*Planned Parenthood v. Casey*, 112 S.Ct. 2791 [1992]). What does such a refusal do to the cultural, symbolic status of the father with reference to his child? American family law has a long way to go to *enforce* the *duties* of the paternal role and *to respect* its very *function*. The individualistic model underlying its decisions *promotes less* than is realistically possible the triangle mother-father-child, which my theoretical conclusions put forth as highly desirable.

I wish to finish by quoting from Genesis. "Male and female He created them" (1, 27). I believe that psychoanalysis in general and Lacan in particular have helped us to understand a little better the depth of difference in gender.

Notes

1. For instance, *S.E.* 19: 143–45, 175–76.

2. For instance, *S.E.* 13: 130–31, 205–6; 18: 154–55; 23: 276–77.

3. For instance, *S.E.* 11: 204–5; 17: 129–32; 19: 178–79; 252–56; 20: 125–29; 23: 193–94; 250–51.

4. Thus, Sara Ruddick ends her beautiful article "Maternal Thinking" with the following wish: "Might we echo the cry of some feminists—there shall be no more 'women'—with our own—there shall be no more 'mothers,' only people engaging in child care? . . . On that day there will be no more 'fathers.' . . . There will be mothers of both sexes who live out a transformed maternal thought in communities that share parental care" (1983, 227).

5. *S.E.* 14: 284: "Anyone . . . compelled to act continually in accordance with precepts which are not the expression of his instinctual inclinations, is living, psychologically speaking, beyond his means, and may objectively be described as a hypocrite, whether he is clearly aware of the incongruity or not."

6. Thus, in a letter to James Jackson Putnam he writes: "It is therefore more humane to establish this principle: 'Be as moral as you can honestly be and do not strive for an ethical perfection for which you are not destined.' Whoever is capable of sublimation will turn to it inevitably as soon as he is free of his neurosis. Those who are not capable of this at least will become more natural and honest" (quoted in Hale 1971, 122). In his technical papers Freud gives this advice: "We are obliged to restrict ourselves . . . to bring about the slow demolition of the hostile super-ego" (*S.E.* 23: 180). Relevant also is Freud's discussion of moral masochism (*S.E.* 19: 169–70).

7. Compare, for instance, *S.E.* 7: 195, with *S.E.* 23: 189–90, 276–77, and 200; and, finally, with *S.E.* 10: 8 n. 2 (footnote added in 1923); and *S.E.* 19: 144 n. 2.

8. *S.E.* 7: 200 n. 2 (cont'd. from p. 199): "For it [the child] knows only one kind of genital: the male one."

9. An early, and still the best, article-length exposition of the often misunderstood relation between anatomical sexuality and personality in Freud and Lacan is Ewens (1976). A longer and more recent study of the problem is the double introduction by Juliet Mitchell and Jacqueline Rose in their *Feminine Sexuality* (1985).

10. Muller (1979). The intellectual origin of this thesis is to be found in Kojève's commentary on Hegel's passage in the *Phenomenology* describing the transition from consciousness to self-consciousness (1969, chap. 1, 3–7, esp. p. 5).

11. See Lacan (1977, 61–68). A possible anthropological basis for Lacan's more sociological or structuralist claim can be found in Freud (*S.E.* 7: 207): "A normal sexual life is only assured by the exact convergence of the affectionate current and the sensual current both being directed towards the sexual object and sexual aim." Lacan himself seems to look in Freud for the theme of compact in sexuality in Freud's studies about Oedipus and Moses and in *Totem and Taboo*. See Lacan (1991, chaps. 6–9).

12. See Ver Eecke (1987). On pp. 326–27 I summarize a number of condi-

tions that can help or hinder the healthy development of the child, according to Freud. Several conditions are central to Lacan's higher-order conceptualization: ability of the child to separate itself from parents, absence of overtenderness by parents, presence of emotional triangle: mother-father-child. The references to Freud are from his *Three Essays on the Theory of Sexuality* (*S.E.* 7, particularly pp. 223–30).

13. See Lacan (1977, 4). The translation uses the word *gaze*.

14. Devra Simiu surveys the revisions of Lacan's mirror stage in: *Disorder and Early Alienation*, chap. 1, "Sea-change: The Theory Transformed" (1986). The positive function of Lacan's theory of the gaze contrasts with Sartre's mainly negative interpretation of the look. Spitz's study of hospitalism provides convincing evidence that the consequences of the child's seeing need to be understood within the emotional context of the child. The later texts of Lacan give a function to the mother. I myself have tried to provide a unified theory of the function of seeing by relating the work of Lacan, Sartre, and Spitz in Ver Eecke (1975, 1985, 1989b).

15. "But the important point is that this form situates the agency of the ego, before its social determination, in a fictional direction, which will only rejoin the coming-into-being . . . of the subject asymptotically, whatever the success of the dialectical syntheses by which he must resolve as *I* his discordance with his own reality" (Lacan 1977, 2).

16. For an articulation of the positive consequences of the presence of the name of the father, see Ver Eecke (1984, 78–84).

17. In Aulagnier's language "a massive castration" (1964, 54). See also, in Mannoni (1972), the case of Jean M. (64) and the case of Mireille (57): "In the absence of her father, Mireille plays for the mother this counterphobic role. If one takes both Mireille and her husband from her, one deprives the mother of all her defenses, and she is thereby endangered." The rest of the case study shows how Mireille is "trapped in the maternal world" (60).

18. See Lacan (1977, 103–4), in which Lacan combines ideas from Freud (*fort-da* game), Heidegger (death and historicity), and Kojève (symbol or word as the murder of the thing).

19. See Lacan (1977, chap. 6). For secondary literature, see: De Waelhens (1978, chap. 4); Ver Eecke (1988 and 1989a).

20. Michèle Montrelay claims that these social processes help to maintain femininity "outside repression" but not so masculine sexuality (1990, 261).

21. A summary of the argument can be found in my review in *Review of Metaphysics* (Ver Eecke 1990, 866–68).

References

Aulagnier, Piera. "Remarques sur la structure psychotique. I. Ego spéculaire, corps phantasmé et objet partiel." *La Psychanalyse* 8 (1964): 47–68.

Chodorow, Nancy. "Family Structure and Feminine Personality." In *Women,*

Culture, and Society, edited by M. Z. Rosaldo and Louise Lamphere. Stanford: Stanford University Press, 1974.

De Waelhens, Alphonse. *Schizophrenia*. Translated by W. Ver Eecke. Pittsburgh: Duquesne University Press, 1978.

Ewens, Thomas. "Female Sexuality and the Role of the Phallus." *Psychoanalytic Review* 63, no. 4 (1976): 615–37.

Freud, Sigmund. *The Standard Edition of the Complete Psychological Works of Sigmund Freud*. Edited and translated by James Strachey. 24 vols. London: Hogarth, 1953–74.

Three Essays on the Theory of Sexuality (1905), vol. 7.

"Analysis of a Phobia in a Five-Year-Old Boy" (1909), vol. 10.

"The Taboo of Virginity" (1918), vol. 11.

Totem and Taboo (1913), vol. 13.

"Fausse Reconnaissance in Psycho-analytic Treatment" (1914), vol. 13.

"Thoughts for the Times on War and Death" (1915), vol. 14.

"On Transformations of Instinct as Exemplified in Anal Erotism" (1917), vol. 17.

"The Psychogenesis of a Case of Homosexuality in a Woman" (1920), vol. 18.

"The Infantile Genital Organization" (1923), vol. 19.

"The Economic Problem of Masochism" (1924), vol. 19.

"The Dissolution of the Oedipus Complex" (1924), vol. 19.

"Some Psychical Consequences of the Anatomical Distinction Between the Sexes" (1925), vol. 19.

Inhibitions, Symptoms and Anxiety (1926), vol. 20.

"Analysis Terminable and Interminable" (1937), vol. 23.

An Outline of Psycho-Analysis (1940), vol. 23.

"Splitting of the Ego in the Process of Defence" (1940), vol. 23.

Glendon, Mary Ann. *Abortion and Divorce in Western Law: American Failures, European Challenges*. Cambridge: Harvard University Press, 1987.

Grosz, Elizabeth. *Jacques Lacan: A Feminist Introduction*. New York: Routledge, Chapman & Hall, 1991.

Hale, Nathan G. F., ed. *James Jackson Putnam and Psychoanalysis*. Cambridge: Harvard University Press, 1971.

Kojève, Alexandre. *Introduction to the Reading of Hegel*. Translated by J. Nichols. New York: Basic Books, 1969.

Kristeva, Julia. *In the Beginning Was Love: Psychoanalysis and Faith*. Translated by Arthur Goldhammer. European Perspectives Series. New York: Columbia University Press, 1987.

Lacan, Jacques. *Ecrits: A Selection*. Translated by Alan Sheridan. New York: Norton, 1977.

———. *L'envers de la psychanalyse. Le séminaire*. Vol. 17. Paris: Editions du Seuil, 1991.

Laplanche, J., and Pontalis, J. B. *The Language of Psychoanalysis*. Translated by Donald Nicholson-Smith. New York: Norton, 1973.

Mannoni, Maud. *The Backward Child and His Mother*. Translated by A. M. Sheridan Smith. New York: Random House, 1972.

Mitchell, Juliet, and Rose, Jacqueline, eds. *Feminine Sexuality: Jacques Lacan and the* école freudienne. Translated by Jacqueline Rose. New York: Norton, 1985.

Montrelay, Michèle. "Inquiry into Femininity." In *The Woman in Question*, edited by Parveen Adams and Elizabeth Cowie. Cambridge: MIT Press, 1990.

Muller, John P. "Lacan's Mirror Stage." *Psychoanalytic Inquiry* 5 (1985): 233–52.

———. "The Analogy of Gap in Lacan's *Ecrits: A Selection*." *Psychohistory Review* 8, no. 3 (1979): 38–45.

Muller, John P., and Richardson, William J. *Lacan and Language: A Reader's Guide to* Ecrits. New York: International Universities Press, 1982.

Nicholson, Linda J., ed. *Feminism/Postmodernism*. New York: Routledge, Chapman & Hall, 1990.

Ortigues, Marie-Cécile, and Ortigues, Edmond. *Oedipe Africain*. Paris: Plon, 1966.

Peraldi, François. "L'attente du père: incidence d'une interprétation sur l'oeuvre de Marguerite Duras." *Etudes Freudiennes* 23 (April 1984): 25–41.

Richardson, William J. "Lacanian Theory." In *Models of the Mind: Their Relationship to Clinical Work*, edited by A. Rothstein. New York: International Universities Press, 1985.

Ruddick, Sara. "Maternal Thinking." In *Mothering: Essays in Feminist Theory*, edited by Joyce Trebilcot. Totowa, N.J.: Rowman & Allanheld, 1983.

Simiu, Devra. *Disorder and Early Alienation: Lacan's Original Theory of the Mirror Stage*. Ph.D. diss., Georgetown University, 1986.

Ver Eecke, Wilfried. "The Look, the Body, and the Other." In *Dialogues in Phenomenology*, edited by Don Ihde and Richard M. Zaner. The Hague: Nyhoff, 1975.

———. *Saying "No": Its Meaning in Child Development, Psychoanalysis, Linguistics, and Hegel*. Pittsburgh, Duquesne University Press, 1984.

———. "Lacan, Sartre, Spitz on the Problem of the Body and Intersubjectivity." *Journal of Phenomenological Psychology* 16 (1985): 73–76.

———. "Sublimation and the Ethical Tradition." *Journal of the American Academy of Psychoanalysis* 47 (1987): 324–30.

———. "Phenomenology and Paternal Metaphor." In *Phenomenology and Psychoanalysis*. The Sixth Annual Symposium of the Simon Silverman Phenomenology Center. Pittsburgh: Simon Silverman Phenomenology Center, Duquesne University, 1988.

———. "Fatherhood and Subjectivity." *Philosophy and Theology* 3 (1989a): 253–64.

———. "Seeing and Saying 'No' within the Theories of Spitz and Lacan." *Psychoanalysis and Contemporary Thought* 12 (1989b): 383–431.

———. Review of *Abortion and Divorce in Western Law: American Failures, European Challenges*, by Mary Ann Glendon. *Review of Metaphysics* 43 (1990): 866–68.

Vergote, Antoine, and Tamayo, Alvaro. *The Parental Figures and the Representation of God*. Leuven: Leuven University Press, 1980.

8   Freud, Race, and Gender

Sander L. Gilman

Freud's "Jewish" identity has long been the topic of scholarly exegesis.[1] Recently Harold Bloom asked:

> What is most Jewish about Freud's work? I am not much impressed by the answers to this question that follow the pattern: from Oedipus to Moses, and thus center themselves upon Freud's own Oedipal relation to his father Jakob. Such answers only tell me that Freud had a Jewish father, and doubtless books and essays yet will be written hypothesizing Freud's relation to his indubitably Jewish mother. Nor am I persuaded by any attempts to relate Freud to esoteric Jewish traditions. As a speculator, Freud may be said to have founded a kind of Gnosis, but there are no Gnostic elements in the Freudian dualism. Nor am I convinced by any of the attempts to connect Freud's Dream Book to supposed Talmudic antecedents. And yet the center of Freud's work, his concept of repression . . . , does seem to me profoundly Jewish, and in its patterns even normatively Jewish. Freudian memory and Freudian forgetting are a very Jewish memory and a very Jewish forgetting. It is their reliance upon a version of Jewish memory, a parody-version if you will, that makes Freud's writings profoundly and yet all too originally Jewish. (1987, 43)

My answer to Bloom's problem is only a very partial one. For Sigmund Freud, an acculturated Jewish medical scientist of late nineteenth-century Vienna, one of the definitions of the Jew that he would have internalized was a racial one, and it is a definition that, whether he consciously sought it or not, shaped the argument of psychoanalysis. Given Freud's own analysis of many of his dreams, the latent or manifest content of which reflects on the question of being "Jewish" in a violently anti-Semitic world, this question seems to have been first raised by Freud himself.[2] Thus, we can respond to Peter Homans's model of a response to an idea of "'Jewishness' after the fashion of a key to its wax impression or a statue to a plaster cast of the statue—psychoanalysis emerged as the negative image, so to speak, of its Jewish surroundings"

(1989, 71). Homans sees the de-idealization of Jewish men, to which Freud had attached himself as the key to this movement; I see this de-idealization, in part, as the result of Freud's struggle with the very definition of science that becomes central to his primary group orientation. The seeming fixation that Freud has on the biological explanation for psychological phenomena, a fixation that has greatly stirred the interest of historians over the past two decades, must be tied to his contemporary understanding of science as a domain in which debates about his own self are carried out.

For Freud in the 1870s the idea of race is a confining, limiting factor, as it implies a biological, immutable pattern of development. After the turn of the century it comes to acquire a more positive valence as a sign of the special status of the Jewish way of seeing the world. It moves from a purely biological category to a purely psychological one. In 1886, about the time Freud was studying with Jean-Martin Charcot in Paris, Gustav Le Bon, the French anti-Semitic sociologist, published his overt discussion of the inheritance of the psychological attributes of race (1886, 1985), which he attributed as much to biology as to social environment.[3] Le Bon's views are central for Freud's later work on the psychology of mass movements, which, though unavowed, are his unstated analyses of anti-Semitism. Freud's experience in Paris was one that was as intensely anti-Semitic as his home in Vienna had been. Freud wants to reject Le Bon's biological view of race as "the innumerable common characteristics handed down from generation to generation, which constitute the genius of a race" (*S.E.* 18: 74).[4] For Le Bon race stands in the "first rank" of those factors that help shape the underlying attitudes of the crowd; racial character "possesses, as the result of the laws of heredity, such power that its beliefs, institutions, and arts—in a word, all the elements of its civilization—are merely outward expressions of its genius" (1960, 83). And yet for the older Freud it is within the psyche, not the body, that the difference between Jew and Aryan exists. Freud does sense that there is a difference, unnameable perhaps, but a difference nevertheless. It is the unknowable essence of the Jew that contemporary anthropologists evoked. Unlike them, Freud provided this essence with a special, positive valence.

In 1926 Freud stated in an address to the B'nai B'rith, on the occasion of being honored on his seventieth birthday, that being Jewish is sharing "many obscure emotional forces [*viele dunkel Gefühlsmächte*], which were the more powerful the less they could be expressed in words, as well as a clear consciousness of inner identity, the safe privacy of a common mental construction [*die Heimleichkeit der gleichen seelischen Identität*]" (*S.E.* 20: 274; *G.W.* 17: 49–53). His contemporaries, such as Theodor Reik (with Freud and Eduard Hintschmann, a psychoanalyst who was a member of the B'nai B'rith), "were especially struck" by these very words as the appropriate central definition of the Jew (Reik 1962, 12).

Freud's version of the ethnopsychology of the Jew twisted Le Bon's claims concerning the biology of race. It evokes the Lamarckianism of William James's view of the transmission of "the same emotional propensities, the same habits, the same instincts, perpetuated without variation from one generation to another" (1890, 2: 678). It is the uncanny nature of the known but repressed aspects of the mental life of an individual, about which Freud wrote in his essay on the uncanny, which haunts his image of the internal mental life that defines the Jew. As Freud writes to his Viennese Jewish "alter ego" Arthur Schnitzler: "Judaism continues to mean much to me on an emotional level" (1955, 100).

The debate about the meaning of what Philip Rieff sees as the Victorian and Edwardian generalities about the "persistent character of the Jews" must be understood as part of the quest of the scientific psychology of the late nineteenth century (1959, 261). For Freud this sense of the psyche of the Jew had not only to do with mental construction of the Jew but also with the Jew's emotional construction. Here he would have found substantial support in the work of William McDougall, whose study *The Group Mind* (1920) played a central role in shaping Freud's own argument about the psychology of the masses (*S.E.* 18: 83–85, 96–97). McDougall sees the fusing of the Hebrew tribes into a nation as having

> played a vital part in its consolidation, implanted and fostered as it was by a succession of great teachers, the prophets. . . . The national self-consciousness thus formed has continued to be not only one factor, but almost the only factor or condition, of the continued existence of the Jewish people as a people, or at any rate the one fundamental condition on which all the others are founded—their exclusive religion, their objection to intermarriage with outsiders, their hope of a future restoration of the fortunes of the nation, and so forth. (159–60)

Jewish self-consciousness leads to the establishment of institutions that preserve this "common mental construction." It is this sense of common purpose, for McDougall but not necessarily for Freud, within the sphere of the political which defines the Jew. Central, however, is that all aspects of the Jewish mind, including all of the affective components, have their root in this common mental construction.

When Freud comments to his fellow "brothers" in the B'nai B'rith about their common mental construction, he is also in a very specific way evoking the presence of the Jewish body. Freud's major association with Jews in the 1870s and 1880s is when he joins (and helps form) a new lodge of the B'nai B'rith in Vienna (see *B'nai B'rith* 1976 and Knoepfmacher 1979). *B'nai B'rith* means "sons of the Covenant." While the name was selected as a replacement for the title "Bundes-Brüder," a German-Jewish lodge founded in New York in 1843, the name evokes, for fin-de-siècle Viennese Jews, a direct association with the image of circumcision. As Theodor Reik commented in 1915:

> the bond which the primordial fathers of the Jews concluded with their god is represented . . . as a glorified and emended account of an initiation ceremony. The connection of the *B'rith* with circumcision is just as little an accident as the covenant meal in which the worshippers of Jahve identified themselves with him; and the giving of the law—*B'rith* can also signify law—which stands in such an intimate relationship to the concluding of the covenant (Sinai) should be set side by side with the procedures of the puberty rites. (1931, 156–57)

The sense of common mental construction is associated closely with the special form of the Jew's body and the ritual bonding that it signifies. Central to this is the act of circumcision. And this is the salient marker of the male Jewish body in fin-de-siècle medicine.

There was a general assumption in the Europe of that time that there was a "Jewish mind" that transcended conversion or adaption,[5] and this was usually understood as being a fault. Ludwig Wittgenstein could comment about Jews such as Freud that "even the greatest of Jewish thinkers is no more than talented. (Myself, for instance.) I think there is some truth to my idea that I really only think reproductively. . . . Can one take the case of Freud and Breuer as an example of Jewish reproductiveness?" (1980, 18–19). The Jewish mind was understood to have no true originality, to be prosaic, as Freud wrote to Emil Fluss in the 1870s: "How well I can imagine your feelings. To leave the native soil, dearly-beloved relatives,—the most beautiful surroundings—ruins close by—I must stop or I'll be as sad as you—and you yourself know best what you are leaving behind. . . . Oh Emil why are you a prosaic Jew? Journeymen imbued with Christian-Germanic fervor have composed beautiful lyrical poetry in similar circumstances" (1978, 426). This view echoes the negative interpretation of the common mental construction of the Jew as expressed in much of the anthropological and cultural debate of the late nineteenth century.

Such views of the Jews are statements about their pathology. Freud concurs on a very basic level with the notion that the Jewish mind-set is pathological. In his lecture on "anxiety" (1917) he evoked the

Lamarckian model of the inheritance of acquired characteristics in order to argue that the "core" of anxiety "is the repetition of some particular significant experience. This experience could only be a very early impression of a very general nature, placed in the prehistory not of the individual but of the species" (*S.E.* 16: 396). Or, one might add, in the prehistory of the race. Freud goes on to see this "affective state . . . constructed in the same way as a hysterical attack and, like it, would be the precipitate of a reminiscence" (396). The anxiety of the Jew is analogous to but not identical with the suffering of the hysteric. The male Eastern Jew is the quintessential hysteric for the medical science of the fin-de-siècle period. It is the psychopathology of the Jew that is impressed through the experience of the collective on the individual.

The roots of this view lie deep in the theories of ethnopsychology as formulated by two Jews, the psychologist Moritz Lazarus and his brother-in-law, the philologist Heymann Steinthal, in the 1860s. In the opening issue of their journal for ethnopsychology and linguistics, *Zeitschrift für Völkerpsychologie und Sprachwissenschaft* (note the link of mind and language), they outlined the assumptions about the knowability of the mind.[6] For Lazarus and Steinthal (1860) the object of study was the "psychology of human beings in groups [gemeinschaft]." Unlike the situation in other fields of psychology of the time, for which laboratory and clinical work was demanded to define the arena of study, ethnopsychology depended on historical and cultural/ethnological data. Their work was highly medicalized: Lazarus had studied physiology with the materialist Johannes Müller and cofounded the Medical-Psychological Society with the Berlin neurologist Wilhelm Griesinger in 1867. While they wish to separate their psychology from materialistic physiology, they are bound by the scientific rhetoric of the materialistic arguments about inheritance. They subscribe to a Lamarckian theory of mnemonic inheritance in the construction of the mind. The great laboratory psychologist Wilhelm Wundt remained the foremost proponent of their views of "universal mental creations" well into the twentieth century (1916, 2). Freud makes extensive use of Wundt's explication of these views in his *Psychopathology of Everyday Life* (1901) and *Totem and Taboo* (1913).[7] The psychology of the individual, as one of Freud's other sources, the Princeton psychologist James Mark Baldwin, commented, recapitulates the history of the "race experience"; one can expect "general analogies to hold between nervous development and mental development, one of which is the deduction of race history epoches from individual history epoches through the repetition of phylogenesis in ontogenesis, called in biology 'Recapitulation'" (1898, 14–15; see *S.E.* 7: 173). The history of the human race was to be found in the development of the individual. But "racial memory" has a very different connotation for a Jewish reader of Wundt and Baldwin.

Freud, like the ethnopsychologists, needed to separate the idea of the psyche from the body, needed to eliminate the image of the fixed, immutable racial composition that determines all thoughts and all actions. For all of these thinkers the psyche was separate from and yet still part of the body. For it seemed to be impossible, even within the needs of such thinkers, to avoid the pitfalls of race, of ever truly separating the mind from the body.

Freud dismisses the Germanic weltanschauung as a "specifically German concept, the translation of which into foreign languages might well raise difficulties" (*S.E.* 22: 158). It is not the rigid paradigm of knowing that appeals to Freud but, rather, the acceptance of the "scientific" model, which, while it accepts the *"uniformity* of the explanation of the universe," only "does so . . . as a programme, the fulfillment of which is relegated to the future" (158–59). It is the scientific mode of seeing the world which is not too Germanic but, rather, allows the Jew to see the world as a scientist (Le Rider 1989). By the mid-1930s Freud can shrug his shoulders at the Nazi burning of his books, sensing that this action represents the German response to his own "common mental construction": "'They told me,' he said, 'that psychoanalysis is alien to their *Weltanschauung*, and I suppose it is.' He said this with no emotion and little interest, as though talking about the affairs of some complete stranger" (Reik 1940, 30). It is Freud the positivist who dominates in his comprehension of the mind-set of the Jews.

These groups are called by Lazarus and Steinthal (1860) "peoples" (*Völker*), but they stress that these groups are constituted by the individuals who comprise them and are not fixed biological "races" (5). "Human beings," as Lazarus observes, "are the creation of history; everything in us, about us, is the result of history; we do not speak a word, we do not think an idea, there is neither feeling nor emotion, which is not in a complicated manner dependent on historical determinants" (1862, 437). The standards for definition of a people are fluid and change from group to group. Thus, the standards for being French are different from those for being German (Lazarus and Steinthal 1860, 35). Even though a "people is a purely subjective construction," it reflects itself in "a common consciousness of many with the consciousness of the group" (35–36). This "common consciousness" exists initially because of the "same origin" and the "proximity of the dwellings" of the members of the group. And "with the relationship through birth, the similarity of physiognomy, especially the form of the body, is present" (37). For them this "objective" fact of biological similarity lays the groundwork for the "subjective" nature of the mental construction of a people (38). But the biological underpinnings of this argument are clear: the Irish eat potatoes as a reflex of being in Ireland, which makes them Irish, and they are Irish because they eat potatoes (39). Could one not argue that Jews are Jews because they circumcise their male infants, and they circumcise their male infants because they are Jews? The place where these acquired characteristics is localized is not the body but within the language of the *Volk*. Lazarus and Steinthal are constituting a definition of group identification that is rooted in a biological (and, therefore, for them observable and demonstrable) relationship but that self-consciously builds upon this basic identity a sense of group cohesion. This is an answer to the argument about race constructing the mentality of the group. Here it is the group that is constituted based on the biological accidents of birth and dwelling, not the inborn identity of blood. And yet it is the observable, the biological, that structures their argument.

Freud sees the construction of the mentality of a group as a reflex of biology tempered by the social context in which the individual finds himself. In *Civilization and Its Discontents* (1930) Freud comments on the subjectivity of happiness: "No matter how much we may shrink with horror from certain situations—of a galley-slave in antiquity, of a peasant during the Thirty Years' War, of a victim of the Holy Inquisition, of a Jew awaiting a pogrom—it is nevertheless impossible for us to feel our way into such people—to divine the changes which original obtuseness of mind, a gradual stupefying process, the cessation of expectations, and cruder or more refined methods of narcotization have produced upon their receptivity to sensations of pleasure and unpleasure" (*S.E.* 21: 89). Freud places himself and the reader (the "us") separate from the victim.[8] This works in terms of the historical images he evokes from antiquity, the seventeenth century, and the sixteenth century, but the image of the pogrom, while obliquely "historical" in that it reflects Russia at the end of the nineteenth century, is also quite immediate to Freud. His view that this mind-set could be constructed at such times of stress separates him out from what was occurring during his own experience, even while he wrote *Civilization and Its Discontents*.

But Freud had rejected traditional definitions of race as a category within the discourse of science. During his analysis of Smiley Blanton he commented: "My background as a Jew helped me to stand being criticized, being isolated, working alone. . . . All this was of help to me in discovering analysis. But that psychoanalysis itself is a Jewish product seems to me nonsense. As a scientific work, it is neither Jewish nor

Catholic nor Gentile" (quoted in Blanton 1971, 43). He wrote in a birthday greeting to Ernest Jones in 1929: "The first piece of work that it fell
to psycho-analysis to perform was the discovery of the instincts that are
common to all men living to-day—and not only to those living to-day
but to those of ancient and of prehistoric times. It called for no great
effort, therefore, for psycho-analysis to ignore the differences that arise
among the inhabitants of the earth owing to the multiplicity of races,
languages and countries" (*S.E.* 21: 249). And this to an individual with
whom he felt a "racial strangeness" (*Rassenfremdheit*) upon first meeting him in 1908.[9] And from whom his first comments elicited the
response: "from the shape of my head I could not be English and must
be Welsh. It astonished me, first because it is uncommon for anyone on
the Continent to know of the existence of my native country, and then
because I had suspected my dolichocephalic skull might as well be
Teutonic as Celtic" (quoted in Jones 1953–57, 2: 42–43).[10] Jones's
response to Freud's remark is couched in the language of racial biology. This use of these categories was simply assumed and in no way
questioned.

What seems to be a contradictory view evinces Freud's complicated
resistance to and restructuring of the idea of a group mentality. His conviction of the compatibility of both neutral science and ethnocentric
perception is found in a letter written on June 8, 1913, to one of his most
trusted Jewish followers, the Hungarian psychoanalyst Sándor Ferenczi:
"Certainly there are great differences between the Jewish and the
Aryan spirit. We can observe that every day. Hence, there would as-
suredly be here and there differences in outlook on art and life. But
there should not be such a thing as Aryan or Jewish science. Results in
science must be identical, though the presentation of them may vary"
(quoted in Jones 1953–57, 2: 168). This difference in "spirit" is present
and yet undefined. Many opponents of political anti-Semitism during
the fin-de-siècle period acknowledged that there were "indeed, many
scientific Jews, but . . . nowhere a Jewish science," to quote Anatole
Leroy-Beaulieu (1895, 51).

Yet it was clear that Freud understood that his own identification as a
Jew both provided the "ground" for the new science of psychoanalysis
and limited access of this new science to the claims of a "neutral science." In 1910 he had confronted his Viennese (read: Jewish) colleagues at the second Psychoanalytic Congress and stated the case
bluntly: "Most of you are Jews, and therefore you are incompetent to
win friends for the new teaching. Jews must be content with the mod-
est role of preparing the ground. It is absolutely essential that I should
form ties in the world of general science. . . . The Swiss will save us"

(quoted in Wittels 1924, 140). But the Swiss—that is, at least C. G. Jung, if not Eugen Bleuler—certainly did not see psychoanalysis as anything but a "Jewish" science. Freud recognized this when he commented to Smiley Blanton in 1930 that he had tried to place Jung at the head of the psychoanalytic movement because "there was a danger that people would consider psychoanalysis as primarily Jewish" (quoted in Blanton 1971, 43). And to Abraham Kardiner he remarked that he hated the idea that "psychoanalysis would founder because it would go down in history as a 'Jewish' science" (quoted in Kardiner 1977, 70). Psychoanalysis had to be freed but could not be freed from the Jewish mind that, at least in Freud's view, had constructed it.

In a 1936 letter (written in English) on the death of his friend and early British supporter Montague David Eder, Freud evoked that common mental construction that sets the Jew apart: "We were both Jews and knew of each other that we carried that miraculous thing in common, which—inaccessible to any analysis so far—makes the Jew" (1960, 443). He uses this rhetoric often in his exchanges with Jews. He can write to Karl Abraham on May 3, 1908, of their common "racial identification" (*Rassenverwandtschaft*) as opposed to the "Aryan" views of C. G. Jung (Freud and Abraham 1980, 47). Freud's letter reflects his anxiety about the labeling of psychoanalysis as a "Jewish national affair."[11] As he later wrote to Jones, science should be beyond such designations but evidently is not. Both Freud and Abraham saw a grain of truth in this charge, a grain rooted in the way Jews were assumed to see the world. Abraham's attitude emerges in this letter to Freud: "I find it easier to go along with you rather than with Jung. I, too, have always felt this intellectual kinship. After all, our Talmudic way of thinking cannot disappear just like that. Some days ago a small paragraph in *Jokes* strangely attracted me. When I looked at it more closely, I found that, in the technique of apposition and in its whole structure, it was completely Talmudic" (Freud and Abraham 1980, 48–49). Freud's response does not deny this but, rather, places the "shared mental construction" into the following terms: "May I say that it is consanguineous Jewish traits [*verwandte, jüdische Zügel*] that attract me to you? We understand each other" (57). Abraham's claim is that the Jews in psychoanalysis share a common discourse, and he evokes, in a positive manner, the traditional negative label of "Talmudic" for this approach. Abraham and Freud both accept (and give a positive value to) the charge that the Jews possess a secret or hidden language, which is manifested in the manner by which Jews use (or, rather, abuse) language. This is the charge, which we have already seen widely stated, that Jews *Mauschel*, that they speak differently from all others.

In July 1912, when the break with Jung is clear, Freud in a letter to Ferenczi despairs of yoking "Jews and *goyim* in the service of psychoanalysis," for "they separate themselves like oil and water" (quoted in Gay 1988, 231). How Freud experiences the "goyim"—that is, Jung—can be seen in a letter to Otto Rank a month later, when the "Jews and *goyim*" become "Jews and anti-Semites" (quoted in Gay 1988, 231). In writing to Jung's former mistress Sabina Spielrein in August 1913, Freud commented: "We are and remain Jews. The others will only exploit us and will never understand or appreciate us" (quoted in Carotenuto 1982, 120–21). Similarly, in writing to Theodor Reik in 1914 about his critique of the Lutheran pastor-psychoanalyst Oskar Pfister's theological understanding of psychoanalysis, Freud says that Reik's comment is "too good for those goyim" (quoted in Reik 1962, 33). Not only are Jews different from Aryans in terms of their mentality, but this is an unbridgeable difference: Jews are unknowable to Aryans.

In Freud's comments on the "resistances to psychoanalysis" he writes in 1925 that "the question may be raised whether the personality of the present writer as a Jew who has never sought to disguise the fact that he is a Jew may not have had a share in provoking the antipathy of his environment to psycho-analysis. . . . Nor is it perhaps entirely a matter of chance that the first advocate of psycho-analysis was a Jew. To profess belief in this new theory called for a certain degree of readiness to accept a situation of solitary opposition—a situation with which no one is more familiar than a Jew" (*S.E.* 19: 222). Even though Freud expresses both pride and fear that psychoanalysis will become identified as a Jewish undertaking, he also writes to the Italian psychiatrist Enrico Morselli,[12] in 1926, that while he does not know whether his "thesis that psychoanalysis as a direct product of the Jewish mind is correct, I would however not be ashamed if it were. Although long alienated from the religion of my ancestors, I have a feeling of solidarity with my people [*Volk*] and think with pleasure of the fact that you are a student of a man of my race [*Stammesgenossen*], the great Lombroso" (1960, 380).

It is not Judaism as a religion (which is "of great significance to me as a subject of scientific interest") with which Freud identifies in a public letter in 1925 but, rather, the "strong feeling of solidarity with my fellow-people [*mit meinem Volk*]" (*S.E.* 19: 291; *G.W.* 14: 556). In his response to the greetings of the chief rabbi of Vienna on the occasion of his seventy-fifth birthday, Freud stresses the communal, psychological identity of the Jew: "Your words aroused a special echo in me, which I do not need to explain to you. In some place in my soul, in a very hidden corner, I am a fanatical Jew. I am very much astonished to discover myself as such in spite of all efforts to be unprejudiced and impartial.

What can I do against my age?" (quoted in Hes 1986, 322).

Indeed, the 1934 preface to the Hebrew edition of *Totem and Taboo* stated the case for a secular, racial (or, at least, ethnopsychological) definition of the Jew quite clearly:

> No reader of [the Hebrew version of] this book will find it easy to put himself in the emotional position of an author who is ignorant of the language of holy writ, who is completely estranged from the religion of his fathers—as well as from every other religion—and who cannot take a share in nationalist ideals, but who has yet never repudiated his people, who feels that he is in his essential nature [*Eigenart*] a Jew and who has no desire to alter that nature. If the question were put to him: "Since you have abandoned all these common characteristics [*Gemeinsamkeiten*] of your countrymen [*Volksgenossen*], what is there left to you that is Jewish?" he would reply: "A very great deal, and probably its very essence." He could not now express that essence clearly in words; but some day, no doubt, it will become accessible to the scientific mind. (*S.E.* 13: xv; *G.W.* 14: 569)

The Transmutation of the Rhetoric of Race into the Construction of Gender

It is not only the Jew who is unknowable within the pantheon of Freud's scientific world. Freud's comments on the unknowability of the Jew are parallel to his claims about the unknowability of the feminine. Just as the scientist does not know what the essence of the Jew is, so too does the scientist not know what the essence of female sexuality is, even to its developmental structure: "Unfortunately we can describe this state of things only as it affects the male child; the corresponding processes in the little girl are not known to us" (*S.E.* 19: 142). This Freud wrote in 1923. It was part of a generally accepted view, echoed by fin-de-siècle sexologists such as Paul Näcke, that "a man can never penetrate [*eindringen*] into the psychology of the female and vice-versa" (1907, 13).[13] But Freud sees the unknowability of the female as a one-sided gender limitation. It is only the feminine that cannot be known. Freud's comment echoes his earlier view, in *Three Essays on the Theory of Sexuality* (1905), that "the significance of the factor of sexual overvaluation can be best studied in men, for their erotic life alone has become accessible to research. That of women—partly owing to the stunting effect of civilized conditions [*Kulturverkümmerung*] and partly owing to their conventional secretiveness [*konventionelle Verschwiegenheit*] and insincerity [*Unaufrichgkeit*]—is still veiled in an impenetrable obscurity [*undurchdringliches Dunkel*]" (*S.E.* 7: 151; *G.W.* 5: 50). The pejorative tone of this description parallels the anti-Semitic rhetoric

about the hidden nature of the Jew and the Jew's mentality widely cir-
culated at the end of the century and common in the medical literature
of the age.

The rhetoric that Freud employs in all of these categories is taken
from the biology of race,[14] with all of its evocation of hidden essences
and unknown forces shaping the actions of an individual. What can be
known is only the essence of the self: "In consequence of unfavourable
circumstances, both of an external and an internal nature, the following
observations apply chiefly to the sexual development of one sex only—
that is, of males" (*S.E.* 9: 211). But is the Jewish male truly a male, or has
Freud constructed a definition of gender, here the male, that would include himself within a category from which Jewish males are excluded?
The assumption of the knowability of the self, as one can glean from
Freud's own remarks, is not extended to the essence of the Jew but only
to the essence of the male. The unknowability of the Jew, the hidden
nature of the Jewish mind, replicated the discourse about the Jewish
body and its diseased and different nature.

The problem of the knowability of the other and the self provides the
rhetoric at the heart of one of the most complex and debated aspects of
Freudian theory, Freud's reading of the meanings of male and female
anatomy.[15] In 1926 Freud, in his essay on lay analysis, referred (in English) to female sexuality as the "dark continent" of the human psyche:
"But we need not feel ashamed of this distinction; after all, the sexual
life of adult women is a 'dark continent' for psychology. But we have
learnt that girls feel deeply their lack of a sexual organ that is equal in
value to the male one; they regard themselves on that account as inferior, and this 'envy for the penis' is the origin of a whole number of
characteristic feminine reactions" (*S.E.* 20: 212). Elsewhere I have
sketched the implications of this phrase in terms of the medicalization
of the black female body during the nineteenth century (Gilman 1985,
76–108). But note Freud's vocabulary concerning the sense of inferiority attributed to the woman because of her "envy for the penis."
The question of the woman's attribution of meaning to the female genitalia, specifically the clitoris, is raised by Freud in this context: "Women
possess as part of their genitals a small organ similar to the male one;
and this small organ, the clitoris, actually plays the same part in childhood and during the years before sexual intercourse as the large organ
in men" (*S.E.* 15: 155). The view that the clitoris is a "truncated penis" is
generally rejected in contemporary psychoanalytic theory. To date, the
only explanation for this view has been found in the arguments about
homologous structures of the genitalia.[16] But little attention has been

given to what Freud could have understood within this generally accepted model.

The image of the clitoris as a truncated penis, as a less than intact penis, reflects the popular fin-de-siècle Viennese view of the relationship between the body of the male Jew and the body of the woman. The clitoris was known in Viennese slang of that time simply as the "Jew" (*Jud*) (Reiskel 1905, 9; Freud makes reference to the periodical volume of this work in *S.E.* 10: 215 n.1). The phrase "for a woman to masturbate" is "to play with the Jew." The "small organ" of the woman becomes a kind of synecdoche for the Jew, with his circumcised, shortened organ. This pejorative synthesis of both bodies because of their "defective" sexual organs reflects the fin-de-siècle Viennese definition of the male as neither female nor Jewish.

But the clitoris, the Jew, becomes a sign of masculinity for Freud. As late as his essay on female sexuality (1931), Freud stressed the need for female sexuality to develop from the early masturbatory emphasis on the masculine genital zone, the clitoris, to the adult sexuality of vaginal intercourse. The clitoris, the Jew, is the sign of the masculine which must be abandoned if and when the female is to mature into an adult woman (*S.E.* 21: 232–33). The Jew is the male hidden within the body of the female for Freud. But it is the definition of the masculine aspect of the woman that must be transcended if she is to define herself antithetically to the male.

The analogy of the body and mind of the Jew to the body and mind of the woman was a natural one at the end of the nineteenth century. Within German high and medical culture this image of the nature of the woman was already present. The entire medical vocabulary applied to the body of the female stressed her physical and mental inferiority to the male. And the terms used were precisely parallel to the discourse about the Jews. Thus, the female, as Elaine Showalter (1985) has so brilliantly shown, is understood as at great risk for mental illness. But the female, like the Jew, also is marked by her smell. The female like the Jew is atavistic in her body and her mind. Cesare Lombroso, the founder of modern forensic anthropology and himself an Italian Jew, provided a reading of the origin of the sense of shame in the "primitive." He remarked that in the Romance languages the term for shame is taken from the root *putere*, which he interpreted as indicating that the origin of the sense of shame lies in the disgust for body smells (1893, 134). This he "proves" by observing that prostitutes show a "primitive pseudoshame," a fear of being repulsive to the male, since they are loath to having their genitalia inspected when they are menstruating. But the association between odor and difference also points quite directly to the image of the source of pollution. The smell of the menses was equated with the stench of ordure, both human and animal, in the public health model of disease which still clung to the popular understanding of illness during the late nineteenth century. Edwin Chadwick, the greatest of the early Victorian crusaders for public sanitation (who built upon the theoretical work of German writers such as E. B. C. Heberstreit) perceived disease as the result of putrefaction of effluvia. For Chadwick "all smell is disease" (Eyler 1979, 100). The link between public sanitation and the image of the corrupting female (and her excreta) is through the agency of smell.

Despite all that is said about the nature of the female, about her body, one also finds the claim that science can never truly capture her essence, which is beyond the understanding of the male. In the later philosophical works of Arthur Schopenhauer and in their medicalization in the work of Freud's contemporary Paul Julius Möbius, the rhetoric of female inferiority was coupled with the charge of unknowability.[17] The ultimate distance between the "neutral" scientific observer and the object observed was the claim that the object could not share in the same perceptual strategies as the observer. Whether Jew or woman was not germane; the central category was the difference in the object's ability to comprehend the world.

In the course of his work on the centrality of human sexuality Sigmund Freud redefined sexuality so as to diminish the stress on sexual anatomy, on the association with the sexuality of the "normal adult." While sexuality came to be defined against the idea of the degenerate, it no longer was possible to recognize the "male" or the "female" on first glance. Sexuality was now part of the mental structure of all human beings. And the bisexual nature of all human beings destroyed any specificity about the meaning of sexual anatomy. Each human being reflected the qualities of mind that were on the spectrum from the purely "masculine" to the purely "feminine":

> In the first place sexuality is divorced from its too close connection with the genitals and is regarded as a more comprehensive bodily function, having pleasure as its goal and only secondarily coming to serve the ends of reproduction. In the second place the sexual impulses are regarded as including all of those merely affectionate and friendly impulses to which usage applies the exceedingly ambiguous word "love." I do not, however, consider that these extensions are innovations but rather restorations: they signify the removal of inexpedient limitations of the concept into which we had allowed ourselves to be led.
> The detaching of sexuality from the genitals has the advantage of al-

lowing us to bring the sexual activities of children and of perverts into the same scope as those of normal adults. The sexual activities of children have hitherto been entirely neglected, and though those of perverts have been recognized it has been with moral indignation and without under-standing. (*S.E.* 20: 38)

By eliminating reproduction as the goal of the sexual, Freud destroyed the argument that Jewish sexual practices (circumcision and endoge-nous marriage) were at the root of the pathology of the Jews. But if we were to substitute the word *Jew* for the word *pervert* in this passage, we would find a restating of the need to incorporate the liminal into the universal of the sexual. "Jews" and "perverts" are virtually interchange-able categories at the end of the nineteenth century.

This phantasm of knowing on the part of the "neutral" observer, as we shall see, is also attributed to the unknowability of the Jew. At about the same time that Freud commented on the unknowability of the Jew he also complained to his friend and analysand Marie Bonaparte, prin-cess of Greece, that he did not know what women wanted.[18] All of these comments point toward the unknowability of the female body as that "object" (in a Freudian sense) which is different from the self. But it also places the Jew (in the slang sense of the clitoris) into the body of the female. But, of course, the essence of the Jewish body is both too well known to be hidden and too well hidden to be known. It is both "canny" and "uncanny" simultaneously.

Freud's contradictions about the meaning and function of race and racial identity and his assumption that race is a category vitiated by the new science of psychoanalysis is a central theme of my work on Freud (see Le Rider 1990, 197–222). The very idea of the Jew within the sci-ence that formed Freud and other Jewish physicians of that time, and which defined the high medical science of his day, is present in images, metaphors, and deep structures of his own theory. It was the case that the image of the male Jew was "feminized" during the course of West-ern (read: Christian) history. Indeed, in accepting the view that the Jews are a single race in 1904, the Elberfeld physician Heinrich Singer comments that "in general it is clear in examining the body of the Jew, that the Jew most approaches the body type of the female" (1904, 9). Singer's view echoes the older anthropological view, such as that of the Jewish ethnologist Adolf Jellinek, who stated quite directly: "In the ex-amination of the various races it is clear that some are more masculine, others more feminine. Among the latter the Jews belong, as one of those tribes which are both more feminine and have come to represent [*repräsentieren*] the feminine among other peoples. A juxtaposition of the Jew and the woman will persuade the reader of the truth of the ethnographic thesis." Jellinek's physiological proof is the Jew's voice: "Even though I disavow any physiological comparison, let me note that bass voices are much rarer than baritone voice among the Jews" (1869, 89–90). The association of the image of the Jew (here read: male Jew) with that of the woman (including the Jewish woman) is one of the most powerful images to be embedded in the arguments about race. And it can be found quite directly in the attacks on Freud and psychoanalysis. In responding to an attack by Felix von Luschan, one of the greatest "experts" on the nature of the Jew, on the new science of psychoanalysis in 1916, Freud can only express himself in racial terms: "an old Jew is tougher than a noble Prussian Teuton" (quoted in Jones 1953–57, 2: 119; see also 2: 398–99). Luschan's attack on Freud, Wilhelm Fliess, and Hermann Swaboda sees them as a pseudoreligious collectivity parallel to Christian Science. He employed a phrase coined by Konrad Rieger for all of these "pseudoscientific" undertakings: "Old Woman—Psychology [*Altweiber-Psychologie*]" (Luschan 1916, 20).

When we turn to Sigmund Freud's internalization of the image of his own difference it is the relationship between ideas of race and ideas of gender at the end of the century that frames Freud's answer. It is through the analysis of the theory in terms of its own critical presuppositions that the repression and projection of the image of the Jew can be found in psychoanalytic theory—not within a theory of race (as is later to be found in the work of C. G. Jung) but within Freud's representation of the image of gender.

Drawing on earlier work published in 1925 and 1931 and on poet Heinrich Heine, Freud wrote about the role of the scientist in resolving the question of gender in his comprehensive *New Introductory Lectures on Psycho-Analysis* (1933):

> To-day's lecture, too, should have no place in an introduction; but it may serve to give you an example of a detailed piece of analytic work, and I can say two things to recommend it. It brings forward nothing but observed facts, almost without any speculative additions, and it deals with a subject which has a claim on your interest second almost to no other. Throughout history people have knocked their heads against the riddle of the nature of femininity—
>
> Häupter in Hieroglyphenmützen,
> Häupter in Turban und schwarzem Barett,
> Perückenhäupter und tausend andre
> Arme, schwitzende Menschenhäupter. . . .
> (Heads in hieroglyphic bonnets,
> Heads in turbans and black birettas,

Heads in wigs and thousand other
Wretched, sweating heads of humans. . . .)

Nor will *you* have escaped worrying over this problem—those of
you who are men; to those of you who are women this will not apply—
you are yourselves the problem. When you meet a human being, the first
distinction you make is "male or female?" and you are accustomed to make
the distinction with unhesitating certainty. Anatomical science shares
your certainty at one point and not much further. (*S.E.* 22: 113)

This argument can be read as part of a rhetoric of race. First, let me
translate the problem, which Freud articulates within the rhetoric of
gender science, into the rhetoric of racial science: "There is an inherent
biological difference between Jews and Aryans and this has a central
role in defining you (my listener) and your culture." The "you" that the
"I" is addressing is clearly the Aryan reader, for the Jewish reader is
understood as but part of the problem. The Aryan is the observer, the
Jew the observed. Upon seeing someone on the street, the first distinction "we" (the speaker and his listener, as Aryans) make is to ask "Jew or
Aryan?" and that distinction can be made with certainty based on inherent assumptions about differences in anatomy. Indeed, according to a
contemporary guidebook, in Vienna the first question one asks about
anybody one sees on the street is "Is he a Jew?" (Hirschfeld 1927, 56).
This biological distinction can be clearly and easily "seen," even through
the mask of clothing or the veneer of civilization. The young American-
Jewish psychoanalyst Abraham Kardiner recounted his rejection by a
young woman he met at a masked ball in Vienna once they unmasked
and it was clear that he was a Jew (1979, 92). But it was not merely
social rejection that could follow. The threat of what it meant to be seen
as a Jew was also articulated on the streets of Vienna. Martin Freud,
Sigmund Freud's eldest son, writes of walking with his aunt Dolfi, his
father's youngest sister, who died in Theresienstadt,: "one day in Vienna
. . . we passed an ordinary kind of man, probably a Gentile, who, as far
as I knew, had taken no notice of us. I put it down to a pathological
phobia, to Dolfi's stupidity, when she gripped my arm in terror and
whispered: 'Did you hear what that man said? He called me a dirty stink-
ing Jewess and said it was time we were all killed' " (1957, 16).
    The false assumption in Freud's text is that the uniformity of the iden-
tity of all males, as opposed to all females, can be made in terms of the
form of their genitalia. Freud continues his argument to show that this
physiological determinant is central in any discussion of the nature of
sexual difference. He identifies himself as a male in this text, quoting a
male author, Heinrich Heine, who represented the Jew as the diseased
feminine in fin-de-siècle culture, in the context of the impossibility of

"knowing" the truth about the dark continent of the feminine (see the discussion of "The Jewish Reader: Freud Reads Heine Reads Freud," in Gilman 1991, 150–68). But Heine's references also evoke quite a different set of associations—especially for the anti-Semitic "Aryan" reader—than they were presumably designed to have in the original text. Heine was (and remains) the primary Jewish writer in the German cultural sphere. Readers finely attuned to Heine's Jewishness would have associated the oriental turbans, Egyptian hieroglyphs, the sweat of ghetto poverty, the wigs of the shaved heads of orthodox Jewish brides, as hidden signs of racial and not merely sexual difference. Here is a Jew (Freud) citing a Jew (Heine) about an essentially Jewish focus, human sexuality. Freud can short-circuit this association only by constructing an image of the male to which he, Heine, and his male, Aryan listeners can all belong. In his lecture on "femininity" Freud's argument continues; he challenges the seeming dichotomy between the male and the female and constructs a universal continuum between these two poles. The distinction between male and female, like the biological distinction between Jew and Aryan, is dissolved, as the seemingly fixed borders are shown to be transitory. Freud's desire to abandon such rigid distinctions in terms of a biology of gender mirrors the acculturated Jew's desire to abandon them in terms of the biology of race.

The voice in Freud's text is that of a male and a participant in the central discourse of the scientific thought-collective about gender science. In my racial rereading the voice would become that of the Aryan and part of the Aryan thought-collective. The fantasy of Freud's identification with the aggressor in my retelling of this passage as one about race seems to be vitiated when Freud transforms the problem of the relationship between the subject and the object into a question of sexual identity. The male is the "worrier" (read: subject), and the female is the "problem" (read: object). But this assumes that Freud's definition of the male body as uniform and constant is the norm within his fin-de-siècle scientific thought-collective. The Jewish male body is different, is marked, in the act of ritual circumcision and in many other ways. It is not that the anatomy of the genitalia created two independent (and antagonistic) categories but that there were three such categories; the male Jew's genitalia were understood as a marker of difference. Freud's need to distance the challenges to the special nature of the Jew's body through his creation of a universal male body transmuted categories of race into categories of gender. The power of these constructs is such that the fact that they are a reaction formation is obscured, and they are accepted as the basis for the discussion of ideas of masculine and feminine gender as primary categories of Freud's system.

Notes

This essay is excerpted from my forthcoming book, *Freud, Race, and Gender* (Princeton: Princeton University Press, 1993).

1. An extensive sample of the literature on this topic follows: Ulla Haselstein, "Poets and Prophets: The Hebrew and the Hellene in Freud's Cultural Theory," *German Life and Letters* 45 (1992): 50–65; Harold Bloom, "Freud: Frontier Concepts, Jewishness, and Interpretation," *American Imago* 48 (1991): 135–52; Yosef Hayim Yerushalmi, *Freud's Moses: Judaism Terminable and Interminable* (New Haven: Yale University Press, 1991); Jerry V. Diller, *Freud's Jewish Identity* (Rutherford, N.J.: Fairleigh Dickinson University Press, 1990); Ken Frieden, *Freud's Dream of Interpretation* (Albany: State University of New York Press, 1990); Gerald Haddad, *L'enfant illegitime: sources talmudiques de la psychanalyse* (Paris: Points hor Ligne, 1990); Emmanuel Rice, *Freud and Moses: The Long Journey Home* (Albany: State University of New York Press, 1990); Jacques Le Rider, *Modernité viennoise et crises de l'identité* (Paris: Presses Universitaires de France, 1990); Renate Böschenstein, "Mythos als Wasserscheide: die jüdische Komponente der Psychoanalyse: Beobachtungen zu ihrem Zusammenhang mit der Literatur des Jahrhundertbeginns," in *Conditio Judaica: Judentum, Antisemitismus und deutschsprachige Literatur vom 18. Jahrhundert bis zum ersten Weltkrieg,* ed. Hans Otto Horch and Horst Denkler (Tübingen: Max Niemeyer, 1989), 287–310; Jacques Chemouni, "Au-delà de la psychanalyse: l'identité juive," *Frenesie* 7 (1989): 9–124; Jakob Hessing, *Der Fluch des Propheten: drei Abhandlung zu Sigmund Freud* (Rheda-Wiedenbrück: Daedalus, 1989); Edward Shorter, "Women and Jews in a Private Nervous Clinic in Late Nineteenth-Century Vienna," *Medical History* 33 (1989): 149–83; Robert S. Wistrich, *The Jews of Vienna in the Age of Franz Joseph* (Oxford: Littman Library of Jewish Civilization/Oxford University Press, 1989), 537–82; Y. H. Yerushalmi, "Freud on the 'Historical Novel'; From the Manuscript Draft (1934) of Moses and Monotheism," *International Journal of Psychoanalysis* 70 (1989): 375–95; Francine Beddock, *L'héritage de l'oubli—de Freud à Claude Lanzmann,* Collection TRAMES (Nice: Z'Editions, 1988); David S. Blatt, "The Development of the Hero: Sigmund Freud and the Reformation of the Jewish Tradition," *Psychoanalysis and Contemporary Thought* 11 (1988): 693–703; Susan Heenen-Wolff, *"Wenn ich Oberhuber hiesse . . . ": die freudsche Psychoanalyse zwischen Assimilation und Antisemitismus* (Frankfurt a. M.: Nexus, 1987); Jerzy Strojonwski, "Polish-Jewish Background of Psychoanalysis," *XXX Congrès International d'Histoire de la Médecine, 1986* (Dusseldorf: n.p., 1988), 1224–30; Paul C. Vitz, *Sigmund Freud's Christian Unconscious* (New York: Guilford Press, 1988); Jacques Chemouni, "Freud interpéte de l'antisemitisme," *Frenesie* 4 (1987): 117–36; Jacques Chemouni, "Freud et les associations juives: contribution à l'étude de sa judéité," *Revue Française de Psychanalyse* 4 (1987): 1207–43; Peter Gay, *A Godless Jew: Freud, Atheism, and the Meaning of Psychoanalysis* (New Haven: Yale University Press, 1987); Mordechai Rotenberg, *Re-biographing and Deviance: Psy-*

chotherapeutic Narrativism and the Midrash (New York: Praeger, 1987); H. Baruk, "Moïse, Freud et le veau d'or," *Revue Historique de la Médecine Hebräique* 37 (1984): 19–23; Harold Bloom, "Grenzbegriffe, Interpretation und jüdisches Erbe bei Freud," *Psyche* 40 (1986): 600–616; L.J. Rather, "Disraeli, Freud, and Jewish Conspiracy Theories," *Journal of the History of Ideas* 47 (1986): 111–31; J. Kirsch, "Jung's Transference on Freud: Its Jewish Element," *American Imago* 41 (1984): 63–84; Elaine Amado Lévy-Valensi, *Le Moïse de Freud ou la référence occulté* (Monaco: Editions Rocher, 1984); Elliott Oring, *The Jokes of Sigmund Freud: A Study in Humor and Jewish Identity* (Philadelphia: University of Pennsylvania Press, 1984); Stanley Rosenman "A Psychohistorical Source of Psychoanalysis—Malformed Jewish Psyches in an Immolating Setting," *Israel Journal of Psychiatry and Related Sciences* 21 (1984): 103–16; Harold Bloom, "Jewish Culture and Jewish Memory," *Dialectical Anthropology* 8 (1983): 7–19; Stanley Rosenman, "The Late Conceptualization of the Self in Psychoanalysis: The German Language and Jewish Identity," *Journal of Psychohistory* 11 (1983): 9–42; Marie Balmery, *Psychoanalyzing Psychoanalysis: Freud and the Hidden Fault of the Father*, trans. Ned Lukacher (Baltimore: Johns Hopkins University Press, 1982); Sigmund Diamond, "Sigmund Freud, His Jewishness, and Scientific Method: The Seen and the Unseen as Evidence," *Journal of the History of Ideas* 43 (1982): 613–34; Peter Gay, "Six Names in Search of an Interpretation: A Contribution to the Debate over Sigmund Freud's Jewishness," *Hebrew Union College Annual* 53 (1982): 295–308; Susan A. Handelman, *The Slaying of Moses: The Emergence of Rabbinic Interpretation in Modern Literary Theory* (Albany: State University of New York Press, 1982), 129–52; Mortimer Ostow, *Judaism and Psychoanalysis* (New York: KTAV, 1982); Theo Pfrimmer, *Freud: lecteur de la Bible* (Paris: Presses Universitaires de France, 1982); Max Kohn, *Freud et le Yiddish: le préanalytique* (Paris: Christian Bourgois, 1982); Dennis B. Klein, *Jewish Origins of the Psychoanalytic Movement* (New York: Praeger, 1981); Justin Miller, "Interpretations of Freud's Jewishness, 1924–1974," *Journal of the History of the Behavioral Sciences* 17 (1981): 357–74; David Aberbach, "Freud's Jewish Problem," *Commentary* 69 (1980): 35–39; C. Musatti, "Freud e l'ebraismo," *Belfagor* 35 (1980): 687–96; Carl E. Schorske, "Freud: The Psycho-archeology of Civilizations," *Proceedings of the Massachusetts Historical Society* 92 (1980): 52–67; Carl E. Schorske, *Fin-de-siècle Vienna: Politics and Culture* (New York: Alfred A. Knopf, 1980), 181–207; Moshe Halevi Spero, *Judaism and Psychology: Halakhic Perspectives* (New York: KTAV, 1980); Fred Grubel, "Zeitgenosse Sigmund Freud," *Jahrbuch der Psychoanalyse* 11 (1979); 73–75; Hugo Knoepfmacher, "Sigmund Freud and the B'nai B'rith," *Journal of the American Psychoanalytic Association* 27 (1979): 441–49; Marianne Krüll, *Freud und sein Vater: die Entstehung der Psychoanalyse und Freuds ungelöste Vaterbindung* (Munich: C. H. Beck, 1979) (in English as *Freud and His Father*, trans. Arnold Pomerans [New York: Norton, 1986]); Avner Falk, "Freud and Herzl," *Contemporary Psychoanalysis* 14 (1978): 357–87; Peter Gay, *Freud, Jews, and Other Germans* (New York: Oxford University Press, 1978), 29–92; N. K. Dor-Shav, "To Be or Not to Be a Jew? A Dilemma of Sigmund Freud," *Acta*

Psychiatrica et Neurologica Scandanavica 56 (1977): 407–20; A. Falk, "Freud and Herzl," *Midstream* 23 (1977): 3–24; Martin S. Bergmann, "Moses and the Evolution of Freud's Jewish Identity," *Israeli Annals of Psychiatry and Related Disciplines* 14 (1976); 3–26; O. Herz, "Sigmund Freud und B'nai B'rith," in *B'nai B'rith Wien, 1895–1975* (Vienna: B'nai B'rith, 1976), 50–56; Robert Gordis, "The Two Faces of Freud," *Judaism* 24 (1975): 194–200; Reuben M. Rainey, *Freud as a Student of Religion* (Missoula, Mont.: American Academy of Religion, 1975); Paul Roazen, *Freud and His Followers* (New York: Alfred A. Knopf, 1975), 22–27; Léon Vogel, "Freud and Judaism: An Analysis in the Light of His Correspondence," trans. Murray Sachs, *Judaism* 24 (1975): 181–93; John Murray Cuddihy, *The Ordeal of Civility: Freud, Marx, Lévi-Strauss, and the Jewish Struggle with Modernity* (New York: Basic Books, 1974); A. L. Merani, *Freud y el Talmud: seguido de critica de los fundamentos de la psicopatologia* (Mexico City: Grijalbo, 1974); Marthe Robert, *D'Oedipe à Moise; Freud et la conscience juive* (Paris: Calmann-Levy, 1974) (in English as *From Oedipus to Moses: Freud's Jewish Identity*, trans. Ralph Manheim [Garden City, N.Y.: Anchor Books, 1976]); S. Rothman, "Men and Ideas: Freud and Jewish Marginality," *Encounter* 43 (1974): 46–54; Max Schur, *Freud: Living and Dying* (New York: International Universities Press, 1972), 22–27; David Singer, "Ludwig Lewisohn and Freud: The Zionist Therapeutic," *Psychoanalytic Review* 58 (1971): 169–82; D. Capps, "Hartmann's Relationship to Freud: A Reappraisal," *Journal of the History of the Behavioral Sciences* 6 (1970): 162–75; M. S. Maravon, *Contribution à l'étude critique de la psychopathologie du juif: psychanalyse du juif* (Paris: Thése, 1969), 25–51: Ignaz Maybaum, *Creation and Guilt: A Theological Assessment of Freud's Father-Son Conflict* (London: Vallentine, Mitchell, 1969); Earl A. Grollman, *Judaism in Sigmund Freud's World* (New York: Appelton-Century, 1965); David Bakan, *Sigmund Freud and the Jewish Mystical Tradition* (New York: Van Nostrand, 1958); Ernst Simon, "Sigmund Freud: The Jew," *Leo Baeck Institute Yearbook* 2 (1957): 270–305; W. Aron, "Notes on Sigmund Freud's Ancestry and Jewish Contacts," *YIVO Annual of Jewish Social Sciences* 2 (1956): 286–95; Karl Menninger, "The Genius of the Jew in Psychiatry," *Medical Leaves* 1 (1937): 127–32 (reprinted in *A Psychiatrist's World: The Selected Papers of Karl Menninger*, ed. Bernard H. Hall [New York: Viking Press, 1959]; Samuel Felix Mendelsohn, *Mental Healing in Judaism: Its Relationship to Christian Science and Psychoanalysis* (Chicago: Jewish Gift Shop, 1936); A. A. Roback, *Jewish Influence in Modern Thought* (Cambridge, Mass.: (Sci-Art Publishers, 1929), 152–97; Enrico Morselli, *La psicanalisi: studii ed appunti critica.* 2 vols. (Turin: Bocca, 1926); A. A. Roback, "Freud, Chassid or Humanist," *B'nai B'rith Magazine* 40 (1926): 118; A. A. Roback, "Is Psychoanalysis a Jewish Movement?" *B'nai B'rith Magazine* 40 (1926): 118–19, 129–30, 198–201, 238–39; Arnold Kutzinki, "Sigmund Freud, ein jüdischer Forscher," *Der Jude* 8 (1924): 216–21.

2. See, for example, Velikovsky (1941); Masson (1978); and Loewenberg (1970, 1971).

3. See the discussion of Le Bon's attitudes toward the Jews in Nye (1975) and Roudinesco (1982), especially Roudinesco's chapters "L'inconscient à la fran-

çaise (de Gustave Le Bon à l'affaire Dreyfus)" (1: 181–221) and "Judéité, isra-élisme, antisémitisme" (1: 395–411).

4. I have compared each quotation with the original as it appears in Sigmund Freud, *Gesammelte Werke: chronologisch geordnet*, 19 vols. (Frankfurt a. M.: S. Fischer, 1952–87); hereafter referred to as *G. W.*

5. See the discussion of this concept, without any reference to the psycholog-ical or medical literature, in Beller (1989, 73–83).

6. See in this context their letters (Lazarus and Steinthal 1971–1986). On the relationship to the medicine of the late nineteenth century, see Schmiedebach (1988, 311–21).

7. On Freud and Wundt, see Tögel (1989, 97–106). For the reciprocal influ-ence, see Elliger (1986) and Scheidt (1986).

8. In this context, see Barnouw (1989) on the question of Freud's construc-tion of fictions of the self.

9. See the Freud and Jung (1974, 71 [in German], 145 [in English]).

10. See also the description of this meeting in his autobiography (Freud 1959, 166).

11. On the context of this exchange, see Homans (1989, 35–41).

12. Morselli was the author of *La psicanalisi: studii ed appunti critici* (1926), which argued that psychoanalysis was a Jewish discovery because of the predisposition of the Jewish to theoretical solutions for material problems. See also his essay "La psicologia etnica e la scienza eugenistica" (1912, 1: 58–62). On Morselli, see Guanieri (1986).

13. See *S.E.* 5: 396.

14. See Diamond (1982). I would also evoke here the work of Jean-François Lyotard on Heidegger and the Jews (1988), in which Lyotard speaks of Heideg-ger's refusal to speak of the Shoah as a form of the refusal to remember, which is closely tied to the role that the Jews play in the cultural world of Christianity, as the ultimate object of projection. The Jew, caught up in such a system of repre-sentation, has but little choice: his essence, which incorporates the horrors projected onto him and which is embodied (quite literally) in his physical being, must forget what he is.

15. See the detailed overview of the psychoanalytic debates concerning "penis envy" in Chehrazi (1986).

16. See, for example, Souchay (1855). This topic is central to the argument in Laqueur (1990).

17. On the image of the woman in fin-de-siècle medicine, see Berna-Simons (1894); on Möbius, see Schiller (1982). Freud distances himself from Möbius's biological work on femininity. Instead, he sees the limitations present within the feminine as a reflex of the suppression of female sexuality in Western cul-ture. See *S.E.* 9: 198–99, for Freud's rebuttal of Möbius.

18. Cited in Jones (1953–57, 2: 468). See Niederland (1989).

References

Baldwin, James Mark. *Mental Development in the Child and the Race.* New York: Macmillan, 1898.

Barnouw, Dagmar. "Modernism in Vienna: Freud and a Normative Poetics of the Self." *Modern Austrian Literature* 22 (1989): 327–44.

Beller, Steven. *Vienna and the Jews, 1867–1938: A Cultural History.* New York: Cambridge University Press, 1989.

Berna-Simons, Lilian. *Weibliche Identität und Sexualität: das Bild der Weiblichkeit im 19. Jahrhundert und in Sigmund Freud.* Frankfurt a. M.: Materialis Verlag, 1984.

Blanton, Smiley. *Diary of My Analysis with Sigmund Freud.* New York: Hawthorn Books, 1971.

Bloom, Harold. *The Strong Light of the Canonical: Kafka, Freud, and Scholem as Revisionists of Jewish Culture and Thought.* City College Papers, no. 20. New York: City College, 1987.

B'nai B'rith: Zwi Perez Chajes Loge, 1895–1975. Vienna: B'nai B'rith, 1976.

Carotenuto, Aldo. *A Secret Symmetry: Sabina Spielrein between Jung and Freud.* Translated by Arno Pomerans, John Shepley, and Krishna Winston. New York: Pantheon, 1982.

Chehrazi, Shahla. "Female Psychology: A Review." *Journal of the American Psychoanalytic Association* 34 (1986): 141–62.

Diamond, Sigmund. "Sigmund Freud, His Jewishness, and Scientific Method: The Seen and the Unseen as Evidence." *Journal of the History of Ideas* 43 (1982): 613–34.

Elliger, Tilman J. S. *Freud und die akademische Psychologie: ein Beitrag zur Rezeptionsgeschichte der Psychoanalyse in der deutschen Psychologie (1895–1945).* Weinheim: Deutscher Studien Verlag, 1986.

Eyler, John M. *Victorian Social Medicine: The Ideas and Methods of William Farr.* Baltimore: Johns Hopkins University Press, 1979.

Freud, Martin. *Glory Reflected: Sigmund Freud—Man and Father.* London: Angus & Robertson, 1957.

Freud, Sigmund. *Gesammelte Werke: chronologisch geordnet.* 19 vols. Frankfurt a. M.: S. Fischer, 1952–87.

———. *The Standard Edition of the Complete Psychological Works of Sigmund Freud.* Edited and translated by James Strachey. 24 vols. London: Hogarth Press, 1953–74.

The Interpretation of Dreams (1900), vol. 5.

The Psychopathology of Everyday Life (1901), vol. 6.

Three Essays on the Theory of Sexuality (1905), vol. 7.

"'Civilized' Sexual Morality and Modern Nervous Illness" (1908), vol. 9.

"On the Sexual Theories of Children" (1908), vol. 9.

Notes upon a Case of Obsessional Neurosis (1909), vol. 10.

Totem and Taboo (1913), vol. 13.

Introductory Lectures on Psycho-Analysis (1916), vol. 15.

General Theory of the Neuroses (1917), vol. 16.

Group Psychology and the Analysis of the Ego (1921), vol. 18.

"The Infantile Genital Organization" (1923), vol. 19.

"The Resistances to Psycho-Analysis" (1925), vol. 19.

"Letter to the Editor of the *Jewish Press Centre in Zurich*" (1925), vol. 19.

An Autobiographical Study (1925), vol. 20.

The Question of Lay Analysis (1926), vol. 20.

"Address to the Society of B'nai B'rith" (1941 [1926], vol. 20.

"Dr. Ernest Jones (on His 50th Birthday)" (1929), vol. 21.

Civilization and Its Discontents (1930), vol. 21.

"Female Sexuality" (1931), vol. 21.

New Introductory Lectures on Psycho-Analysis (1933), vol. 22.

———. "Briefe an Arthur Schnitzler." *Neue Rundschau* 66 (1955): 100.

———. *Briefe, 1873–1939.* Edited by Ernst and Lucie Freud. Frankfurt a. M.: S. Fischer, 1960.

———. "Some Early Unpublished Letters." Translated by Ilse Scheier. *International Journal of Psychoanalysis* 59 (1978): 426.

Freud, Sigmund, and Abraham, Karl. *Sigmund Freud—Karl Abraham: Briefe, 1907–1926.* Edited by Hilda C. Abraham and Ernst L. Freud. Frankfurt a. M.: S. Fischer, 1980.

Freud, Sigmund, and Jung, Carl G. *Sigmund Freud—C. G. Jung: Briefwechsel.* Edited by William McGuire and Wolfgang Sauerländer. Frankfurt a. M.: S. Fischer, 1974. *The Freud/Jung Letters: The Correspondence between Sigmund Freud and C.G. Jung.* Edited by William McGuire. Translated by Ralph Mannheim and R.F.C. Hull. Princeton: Princeton Unviersity Press, 1974.

Gay, Peter. *Freud: A Life for Our Time.* New York: Norton, 1988.

Gilman, Sander L. *Difference and Pathology.* Ithaca: Cornell University Press, 1985.

———. *The Jew's Body.* New York: Routledge, 1991.

Guanieri, Patrizia. *Individualità difformi: la psichiatria antropologica di Enrico Morselli.* Milan: F. Angeli, 1986.

Hes, Josef Philip. "A Note on an as yet Unpublished Letter by Sigmund Freud." *Jewish Social Studies* 48 (1986): 322.

Hirschfeld, Ludwig. *Was nicht im Baedeker steht: Wien und Budapest.* Munich: R. Piper, 1927.

Homans, Peter. *The Ability to Mourn: Disillusionment and the Social Origins of Psychoanalysis.* Chicago: University of Chicago Press, 1989.

James, William. *The Principles of Psychology.* 2 vols. New York: Henry Holt, 1890.

Jellinek, Adolf. *Der jüdische Stamm: ethnographische Studien.* Vienna: Herzfeld & Bauer, 1869.

Jones, Ernest. *The Life and Work of Sigmund Freud.* 3 vols. New York: Basic Books, 1953–57.

———. *Free Associations: Memories of a Psycho-Analyst.* London: Hogarth Press, 1959.

Kardiner, Abraham. *My Analysis with Freud: Reminiscences.* New York: Norton, 1977.

Knoepfmacher, H. "Sigmund Freud and the B'nai B'rith." *Journal of the American Psychoanalytic Association* 27 (1979): 441–49.

Laqueur, Thomas. *Making Sex: Body and Gender from the Greeks to Freud.* Cambridge: Harvard University Press, 1990.

Lazarus, Moritz. "Uber das Verhältnis des Einzelnen zur Gesamtheit." *Zeitschrift für Völkerpsychologie und Sprachwissenschaft* 2 (1862): 437.

Lazarus, Moritz, and Steinthal, Heymann. "Einleitende Gedanken über Völkerpsychologie." *Zeitschrift für Völkerpsychologie und Sprachwissenschaft* 1 (1860): 1–73.

———. *Moritz Lazarus und Heymann Steinthal: die Begründer der Völkerpsychologie in ihren Briefen*, edited by Ingrid Belke. 2 vols. Tübingen: Mohr, 1971–86.

Le Bon, Gustae. "Applications de la psychologie à classification des races." *Revue philosophique* 22 (1886): 593–619.

———. *The Crowd: A Study of the Popular Mind.* New York: Viking Press, 1960.

———. *Role des Juifs dans la civilisation.* Paris: Amis de Gustave Le Bon, 1985.

Le Rider, Jacques. "Freud zwischen Aufklärung und Gegenaufklärung." In *Aufklärung und Gegenaufklärung in der europäischen Literatur, Philosophie und Politik von der Antike bis zur Gegenwart*, edited by Jochen Schmidt. Darmstadt: Wissenschaftliche Buchgesellschaft, 1989.

———. *Modernité viennoise et crises de l'identité.* Paris: Presses Universitaires de France, 1990.

Leroy-Beaulieu, Anatole. *Israel among the Nations: A Study of the Jews and Antisemitism.* Translated by Frances Hellman. New York: G. P. Putnam's, 1895.

Loewenberg, Peter. "A Hidden Zionist Theme in Freud's 'My Son, the Myops . . .' Dream." *Journal of the History of Ideas* 31 (1970): 129–32.

———. "'Sigmund Freud as a Jew': A Study in Ambivalence and Courage." *Journal of the History of the Behavioral Sciences* 7 (1971): 363–69.

Lombroso, Cesare, and Ferro, Guglielmo. *La donna deliquente.* Turin: Roux, 1893.

Luschan, Felix von. "Altweiber-Psychologie." *Deutsche medizinische Wochenschrift* 42 (January 6, 1916): 20.

Lyotard, Jean-François. *Heidegger et "les juifs."* Paris: Galilée, 1988.

Masson, Jeffrey. "Buried Memories on the Acropolis: Freud's Response to Mysticism and Anti-Semitism." *International Journal of Psychoanalysis* 59 (1978): 199–208.

McDougall, William. *The Group Mind.* New York: Cambridge University Press, 1920.

Morselli, Enrico. "La psicologia etnica e la scienza eugenistica." *International Eugenics Congress—1912.* 2 vols. London: Eugenics Education Society, 1912.

———. *La psicanalisi: studii ed appunti critici.* Turin: Bocca, 1926.

Näcke, Paul. "Uber Kontrast-Träume und speziell sexuelle Kontrast-Träume." *Archiv für Kriminal-Anthropologie und Kriminalistik* 28 (1907): 1–19.

Niederland, William G. "The Source of Freud's Question about What Women Want." *American Journal of Psychiatry* 146 (1989): 409–10.

Nye, Robert. *The Origins of Crowd Psychology: Gustave Le Bon and the Crisis of Mass Democracy in the Third Republic.* Beverly Hills, Calif.: Sage, 1975.

Reik, Theodor. "Die Pubertätsriten der Wilden: Uber einige Ubereinstimmungen im Seelenleben der Wilden und der Neurotiker." *Imago* 6 (1915–16): 125–44, 189–222.

———. *Ritual: Psycho-Analytic Studies.* Translated by Douglas Bryan. London: Hogarth Press, 1931.

———. *From Thirty Years with Freud.* Translated by Richard Winston. New York: Farrar & Rinehart, 1940.

———. *Jewish Wit.* New York: Gamut Press, 1962.

Reiskel, Karl. "Idioticon viennense eroticum." *Anthropophyteia* 2 (1905): 1–13.

Rieff, Philip. *Freud: The Mind of the Moralist.* New York: Viking Press, 1959.

Roudinesco, Elisabeth. *La bataille de cent ans.* 2 vols. Paris: Ramsay, 1982.

Scheidt, Carl Eduard. *Die Rezeption der Psychoanalyse in der deutschsprachigen Philosophie vor 1940.* Frankfurt a. M.: Suhrkamp, 1986.

Schiller, Francis. *A Möbius Strip: Fin-de-Siècle Neuropsychiatry and Paul Möbius.* Berkeley: University of California Press, 1982.

Schmiedebach, Heinz-Peter. "Die Völkerpsychologie von Mortiz Lazarus (1824–1903) und ihre Beziehung zur naturwissenschaftlichen Psychiatrie." *XXX Congrès International d'Histoire de la Médecine, 1986.* Düsseldorf: N.p., 1988.

Showalter, Elaine. *The Female Malady: Women, Madness, and English Culture, 1830–1980.* New York: Pantheon, 1985.

Singer, Heinrich. *Allgemeine und spezielle Krankheitslehre der Juden.* Leipzig: Benno Konegen, 1904.

Souchay, F.D.F. *De l'homologie sexuelle chez l'homme.* Paris: Rignoux, 1855.

Tögel, Christfried. "Freud und Wundt: von der Hypnose bis zur Völkerpsychologie." In *Freud und die akademische Psychologie: beiträge zu einer historischen Kontroverse,* edited by Bernd Nitzsche. Munich: Psychologie Verlags Union, 1989.

Velikovsky, Emmanuel. "The Dreams Freud Dreamed." *Psychoanalytic Review* 30 (1941): 487–511.

Wittels, Fritz. *Sigmund Freud: His Personality, His Teaching, and His School.* Translated by Eden and Ceder Paul. London: Allen & Unwin, 1924.

Wittgenstein, Ludwig. *Culture and Value.* Edited by G. H. von Wright and Heikki Nyman. Oxford: Blackwell, 1980.

Wundt, Wilhelm. *Elements of Folk Psychology: Outlines of a Psychological History of the Development of Mankind.* Translated by Edward Leroy Schaub. London: Allen & Unwin, 1916.

9   Gender Stereotyping as a Way of Not Knowing

Barbara Shapard

In relating to each other, men and women have a tendency to polarize individuation and attachment by gender. This polarization can be seen through the process of projection and introjection in communication between men and women. The psychoanalytically oriented feminist literature discusses characteristics and tendencies along gender lines (Benjamin 1988; Chodorow 1989, 23–65, 69–78, 88; Dinnerstein 1976, 42–75, 164–73, 229–78; Gilligan 1982, 12–63; Josselson 1987, 168–91; Tannen 1990, 24–48, 77–78). Identifying certain characteristics as typically feminine or typically masculine can itself foster gender stereotyping. Certain characteristics are not innately and unchangeably tied to gender as much as they are the product of the culture in which they are observed. Clinical work, however, requires knowledge of gender issues, including the gender stereotyping of a given culture. Understanding the stereotyping that individuals and couples subscribe to can be a step toward alleviating the defensive use of that stereotyping.

I believe that in this culture at this time women are still primarily valued and envied for their containment and expression of need, and men are still primarily valued and envied for their separate activity. Women have made considerable gains asserting themselves in the public arena. These women are often overfunctioning, containing the domestic arena as well as pursuing their separate activity in the world (Hochschild 1986, 28, 109, 180). I think men still prefer to value women for their nurturing functions and feel threatened by women's mastery of the public arena. Women attach to men and women by overidentifying with them. This can result in depletion of their own separate selves and activity. Women express this kind of connection with others in much the same way as they experience more or less con-

163

flicted love for, need for, and identification with mother. Men repress their awareness of needing mother and identify with father and his separate activity away from mother and the home. Men put their own need into women and withdraw from women into separate activity. In contrast to the high proportion of women in Western cultures who fill both the containing and public roles, relatively few men have moved away from the singular obligation toward the high performance that is necessary to sustain a family financially.

Denigration and envy between the sexes results from the polarization of: (1) the idealization of being or longing for the primary mother, with fear of separateness (more commonly found in women); and (2) the fear of longing for the primary mother and the idealization of separateness (commonly found in men). Elsewhere in this volume Joseph Smith describes the yearning for and fear of remerger with the mother as well as the pain and growth related to knowing and mourning mother. Men dread and withdraw from this wordless unmourned loss of mother when confronting women, and women try to become the unmourned lost ideal mother in relation to men (Lazar 1990). Women seem to complain actively as a way of connecting to the conflicted mother or father, displaced then onto men. Men withdraw and remove themselves from the conflicted mother or father, who is then displaced on women. In this chapter I want to show, from my clinical work with couples, the polarization of men urgently withdrawing and women desperately connecting. I believe this to be a collusive defense against knowing the mother or father, which, in turn, defends against each partner mourning the mother or father. Below are examples of couples' dialogues that trace this projective-introjective process, further polarizing individuation and attachment to gender qualities.

Who Demands, Who Withdraws?

The couple in my first example, both high-level government administrators, good parents, with many friends and interests, were frozen in relation to each other. She felt the loss of her nurturing, protective father most intensely in her husband's presence. He felt most inadequate and guilty about his separate functioning in her presence. The guilt and loss were polarized, so that she couldn't tackle the guilt of her prized position with her father, and he couldn't know his loss of his mother, who had died when he was in his teens.

She complained about their weekend at the beach, during which he played golf and watched TV instead of paying attention to her, told her uncaringly what to do about a worry she had at work, then wanted to have sex. She felt ignored and used as she cleaned up the house, cooked, and shopped for him.

He said he had played golf just one afternoon and had spent a lot of time out on the beach with her when she was in a bad mood. He felt he was trying to be helpful in his suggestion about her work worry, and he wanted to make love because he felt relaxed by the holiday. She said that she wanted yogurt, and he, in his usual way of being difficult, wanted to go down the boardwalk and get ice cream instead. He said, "You can have your yogurt, me my ice cream, without being angry with me." She cried and told him that her father had always considered her mother until he died, "but you go out of your way not to consider me." He said, "I try to help you out a lot, and you are still in a bad mood, and I give up."

This is the couple's theme: she feels envious of his separateness and feels abandoned, as she did when the good father had abandoned her and her mother by dying. She feels very entitled to his attentions, to make up for her and her mother's loss of a good father. She is silently doing chores for him, and she expects the same silent, knowing attention from him. Unowned guilt and anxiety inhibit her own separate activity. Although he feels entitled enough to pursue his separate activity (i.e., play golf, watch TV, and eat ice cream), he feels guilty about not being able to please her, as he was unable to please his mother. In resignation he withdraws from her and from his failure to please her. Ultimately, this inability to own his needing something from her reflects his inability to acknowledge the need of, and to mourn, his mother. Similarly, there is no space for her to mourn the loss of her father and then deal with her guilt toward her mother. She demands to be mothered by her husband in part to defend against her guilt and anxiety around separation from her parents. They polarize needing and withdrawing from the need as a defense against knowing and mourning the loss of the nourishing parent.

If You Won't Be Mommy, I Won't Play

Below is a conversation between a man and wife in Erica Jong's novel *Fear of Flying* (1973). (The bracketed "She" and "He" have been added for clarity.)

> [SHE]: Why do you always have to do this to me? You make me feel so lonely.
> [HE]: That comes from you.
> [SHE]: What do you mean it comes from me? Tonight I wanted to be happy. It's Christmas Eve. Why do you turn on me? What did I do?

(*Silence.*)

[SHE:] What did I do?

(*He looks at her as if her not knowing were another injury.*)

[HE:] Look, let's just go to sleep now. Let's just forget it.

[SHE]: Forget what?

(*He says nothing.*)

[SHE]: Forget the fact that you turned on me? Forget the fact that you're
punishing me for nothing? Forget the fact that I'm lonely and cold, that
it's Christmas Eve and again you've ruined it for me? Is that what you
want me to forget?

[HE]: I won't discuss it.

[SHE]: Discuss what? *What* won't you discuss?

[HE]: Shut up! I won't have you screaming in the hotel.

[SHE]: I don't give a fuck what you won't have me do. I'd like to be treated
civilly. I'd like you to at least do me the courtesy of telling me why
you're in such a funk. And don't look at me that way. . . .

[HE]: What way?

[SHE]: As if my not being able to read your mind were my greatest sin. I
can't read your mind. I *don't* know why you're so mad. I *can't* intuit
your every wish. If that's what you want in a wife you don't have it in me.

[HE]: I certainly don't.

[SHE]: Then what is it? Please tell me.

[HE]: I shouldn't have to.

[SHE]: Good God! Do you mean to tell me I'm expected to be a mind
reader? Is that the kind of mothering you want?

[HE]: If you had any empathy for me . . . .

[SHE]: But I *do*. My God, you don't give me a chance.

[HE]: You tune out. You don't listen.

[SHE]: It was something in the movie, wasn't it?

[HE]: What, in the movie?

[SHE]: The quiz again. Do you have to quiz me like some kind of criminal?
Do you have to *cross-examine* me? . . . It was the funeral scene. . . . The
little boy looking at his dead mother. Something got you there. That was
when you got depressed.

(*Silence.*)

[SHE]: Well, *wasn't* it?

(*Silence.*)

[SHE]: Oh come on, Bennett, you're making me *furious*. Please tell me.
Please.

[HE]: (*He gives the words singly like little gifts. Like hard little turds.*)
What was it about that scene that got me?

[SHE]: Don't quiz me. Tell me! (*She puts her arms around him. He pulls
away. She falls to the floor holding onto his pajama leg. It looks less
like an embrace than like a rescue scene, she sinking, he reluctantly
allowing her to cling to his leg for support.*)

[HE]: Get up!

[SHE]: (*Crying*) Only if you tell me.
[HE]: (*He jerks his leg away.*) I'm going to bed.

Deborah Tannen points out the painful interaction of the two styles, her insistence on connecting, his passive-aggressive withdrawal (1990, 229). The man's inability to acknowledge his loss of "the dead mother" and need for her comfort evokes her desperate reaction to become the maternal ideal, fulfilling his unspoken needs, sending her clinging to him as she falls to the floor. His shame in needing mother became her shame in not giving, not being the understanding mother, turning her into the desperate, needy child. They both defend against sharing the grief of the dead mother by continuing the desperation/withdrawal hostile exchange. The polarization of her desperate awareness of need and his withdrawal from need keeps them from knowing the need and knowing they can mourn the loss of the mother.

In the next two conversations both couples, after painstaking therapeutic work, find the words to admit need for the parent, allowing for the potential space to understand and love each other. I am referring here to Smith's idea (in this volume) of owning one's own struggle with the ambivalence toward mother in order to reclaim a sense of worthiness. Love can then be shared.

Inadequacy Projected, Inadequacy Owned

In the following dialogue a wife tries to connect to her husband, who has withdrawn out of shame at his anxiety and fear of rejection.

SHE: I've missed you, feel you are cutting me off, drinking more, withdrawing.

HE: You're egocentric. You just care about how my drinking affects you and are just critical of it. I feel you are the enemy I have to hide from.

SHE: I'm hurt.

HE: I don't intend to hurt you. See, you are thinking of yourself again.

SHE: I don't know who you are when you are this way. Why is it I feel so bad when I started out saying I missed you?

HE: I feel like you don't care enough about me.

SHE: I do, but if you withdraw, disconnect, it is hard to show I care. And if you don't talk about what you need me to care about then I can't show I care.

HE: I feel like I have so much going on between work and trying to sell those houses, I drink to calm down.

SHE: Really, I didn't have any idea you were stressed out.

HE: I was afraid you would be angry that some of my worries are so neurotic that you would throw them up in my face.

SHE: Well, I wish you would take the risk and share your worries before you decide that I am your critical enemy and then cut me off. I get hurt.

HE: I am sorry I hurt you that way: I cut you off and blame you when I am feeling insecure.

She expresses for both of them the feeling of being cut off from the other, missing the other's caring. Both had demanding, self-involved mothers. She is trying to connect with him, in the same way that she tries to connect with her self-involved mother. He shames her for her self-involved need, denigrates her for not thinking of him. He feels hopeless about her and his mother's capacity to think of him. He then projects his mother's shame and hatred for his needful self into her.

Rather than her wordlessly identifying with the self-involved mother with shame and self-hatred, she expresses her awareness that her feeling bad is his feeling bad put into her. Her clarity about what is her hurt and what is his hurt evokes reparation from him and then compassion for him. For the moment they diminish the gender split. Both know of the mothers' love they seek and of what they missed. At such a moment they refind each other as loving and lovable.

No Valentine for Mother

The following dialogue is about a stingy husband's reaction to a giving wife.

She gives him a card, a tie, and one rose.
He says, "That is nice," doesn't look at her, and goes back to reading his paper.
She says, "Let's do something special and go out for dinner tonight."
He says, "I have to work late. You know I have to get up early in the morning. I don't know what it is you expect of me." He leaves in a huff.
She cries.

The couple work very hard on this exchange and reach the following understanding. His inability to give her a valentine expresses anger at deprivation felt at the hands of his mother. His inability to appreciate her valentine present is like his inability to admit he felt hurt by his ungiving mother. His anger at her is for her having evoked anger and deprivation regarding his mother. Her giving evoked his guilt at not being able to give her what she expects. All the feelings he can't feel toward his mother he put into his wife, and initially she accepted them. In this session he began to learn to know his mother and own his conflicted relationship to her. In a later session she realizes that her containment of his conflicted relationship with his mother is a defense against knowing her own conflict with an ungiving mother. She became the giving mother for both of them as a defense against their knowing and mourning their mothers.

Being biologically and culturally sensitive to others, women tend to intuit and provide what men and other women want from them. Women's oversensitivity to men and undersensitivity to self result in restricting the space for either to know themselves and grow.

Jill Scharff illustrates this point when describing her introjective ability in working with a nine-year-old boy. Scharff experiences the boy crawling under the rug as the boy's wish to be her baby and crawl under her maternity sweater. Understanding his wish, she says, "You do not want to give me your words but want . . . to be perfectly held and cared for and fed effortlessly." Jill then becomes aware of being afraid of her own words, as if they are dangerous, producing too much separation anxiety. She realizes that she is identifying with the "boy's fear of words" and finds herself resorting to feverish guessing at the boy's internal experience. Scharff then understands that her feverish guessing is like that of the boy's overzealous mother. By overidentifying with the boy's fear of words and his overzealous mother, Scharff realizes that she is crowding the boy's separate internal experience of himself. She then explains how she extricates herself from the boy's internal world by "emptying myself of desire" to know him. She then entertains herself with her own thoughts, "instead of focusing on his response or confirmation." This internal shift on her part also frees the boy for autonomous play and individuation without annihilation (Scharff 1992, 312–13).

In this example Scharff offers women a model of internally detaching from significant others so as to give themselves and others more autonomy to play and work. When Scharff stops being the mother, the boy can play in a space that allows him to know and mourn the loss of his real mother. Women have a tendency to introject needs in attaching to men, as men project needs in attaching to women. Polarization of gender by introjecting and projecting needs reflects defenses against being separate whole people with longings and limits.

In conclusion I would suggest that a major developmental task for a man in this culture at this time is to tolerate his need/desire for woman/ mother while retaining his separate activity. Men can learn to be aware of the tendency to denigrate women as a way of controlling their desire, envy, and fear of women. Men can observe their passive-aggressive withdrawal as, in part, a reaction to fears of engulfment and shame over needing women. The analogous developmental task for women in this culture at this time is to tolerate their own guilt and anxiety around separate selfhood and activity while still connecting to men. Women can learn to be aware of their wish to control men as a defense against envy, guilt, and separation anxiety. Women can recognize their aggressive complaining as partly a reaction to guilt and anxiety around their own selfhood and activity (separate from mother).

Generally, we, women and men, need to be aware of our defensive use of each other in surviving loss and confronting death. Polarizing and idealizing attachment or individuation along gender lines are instances of such defensive use. Beyond such stereotyping the dialogue between individuation and attachment in ourselves and with each other is toleration of loss and death, paradoxically affording a richer, fuller life. Lacan suggests that the developmental task is to acknowledge our longings and tolerate the disappointment and incompleteness without demand or retaliation (quoted in Smith 1991, 54–56). I would suggest that this developmental task applies to our longings for separateness from as well as attachment to others. In individuating as well as in attachment, the sharing of guilt, anxiety, and loss between the genders minimizes the need for projection or introjection, allowing for fuller selfhood, separate activity, and relating to the other.

References

Benjamin, Jessica. *The Bonds of Love*. New York: Pantheon Books, 1988.

Chodorow, Nancy J. *Feminism and Psychoanalytic Theory*. New Haven: Yale University Press, 1989.

Dinnerstein, Dorothy. *The Mermaid and the Minotaur*. New York: Harper & Row, 1976.

Gilligan, Carol. *In a Different Voice*. Cambridge: Harvard University Press, 1982.

Hochschild, Arlie. *The Second Shift*. New York: Viking Press, 1986.

Jong, Erica. *Fear of Flying*. New York: Henry Holt, 1973.

Josselson, Ruthellen. *Finding Herself*. San Francisco: Jossey-Bass, 1987.

Lazar, Susan. "Men's Views of Women: The Gender Roots of Male Chauvinism in Women and Men." Presented at Meeting of the American Academy of Psychoanalysis, New York City, 1990.

Scharff, Jill Savege. *Projective and Introjective Identification and the Use of the Therapist's Self*. Northvale, N.J.: Jason Aronson, 1992.

Smith, Joseph H. *Arguing with Lacan: Ego Psychology and Language*. New Haven: Yale University Press, 1991.

Tannen, Deborah. *You Just Don't Understand*. New York: William Morrow, 1990.

Index

171

Library of Congress Cataloging-in-Publication Data

Psychoanalysis, feminism, and the future of gender / Joseph H. Smith, editor ; Afaf M.
  Mahfouz, associate editor.
        p.   cm. — (Psychiatry and the humanities ; v. 14)
    Includes bibliographical references and index.
    ISBN 0-8018-4711-7 (alk. paper). — ISBN 0-8018-4786-9 (pbk. : alk. paper)
    1. Psychoanalysis and feminism.   2. Women and psychoanalysis.   3. Sex (Psychol-
ogy).   I. Smith, Joseph H., 1927–   .   II. Mahfouz, Afaf M.   III. Series.
RC321.P943   vol. 14
[BF 175.4.F45]
616.89 s—dc20
[150.19'5'082]   93-26632